QUEER ACTIVISM AFTER MARRIAGE EQUALITY

Queer Activism After Marriage Equality focuses on the implications of legal same-sex marriage for LGBTQ social movements and organizing. It asks how the agendas, strategies, structures, and financing of LGBTQ movement organizations are changing now that same-sex marriage is legal in some countries.

Building on a major conference held in 2016 entitled "After Marriage: The Future of LGBTQ Politics and Scholarship," this collection draws from critical and intersectional perspectives to explore the questions and issues facing the next chapter of LGBTQ activism and social movement work. It comprises academic papers, international case studies, edited transcripts of selected conference sessions, and interviews with activists. These take a critical look at the high-profile work of national and state-wide equality organizations, analyzing the costs of winning marriage equality and what that has meant for other LGBTQ activism. In addition to this, the book examines other forms of queer activism that have existed for years in the shadow of the marriage equality movement, as well as new social movements that have developed more recently. Finally, it looks to examples of activism in other countries and considers lessons U.S. activists can learn from them.

By presenting research on these and other trends, this volume helps translate queer critiques advanced during the marriage campaigns into a framework for ongoing critical research in the after-marriage period.

Joseph Nicholas DeFilippis is the founder and former Executive Director of Queers for Economic Justice, and worked as an activist for over two decades. He is currently Assistant Professor of Social Work at Seattle University, U.S.A., and has written about queer social movements, poverty, and marriage politics.

Michael W. Yarbrough is an interdisciplinary social scientist whose work explores the intersection of law, culture, and family. He is Assistant Professor of Law and

Society in the Political Science Department of John Jay College of Criminal Justice (CUNY), U.S.A., and a Research Associate in the Department of Sociology, Faculty of Humanities, at the University of Johannesburg, South Africa.

Angela Jones is Associate Professor of Sociology at Farmingdale State College, SUNY, USA. Her research interests include African American political thought and protest, gender, and sexuality. Jones is the author of four books and numerous scholarly articles in peer-reviewed journals.

QUEER ACTIVISM AFTER MARRIAGE EQUALITY

*Edited by Joseph Nicholas DeFilippis,
Michael W. Yarbrough, and Angela Jones*

Routledge
Taylor & Francis Group

LONDON AND NEW YORK

First published 2018
by Routledge
2 Park Square, Milton Park, Abingdon, Oxon OX14 4RN

and by Routledge
711 Third Avenue, New York, NY 10017

Routledge is an imprint of the Taylor & Francis Group, an informa business

British Library Cataloguing-in-Publication Data
A catalogue record for this book is available from the British Library

Library of Congress Cataloging-in-Publication Data
A catalog record has been requested for this title.

ISBN: 978-1-138-55749-9 (hbk)
ISBN: 978-1-138-55750-5 (pbk)
ISBN: 978-1-315-15109-0 (ebk)

Typeset in Bembo
by Sunrise Setting Ltd, Brixham, UK

CONTENTS

PREFACE

Two Junes, a year apart, frame the mission of this collection. In June 2015, the U.S. Supreme Court ruled that that country's constitution forbids the exclusion of same-sex couples from legally recognized marriage. Arriving after a hard and often painful fight, the ruling seemed to many to mark a new kind of inclusion. Rainbows wrapped many of our public spaces, from profile pics to the White House, in triumphant celebration.

One year later, in June 2016, a massacre on Latin night at Pulse nightclub in Orlando shocked the nation and the world. Many felt the shock of disbelief. But many LGBTQ people, especially LGBTQ people of color, felt the shock of recognition at a familiar violence that marriage did little to address.

Fiercely debated for many years, same-sex marriage has become a legal reality in a rapidly growing number of jurisdictions around the world. First enacted in 2001 in the Netherlands, same-sex marriage is now legally recognized in over 20 countries,[1] approximately three-quarters of which legalized it in the past half-decade. At the same time, these sweeping gains have often triggered significant backlash both where they have occurred and elsewhere. Homosexual acts are currently criminalized in 75 countries, including ten where they can be punished by death. Such violent backlash is an especially visible manifestation of a complex range of consequences that have accompanied same-sex marriage. In the United States, for example, same-sex marriage has channeled the priorities of national LGBTQ and state-wide equality organizations away from other issues, reduced the availability of other forms of legal recognition for families, and generally reinforced mainstream family norms.

The time is thus ripe to (1) examine this key moment in the ongoing history of LGBTQ communities; (2) interrogate predictions by scholars and activists about what social changes same-sex marriage would produce; and (3) consider paths forward for LGBTQ scholarship and politics.

The *After Marriage Equality* collection was designed to tackle these three broad themes. *Queer Families and Relationships After Marriage Equality* focuses on the legal, material, and cultural impacts of legal marriage equality on diverse queer families and relationships. *Queer Activism After Marriage Equality* focuses on the implications of legal same-sex marriage for LGBTQ social movements and examines what queer activism looks like now that the national gay and lesbian organizations have succeeded in achieving their main priorities. *The Unfinished Queer Agenda After Marriage Equality* focuses on dire issues facing LGBTQ individuals and communities that were eclipsed by the marriage equality movement, such as policing, immigration, health care, homelessness, violence, poverty, and more.

All three titles draw their materials from a major conference held at John Jay College of Criminal Justice on October 1–2, 2016 and organized by CLAGS: The Center for LGBTQ Studies, based at the City University of New York (CUNY). This conference, entitled "After Marriage: The Future of LGBTQ Politics and Scholarship," staged an open, diverse, and critical conversation among over 175 academic, activist, and artist speakers. Approximately 450 people attended, and the conference was also streamed online. Building on similar conversations LGBTQ activists have been having among themselves for some time, this was to our knowledge the largest public conversation focused on this theme, and the only one combining critical and intersectional perspectives with extensive dialogue among both scholars and activists. The conference was supported in part by a grant from the American Sociological Association and the National Science Foundation, by the Office for the Advancement of Research at John Jay College of Criminal Justice, and by the Center for the Study of Gender and Sexuality at New York University. We would like to thank our colleagues on the CLAGS staff and the conference organizing committee who helped make the conference a reality: Yana Calou, Stephanie Hsu, Bianca Laureano, Kevin Nadal, Noam Parness, Jasmina Sinanovic, Andrew Spieldenner, Nicole Vitrit, and Kalle Westerling. In addition, we are so grateful to our editor at Routledge, Alexandra McGregor, whose support and enthusiasm for this project was unwavering. We would be remiss if we did not thank our editorial assistant at Routledge, Kitty Imbert, who shepherded us through the entire publication process.

Joseph would also like to offer his personal thanks to several people. My family has always been unwavering in their support, and I am in their debt for more than I could ever acknowledge. I am grateful to Ben Anderson-Nathe, Miranda Cunningham, Thuan Duong, and Gita Mehrotra for their invaluable feedback and suggestions for my own writings in this volume. I want to acknowledge Paul Beshire and Cal Garrett for their reliable and thoughtful work as research assistants. I thank Terry Boggis, Hiram Perez, and Jessica Stern, for encouraging me when I wanted to throw in the academic towel. And, finally, I want to thank Angela Jones and Michael W. Yarbrough for their great work on the inspiring conference that birthed this project, for reaching out to me and asking me to join them on this book collection, and for being lovely collaborators.

All three titles use critical and intersectional lenses, focusing on the problems and limits of marriage and on those queer and trans people also disadvantaged by racism, immigration status, socioeconomic class, and other intersecting factors. The rapid spread of legal same-sex marriage increases the relevance of long-standing queer critiques of marriage, thus many of the chapters in this collection use as a starting point queer critiques of the same-sex marriage movement, investigating their implications now that marriage is legal. By presenting research on these and other trends, these volumes help translate queer critiques advanced during the marriage campaigns into a framework for ongoing critical research in the after-marriage period.

In light of these important intersectional and queer critiques of marriage, we would like to address the problematic titles of these books. We originally proposed the books to have the same title as the conference, *After Marriage*. In working with the publisher, there was concern that some readers might become confused, associating the phrase "After Marriage" with newly-weds or with divorce. We needed to find a framework that would be easily recognizable to a mainstream audience, and "marriage equality" had become the dominant frame used by same-sex marriage rights advocates in the United States and many other countries. We want to reassure our readers that we both recognize and reject the implication in the title *After Marriage Equality* that the *Obergefell* decision created equality for LGBTQ communities. Not only is that emphatically not true, but the central point of the conference and these volumes is to highlight the reality that so many queer and trans people, particularly queer immigrants and queer people of color, know all too well—that legally sanctioned, same-sex marriage did not create equality or address the myriad issues facing them. *Obergefell* did not foster economic justice; it did not address poverty; it did not address racist and heterosexist policing; it did not address a bigoted immigration system; it did not address a broken health care system; it did not address systemic violence and any of the other ominous issues facing queer and trans people that were ignored by the marriage equality movement. It did not even provide legal protections for most LGBTQ families.

Despite the issues we had with the title *After Marriage Equality*, we do believe that this framing can help bring in readers who may not be familiar with queer critiques of marriage equality. To help open these volumes up to such readers, we use a variety of materials, including research studies, essays, interviews, and transcripts from the conference. Our contributors include activists working on a wide range of issues and scholars from numerous disciplines, both in the United States and around the world. We also asked contributors to write in accessible language suitable for undergraduate students in a variety of courses (including LGBTQ studies, gender studies, social movements, social work, family studies, law and society, and political science), as well as for a wide range of audiences outside the academy. Finally, each of the three volumes was designed so that it could be read individually as a stand-alone book, but also to complement and build on the others so that they could be used together as a complete set.

We see this moment as an opportunity to reorient the direction of LGBTQ thought and action. We hope that the diverse perspectives found in this book collection will open up conversations among students and community members about what can or should happen next for LGBTQ families, activists, and communities.

Joseph Nicholas DeFilippis, Michael W. Yarbrough, and Angela Jones

Note

1 While not an exhaustive list, as same-sex marriage laws are constantly changing, nations that have legalized same-sex marriage include: Argentina, Belgium, Brazil, Canada, Denmark, England and Wales, Finland, France, Germany, Iceland, Ireland, Luxembourg, the Netherlands, New Zealand, Norway, Portugal, Scotland, South Africa, Spain, Sweden, the United States, Uruguay, and many states in Mexico. As the collection was going to press, Taiwan, Chile and Australia both took steps moving toward legalization.

CONTRIBUTORS

Myrl Beam is an Assistant Professor in the Department of Gender, Sexuality, and Women's Studies at Virginia Commonwealth University. His book, *Activism, Incorporated: Neoliberalism and the Non-Profitization of Queer Social Movements,* will be released in the fall of 2018 by the University of Minnesota Press. The book analyzes the expansion of the non-profit system in the U.S. since the mid-1960s and the impact that expansion has had on queer politics. He completed his PhD in American Studies at the University of Minnesota in 2014. Myrl's activist work centers on prison abolition, homelessness, and supporting the leadership of trans youth in movements for justice.

Hugo Bouvard is a political sociologist. An alumnus of the École Normale Supérieure in Paris and a former Lecturer in French at Duke University, he was Visiting Scholar at the Institute of French Studies (New York University) from 2015 to 2018, where he taught courses on gender, sexuality, and politics in contemporary France. He is currently completing doctoral work in Political Science at Paris-Dauphine University. His research focuses on the sexual norms of political life and looks in particular at LGBT elected officials in France and in the United States. He also recently co-published an article on voting indiscipline within the majority group in the French National Assembly (*Politix*, 117, 2017).

Jara M. Carrington is an academic and has previously worked with several immigrant rights-focused NGOs, including Human Rights Initiative of North Texas and Immigration Equality.

Claudia Cojocaru is a researcher focusing on sex work, trafficking in the sex industry and policing. She teaches at John Jay College of Criminal Justice in New York, and serves as an expert witness in criminal trafficking cases.

Courtenay W. Daum is an Associate Professor of Political Science at the Center for Women's Studies and Gender Research, Colorado State University. Daum's research focuses on the interactions among law and society, including LGBTQ politics, feminist legal theory, and organized interests' political mobilization and litigation strategies. Recent publications and research include "Marriage Equality: Assimilationist Victory or Pluralist, Defeat? What the Struggle for Marriage Equality Tells Us About the History and the Future of LGBTQ Politics," in *LGBTQ Politics: A Critical Reader*, eds. Susan Burgess, Marla Brettschneider and Cricket Keating (New York University Press, 2017), "Counterpublics and Intersectional Radical Resistance: Agitation as Transformation of the Dominant Discourse" (*New Political Science*, 2017), and a book manuscript on the limitations of rights-based litigation and reform strategies as mechanisms for advancing the interests of trans communities.

Joseph Nicholas DeFilippis is Assistant Professor of Social Work at Seattle University. He received his BA at Vassar College, a masters' degree in community organizing at the Hunter College School of Social Work, and a PhD in Social Work and Social Research from Portland State University. His teaching has focused on social welfare policy, social justice, public policy, family law, sexuality, political economy, and community organizing. In addition to his teaching, Joseph has over 15 years' practice in community-based work. He spent years doing volunteer work as a welfare-rights organizer, and then served for four years as the Director of SAGE/Queens, an organization for LGBT senior citizens. In 2003, Joseph became the founding director of Queers for Economic Justice, an organization working with low-income and homeless LGBT people, and led the organization for six years. He has published numerous articles on a range of issues, including LGBT communities, poverty, marriage politics, and feminist research. He is one of the primary authors of the infamous 2006 *Beyond Same-Sex Marriage* (which publicly critiqued the direction of the marriage equality movement), and one of the editors of *A New Queer Agenda* published in 2012 by the Barnard Center for Research on Women. Joseph was born and raised in New York City. He is the bi-racial son of two immigrants.

Gabriel Foster is the co-founder and Executive Director of the Trans Justice Funding Project. He is a black, queer, trans, "momma's boy" living and loving in New York. Prior to making his way to the Eastern Time Zone, he worked in Seattle, WA, with the Northwest Network of bisexual, trans, lesbian and gay survivors of abuse helping to create their youth programming. From age 15 to 26, he worked with the American Friends Service Committee's GLBTQ Youth Program. Before arriving in New York, he worked at SPARK Reproductive Justice Now with LGBTQ youth of color and allies in Atlanta, GA. He also worked for the Leeway Foundation, supporting women and trans people creating art and social change in Philadelphia, PA, and provided outreach for the Johnathan Lax Fund at the Bread and Roses foundation in Philadelphia, PA. Gabriel is also a former staff member of the Sylvia Rivera Law Project.

Jennicet Gutiérrez is a transgender activist and organizer from México. She is best known for shedding light on the plight of transgender women in immigrant detention centers through the organization Familia: Trans Queer Liberation Movement. She burst onto the national scene when she interrupted former President Obama in the summer of 2015 during his White House speech in honor of Pride month, calling attention to the struggles of trans immigrant women. She believes in the importance of uplifting and centering the voices of trans women of color in all racial justice work. Jennicet will continue to organize in order to end the deportation, incarceration, and criminalization of immigrants and all people of color. She currently resides in Los Angeles.

Jorge Gutierrez is an UndocuQueer activist born in Nayarit, Mexico, and was raised in Santa Ana, California. He is a graduate of the California State University, Fullerton, with a Bachelor's Degree in English. Currently, he is the National Coordinator and founder of Familia: TQLM. In addition, he has co-founded various organizations focused on social justice for the LGBTQ and immigrant communities: DeColores Queer Orange County, the California Immigrant Youth Justice Alliance (CIYJA), and was the founder of the Queer Undocumented Immigrant Project (QUIP).

Jamila Hammami is the founding Executive Director of the Queer Detainee Empowerment Project. They are a North African first generation Queer genderqueer American and have first-hand experience with the carceral system.

Caner Hazar, MA, is a doctoral student in the Department of Sociology at the University of Connecticut. His primary research interests are religion, social movements, sexuality and gender in Turkey. He explores them in a relational framework which considers culture, institutions, and history simultaneously.

Paulina Helm-Hernandez is a queer femme artist, trainer, political organizer, strategist and trouble-maker-at-large from Veracrúz, Mexico. This Chicana grew up in rural North Carolina, and is currently growing roots in Atlanta, GA. Paulina was the Co-Director of Southerners on New Ground (SONG) for 11 years, having joined the staff after coordinating the Southern regional youth activism program at the Highlander Research & Education Center for over four years. Paulina has a background in farm worker and immigrant/refugee rights organizing, cultural work, youth organizing, anti-violence work, and liberation work that centers people most affected by violence, poverty, war and racism. Paulina currently sits on the Board of Directors of the GA Latino Alliance for Human Rights Political Research Associates, the Vision and Strategies Council of Kindred Southern Healing Justice Collective, and is always exploring ways to deepen political unity with people willing to fight and organize for collective liberation.

Angela Jones is Associate Professor of Sociology at Farmingdale State College, State University of New York. Jones obtained her PhD from the New School for Social Research. Her research interests include: African American political thought and protest, gender, and sexuality. Her current research is on online sex work. Specifically, she is conducting a mixed method study of adult webcam performers and her book based on this research is forthcoming with NYU Press. Jones is the author of three books: *African American Civil Rights: Early Activism and the Niagara Movement* (Praeger, 2011), *The Modern African American Political Thought Reader: From David Walker to Barack Obama* (Routledge, 2012), and *A Critical Inquiry into Queer Utopias* (Palgrave, 2013). She is also the author of numerous scholarly articles, which have been published in peer-reviewed journals.

Siobhán McGuirk is an academic, co-founder of the LGBT Freedom and Asylum Network, and an activist with No Justice No Pride (DC), among other groups.

Robyn Ochs is an educator, speaker, award-winning activist, and editor of the *Bi Women Quarterly*, the 42-country anthology, *Getting Bi: Voices of Bisexuals Around the World* (Bisexual Resource Center, 2005) and the new anthology *RECOGNIZE: The Voices of Bisexual Men* (Bisexual Resource Center, 2014). Her writings have been published in numerous bi, women's studies, multicultural, and LGBT anthologies. Robyn has taught courses on LGBT history and politics in the United States, the politics of sexual orientation, and the experiences of those who transgress the binary categories of gay/straight, masculine/feminine, black/white and/or male/female. An advocate for the rights of people of all orientations and genders to live safely, openly and with full access and opportunity, Robyn's work focuses on increasing awareness and understanding of complex identities, and mobilizing people to be powerful allies for one another within and across identities and social movements. Robyn served for 12 years on the Board of Directors of MassEquality, Massachusetts' state-wide equality organization and for three years on the Massachusetts Commission on LGBTQ Youth.

Cara Page is a Black queer feminist cultural worker & organizer. She comes from a long ancestral legacy of organizers and cultural workers from the southeast to the northeast. For the past 20+ years she has worked within the queer and trans liberation movement, reproductive justice movement, the racial and economic justice movements and the National People's Movement Assembly. She continues to organize, create cultural and political spaces that honor our leaders, movements, communal legacies, and mobilize transformative spaces for the safety and well-being of our communities. Cara is the former Executive Director of the Audre Lorde Project. She is also co-founder and former Coordinator of the Kindred Collective, which is a southeastern network of healers, health practitioners and organizers seeking ways to respond to and intervene on state violence and generational trauma. She is the former National Director of the Committee on Women, Population & the Environment and a proud member of Southerners on New Ground, Project South, and INCITE! Women of Color Against Violence.

Raha Iranian Feminist Collective Mission Statement: We are an NYC-based collective that started with a group of Iranian and Iranian-American women in New York City. Raha is open to people of all genders committed to working as a collective combating patriarchy both in our work and in our process. We work to raise awareness about movements for justice in Iran and the U.S. through internal education, creative messaging, solidarity actions and public education. We seek to support the aspirations of the democratic movements in Iran whilst also opposing U.S. economic and military intervention. We also seek to counter misconceptions about Iran and what it means to be anti-imperialist. Understanding that patriarchy and militarism go hand-in-hand, we seek to challenge the different ways they operate in both the U.S. and Iran. We see this work as inextricably linked to a diverse range of grassroots movements for economic, racial, gender, and sexual justice with which we seek to build alliances. We believe that all genuine liberation comes from below.

Chriss V. Sneed is a Sociology PhD student at the University of Connecticut and the 2017–2018 Student Representative on Council of Sociologists for Women in Society. As a young scholar working at the intersections of race, gender, and sexuality, Chriss relies on queer of color critique and critical feminist analytics to examine inequality within our social world. Much of their recent work stems from the contradictions of identity formation, resistance against inequality, and the precarious negotiation of inclusion within social justice activism. Outside of research, Chriss is the founder and lead organizer of the interdisciplinary conference "Borderlands: A Critical Graduate Symposium" held each year at University of Connecticut. Additionally, Chriss has served as President of the Graduate Student Senate and a student representative for the University Senate's Executive Committee, Diversity Committee, and the Task Force on Free Speech and Civility while attending UConn. Beyond and within the academy, Chriss is committed in fostering everyday Afro-futures and liberation.

Steven William Thrasher is a Contributing Editor at BuzzFeed and is the 2012 National Lesbian & Gay Journalist Association's Journalist of the Year. Steven spent three years as a staff writer for the *Village Voice*, where he wrote long format features and investigative articles, including 20 cover stories. His writing has appeared in the *New York Times*, *Out*, *Rolling Stone*, the *Daily Beast*, the *Advocate*, and *Time Out New York*. As a radio reporter and producer, he regularly contributes to *Marketplace* and is a guest host for the *Michelangelo Signorile Show* on SiriusXM QutQ 108. In 2007, Steven spent a year traveling America recording oral history for the NPR StoryCorps project, and his radio work has been heard on *Morning Edition*, *All Things Considered* and *News and Notes*. Much of his work discusses the intersections of race, class, sexual identity, religion and politics. Steven was trained in writing and film-making at NYU's Tisch School of the Arts, where he was a University Scholar and received his BFA. Steven is a Sloan Foundation Science Writing Fellow and a 2010 recipient of the Anti-Violence Project's Courage Award. That year, he also penned the viral internet hit "White America Has Lost Its Mind," which was read by over a million people and was translated into Polish. In 2011, he won the James Aronson Award for Social Justice Journalism from Hunter College for his story "Ronnie's Kids," as well as a Feature Writing Award from the Association of Alternative Newsweeklies for his profile of "Bad Lieutenant" Dan Choi.

Gracia Trujillo is Associate Professor of Sociology at the University of Castille-La Mancha, and queer and feminist activist based in Madrid. She has been involved in research projects and has published widely on social movements, feminist and LGTBI queer theories and political practices, and gender and sexuality issues with an intersectional perspective, including queer pedagogies and reproduction and kinship. Some of her publications are *Identities and Collective Action* (Juan March Institute Press, 2007), *Desire and Resistance. Thirty years of Lesbian Mobilization in Spain (1977–2007)* (Egales, 2009), and she has participated in collective works such as *A Universal Discrimination. Homosexuality in Francoism and in the Transition to Democracy* (Egales, 2008); *Political Bodies and Agency. Feminist Analysis on Body, Work and Colonial issues* (University of Granada Press, 2011); *Lesbian and Queer Feminisms. Visibility, Politics and Representation* (Plaza y Valdés, 2013); *Hispanic (LGT) Masculinities in Transition* (Peter Lang Publishing Group, 2014); and *Queering Narratives of Modernity* (Peter Lang Publishing Group, 2016), among others.

Urvashi Vaid is an attorney and organizer whose leadership in the lesbian, gay, bisexual and transgender (LGBT), and social justice movements spans legal, advocacy, philanthropic, and grassroots organizations. Vaid is CEO of The Vaid Group LLC, a social innovation firm that works with global and domestic organizations to advance equity, justice and inclusion. From 2011 to 2015, Vaid was Senior Fellow and Director of the Engaging Tradition Project at Columbia Law School's Center for Gender and Sexuality Law. Prior to joining Columbia, Vaid was Senior Fellow at the City University of New York Graduate Center. From 2005 to 2010, Vaid was Executive Director of the Arcus Foundation. She served as Deputy Director of the Governance and Civil Society Unit of the Ford Foundation from 2001 to 2005. Over a ten-year period, Vaid worked at the National Gay and Lesbian Task Force as its Executive Director and Director of its think tank, the Policy Institute. She was staff attorney at the National Prison Project of the American Civil Liberties Union. Vaid is the author of *Irresistible Revolution: Confronting Race, Class and the Assumptions of LGBT Politics* (Magnus Books, 2012); and *Virtual Equality: The Mainstreaming of Lesbian and Gay Liberation* (Anchor Books, 1996). She co-edited an anthology titled *Creating Change: Public Policy, Sexuality and Civil Rights* (St. Martin's Press, 2000). She is co-author of *A Roadmap for Change: Federal Policy Recommendations Addressing the Criminalization of LGBT people and People living with HIV* (Center for Gender and Sexuality Law at Columbia Law

School, 2014). She is founder and Board member of LPAC, the lesbian SuperPAC; a co-founder of *the Creating Change Conference*; Board member of the Planned Parenthood Action Fund, and a former Board member of the Gill Foundation. Vaid is a graduate of Northeastern University School of Law and Vassar College.

Michael W. Yarbrough is an interdisciplinary social scientist whose work examines the intersection of law, culture, and family. He is especially interested in the ways people define their relationships to each other, and how these definitions both reflect and shape struggles for power. His current book manuscript pursues these questions through comparative ethnographic research among two groups recently incorporated into South African marriage law: people living in communities that observe African customary law; and people who identify as lesbian, gay, bisexual, and/or transgender. His research has been published in *Social Politics*, *Law & Social Inquiry*, *Sexualities*, and the *Yale Journal of Law & Feminism* and has received a Fulbright-Hays Fellowship and other awards. Yarbrough is currently an Assistant Professor of Law and Society in the Political Science Department of John Jay College of Criminal Justice (CUNY), where he received a Distinguished Teaching Award in 2015. He also serves as a Research Associate in the Department of Sociology, Faculty of Humanities, at the University of Johannesburg, and he is a former member of the Board of Directors of CLAGS: The Center for LGBTQ Studies.

Hari Ziyad is an artist and writer. They received their BFA from New York University, where they concentrated on Film and Television and Psychology. Their work is informed by their passion for storytelling and wrestling with identity as a Black, non-binary child of Muslim and Hindu parents while growing up in Cleveland. Hari primarily creates art engaging with identity, race, gender and sexuality, ally politics, and the arts. Their work has been featured on *Gawker, Out, Ebony, Mic, The Guardian, Colorlines, Paste Magazine, Black Girl Dangerous, The Feminist Wire,* and in the peer-reviewed journal *Critical Ethnic Studies* (upcoming 2017). They are also Deputy Editor for Black Youth Project, an Assistant Editor for *Vinyl Poetry & Prose*, and writer for *AFROPUNK*.

Marzena Zukowska works at the National Domestic Workers' Alliance, is a member of the Radical Communicators Network, and is a proud formerly undocumented queer woman.

INTRODUCTION

Joseph Nicholas DeFilippis

On March 10, 2010, the Centers for Disease Control and Prevention (CDC) released a report that found that gay men were 44 times more likely to have HIV than anyone else in the United States (Gay Men's Health Crisis, 2010). Shortly thereafter, staff from GLAAD (the Gay and Lesbian Alliance Against Defamation) met with representatives from several prominent AIDS organizations to discuss this news. Much to the surprise of these AIDS activists, GLAAD pressured their organizations to avoid any press or public work about the new CDC data, indicating that they saw it as a negative depiction of gay men that undermined the narrative they were trying to produce about same-sex marriage. According to one veteran African-American HIV activist who described this meeting to me in an interview, this new data "fucked with GLAAD's messaging about the gay community being 'just like everyone else so we deserve these marriage rights'." Even though AIDS was still killing gay men, particularly gay men of color, the leaders of one of the most well-known and well-funded LGBTQ organizations decided that securing marriage rights was more important than combating a life-threatening medical epidemic. This incident illustrates much of what transpired in mainstream LGBTQ activism in the United States in the twenty-first century. The organizations that had the resources to set the agenda prioritized the pursuit of same-sex marriage above all of the other issues (no matter how urgent) that were impacting our communities.

A history of tensions about marriage

For most of the twenty-first century, LGBTQ funders, national LGBTQ organizations, and the state-wide equality groups (which collectively I refer to here as the mainstream gay rights movement) made the legalization of same-sex marriage the number one priority on their "gay agenda." On June 26, 2015, their work came to fruition with the U.S. Supreme Court ruling in *Obergefell v. Hodges* that same-sex couples have the right to marry. Not all LGBTQ activists, however, celebrated this victory. In the preceding two decades, numerous activists and scholars loudly critiqued the mainstream gay rights movement's prioritization of same-sex marriage rights and pursuit of legal equality, rather than broader social justice. These critiques are well-documented, and the anthology *Against Equality: Queer Critiques of Gay Marriage* (Conrad, 2010) offers a good representation of them. I provide only a brief overview in order to set the context for this book and to provide suggested readings for those new to this material.

Resistance to the gay marriage agenda came from multiple fronts. Some critics argued that numerous family formations, created outside of romantic couplings, would remain unprotected by marriage (see works by Terry Boggis, Nancy Polikoff, Queers for Economic Justice, and *Queer Families and Relationships After Marriage Equality*, Routledge 2018). Others voiced concern that the gay marriage agenda excluded and further stigmatized queer people who do not comply with dominant notions of normality and sexual monogamy (see Mattilda Bernstein Sycamore and Michael Warner). Other critics claimed that the conservative rhetoric of gay marriage demeaned unmarried people, single mothers, and Black families, and served to control them (see Lisa Duggan, Kenyon Farrow, Priya Kandaswamy, and Tamara Nopper). Another line of critique claimed that marriage is a conservative tool of neoliberalism (placing caregiving work on the family rather than on the government), and that such narrow pursuits of formal equality (rather than broader structural change) did nothing to challenge oppressive structures (see Lisa Duggan, Angela P. Harris, Darren Lenard Hutchinson, and Yasmin Nair). Finally, many activists and scholars worried about the resources and energy that were diverted away from other critical issues facing LGBTQ communities and were instead directed toward the pursuit of marriage (see *The Unfinished Queer Agenda After Marriage Equality*, Routledge 2018).

Same-sex marriage is now legal, and it is time to analyze the movement and determine the continued relevance of the above critiques. This specific book uses some of those critiques of "marriage equality" as a starting point to examine the state of LGBTQ activism now that the campaigns for same-sex marriage are over. In the rest of this introduction, I would like to offer some context about the current state of LGBTQ activism, and issues to consider about its future, before providing an overview of the contents of this book.

How marriage become the priority

Wealthy funders have played a huge role in directing the work of LGBTQ activism in the United States, and in recent decades that has meant steering the work towards a focus on marriage rather than on other issues that were of greater importance to people of color, transgender people, and low-income people. For the most part, "gay issues" have been determined by those people with the most resources and for whom the inability to get married was the only real form of discrimination they faced. There are some important reasons for this.

LGBTQ activism of the past several decades has been shaped by a larger trend found among all social movements – the rise of the 501(c)3 non-profit structure as the vehicle through which activism is centered. The gay rights movement began as completely grassroots, but is now overwhelmingly dominated by 501(c)3 corporations. Many activists and scholars have written about the limits of social movement work when it is based in nonprofits (e.g., INCITE's "The revolution will not be funded").[1] In particular, critics claim that the non-profit structure limits the scope of activists' work (i.e., their political agenda), and it subjects social movements to various forms of state control. In addition, observers and participants alike have voiced tremendous concern about how the structure of non-profits restricts access to social change work, requiring college-educated, middle-class leadership, while also allowing these leaders to remain unaccountable to the communities which they purport to represent. Finally, community members express alarm over LGBTQ organizations being in bed with corporations, foundations, and wealthy donors, contending that corporate sponsorships are antithetical to progressive activism.

One of the primary methods of sustaining these LGBTQ 501(c)3 organizations in the U.S. is the philanthropic support that has been provided to the movement, which continues to grow each year. In the 40 years between 1970 and 2010, hundreds of foundations invested more than $771 million towards LGBTQ issues, 86 percent of which ($663 million) were awarded from 2000 to 2010 (Funders for LGBTQ Issues, 2012). This is an astonishing increase in a very short time. In 2015, $160.7 million was given by foundations to LGBTQ organizations, the largest amount ever in one year (Funders for LGBTQ Issues, 2017). However, for LGBTQ people of color (POC), funding is more difficult. They receive only 14 percent of the overall annual philanthropic support that goes to LGBTQ issues (Funders for LGBTQ Issues, 2017). In addition, much of that money goes to "outreach" efforts, which are generally attempts to bring people of color into white-dominated organizations, rather than funding POC organizations that determine their own agendas. Nevertheless, LGBTQ non-profits continue to grow. Today, there are more than 500 organizations across the country working on LGBTQ issues, with a combined annual budget of about $530 million, and with thousands of employees (Movement Advancement Project, 2016).

A movement so dependent upon philanthropic support ends up beholden to funders, and those funders end up dictating the direction of the movement. One significant example worth particular consideration is the Civil Marriage Collaborative (CMC). Created in 2004, the CMC is a consortium of about a dozen foundations working together (and housed by the Proteus Fund) to prioritize and guide marriage equality campaigns across the country. Individually and collectively, from 2004 to 2015 the funders in the CMC invested $153 million in marriage equality work (Foreman, 2015). When they began, they held an initial consultation with the leaders from the largest gay rights organizations. However, grassroots organizations and activists were excluded, and even the large groups that were consulted held less power than their major funders. This small group of funders directed the work of the movement for over a decade. In their own words, they worked to make sure that the movement utilized "a shared strategy" in pursuit of same-sex marriage state-by-state and then nationwide (Foreman, 2015). According to Andrew Lane of the Johnson Family Foundation, "the CMC created efficiency, focus, clarity and strategic alignment in the funding" (Lewis, 2015, p. 16). When powerful funders agree that there should be a "shared strategy" and "strategic alignment" on an issue, the result is often that groups that approach the subject from a different perspective go unfunded. Indeed, the CMC's Request for Proposal (RFP) was "by invitation only," so activist organizations could not even submit funding proposals to present their ideas. Instead, the small group of people running the CMC hand-picked the organizations that would lead the activism on their pre-determined issue and implement the strategies that the funders had identified.

In the course of my own research, I have interviewed queer activists from across the United States. Many of them conveyed that although they knew where the funding was going and suspected that funders were working together to prioritize marriage, they were previously in the dark about how and where these decisions were being made. In fact, to my knowledge, it was not until after the Supreme Court verdict in *Obergefell*, that the Collaborative actually went public. In 2015, when the Proteus Fund wrote about the work of the CMC, it described it as having played "a critical, and *largely unknown*, role" in the legalization of same-sex marriage (Lewis, 2015, p. 1, emphasis added).

One of the organizations that benefited most from the CMC's largesse was Freedom to Marry, whose sole purpose was the pursuit of legalized same-sex marriage. The CMC's member foundations provided Freedom to Marry with its initial funding, and then quickly decided to expand its work. Within a very short period of time, and largely with CMC support, Freedom to Marry went from a five-person to a 40-person organization and saw its annual budget grow from about $3 million to more than $12 million (Lewis, 2015). The budget and size of Freedom to Marry dwarfed those of well-respected, long-time queer organizations such as The Audre Lorde Project, Southerners on New Ground, and the Sylvia Rivera Law Project. [2] These grassroots groups were working on a completely different set of issues (focused on racial and economic justice), and doing so with budgets that, even when combined, were smaller than Freedom to Marry's alone.

This imbalance of organizational power and resources is the result of a small group of funders meeting in secret to determine the priorities, strategies, and leadership of the LGBTQ movement. As the Audre Lorde Project's Cara Page said to me in one interview, these foundations were building a "funding empire" that held an astonishing amount of control over the movement's direction and strategies. If it sounds as if I have been trying to draw a picture of a handful of powerful elites perniciously meeting in secret and determining the direction of entire communities based on their own personal values and preferences, well, that is because I am.

The power of race and class

It is worth noting that the people making these secret decisions and leading the U.S. movement are disproportionately white. For example, of the 15 groups that were part of the powerful Civil Marriage Consortium, 86 percent of their leaders were white. The same was true of the leaders of the organizations in the mainstream gay rights movement during the two decades of work for same-sex marriage. In a 2011 survey of the 40 largest national LGBTQ advocacy organizations, only two were led by people of color and both of those were POC-specific organizations (Vaid, 2012), and as I write this six years later, 75–80 percent of the leaders of 50 of the largest LGBTQ/AIDS organizations are white.

These white, middle-class funders and leaders prioritized the issues that they cared about over the issues that were most important to other queer people. LGBTQ people who are people of color, low income, senior citizens, and/or transgender have repeatedly identified concerns that are very different from those expressed by the mainstream gay rights movement. In numerous surveys, they have prioritized housing and homelessness, violence and discrimination, legal services, HIV/AIDS, health care and welfare benefits, job access and job training, and access to education (DeFilippis, 2016). Nevertheless, mainstream gay rights organizations have done little work on racial and economic justice issues. Numerous activists have claimed that these issues are ignored because the leaders do not reflect the diversity of the communities they claim to represent, and thus do not understand their needs.

The result has been that many LGBTQ communities feel unrepresented by the national organizations and state-wide equality groups, voicing frequent criticism of the "gay agenda." In addition to expressing frustration about the emphasis on gay marriage over racial and economic justice issues, grassroots activists have also debated movement leaders about hate crime legislation, access to the military, employment discrimination, and adoption. Each of these issues, also prioritized by the mainstream gay rights movement, has been subject to critique from progressive queer activists through racial and economic justice lenses.

Empty promises

Many U.S. same-sex marriage activists rebuked their critics, insisting that it was not a zero-sum game; they argued that it was possible to work on other issues too, while also working towards same-sex marriage rights. The reality, however, is that this did not happen. Funding did not get equally directed towards racial or economic justice issues.

Other promises by the same-sex marriage leaders proved equally hollow. One common critique of the same-sex marriage movement was that it failed to challenge marriage as the vehicle through which rights and protections are offered in the first place. Consequently, marriage equality still leaves the majority of U.S. households (including LGBTQ families) that are not centered around married couples unpro-tected (U.S. Census, 2016). Critics, including the authors of a 2006 statement signed by hundreds of LGBTQ leaders and scholars, called "Beyond Marriage" (reprinted in *Queer Families and Relationships After Marriage Equality*, Routledge 2018), advocated for multiple forms of legal recognition to protect all varieties of family formations, rather than merely extending marriage privileges to same-sex couples. Marriage activists repeatedly claimed that they agreed with this argument, and said they did not see marriage campaigns as precluding those other efforts to protect other families. For example, Freedom to Marry's Evan Wolfson, the most prominent leader of the same-sex marriage movement, told numerous newspapers that he agreed with the 2006 Beyond Marriage statement. Yet, as numerous states began to pass gay marriage, local municipalities and businesses subsequently revoked other forms of family recognition (i.e., domestic partnerships). This happened because marriage activists had denigrated them as "second-class marriages" and they falsely claimed they were not needed if marriage was available. Neither Wolfson's group nor other marriage organizations fought to retain these other forms of family recognition. In fact, when marriage victories happened on a state-by-state level, these groups discontinued their work, rather than expanding it to focus on other types of queer families. For instance, Connecticut's Love Makes a Family closed in 2009 after defeating an anti-gay marriage ballot initiative. When marriage equality passed nationally in 2015, major organizations declared their work done and shut down. These organizations included Marriage Equality U.S.A., New York's Empire State Pride Agenda, the Vermont Freedom to Marry Task Force, and, yes, Freedom to Marry.

The focus on marriage did more than direct financial resources and energy toward the issue of greatest concern to its white leaders and funders. It also dominated the national discourse on LGBTQ issues and limited the public imagination. The mainstream gay rights movement was so persuasive in its framing that, as a result, all other forms of family recognition were derided as "second-class status," despite being preferred by thousands of families. Further issues, such as poverty, immigration, or police violence, became "other issues" that were not considered "gay issues." This created a narrative for heterosexual society, including for straight social justice activists, that marriage was all that mattered to our movement, thus limiting the invitations for collaboration and coalition with other movements. The marriage work dominated the public discourse and shaped the national conversation.

Although some liberals agreed that same-sex marriage was insufficient, they believed it was a step in the right direction, offering some gains to certain people, and hurting no one. However, others strongly disagreed with this assessment. In the words of one activist:

> (In actuality) gay marriage efforts over the last decade actively discouraged strategies that aspired to broader change, diverted millions of dollars and immeasurable other resources away from the neediest LGBT communities, rendered unintelligible a host of other social concerns, and helped build increasingly narrow cultural and legal parameters of family, intimacy, and

human worth. The problem isn't that gay marriage has passively ignored "other issues," it's that it helped shape them into their present incarnations and contributed to the hardiness of much social inequality today.

A. J. Lewis, personal communication, March 26, 2013

This shaping of the public imagination was intentional, as evidenced by GLAAD's response to the AIDS data that they thought undermined their marriage work. The chapters in this book authored by Myrl Beam and Chriss Sneed both examine the larger cultural impact of the rhetoric deliberately deployed by marriage equality organizations.

Global activism

During the two decades in which the U.S. mainstream movement was focused on same-sex marriage, activists in other countries pursued similar goals. In 2001, the Netherlands became the first country to legalize same-sex marriage, and since then another 20 countries have done the same. In addition, numerous countries have implemented other forms of legal protection for LGBTQ people. However, in what scholars and activists have termed "pink-washing," some governments herald their gay rights laws in order to claim they are "gay-friendly" and progressive, effectively serving as distractions from their other civil rights infractions and colonialism (Puar, 2007).

There are, however, also many countries where LGBTQ activists are still fighting for basic rights. Same-sex sexual behavior is illegal in 75 countries, including some where they are punishable by death. Activists across the globe are fighting for their physical safety, legal rights, the ability to create families, and the end of government harassment. For example, in the summer of 2017, 141 men were arrested in a gay sauna in Jakarta, the capital of Indonesia, and charged with violating "pornography" laws.

Of particular relevance to this volume is another issue, which OutRight Action International[3] describes as "crackdowns on activism." Numerous governments regularly shut down LGBTQ organizations, confiscate and censor materials, and ban public demonstrations, including Pride marches and other attempts to organize LGBTQ communities (OutRight Action International, n/d). In such a context, LGBTQ activism can be difficult and dangerous.

At the same time, the U.S. and other governments use those anti-LGBTQ policies as justification for imperialism. "Protecting the gays" has become a surprising rationalization for military intervention, often by governments, such as ours, that ignore the lack of real equality or justice in their own countries (Puar, 2007). Whether or not a country has legalized same-sex marriage has become a gauge by which we measure its progressiveness. By weaponizing marriage in this way, U.S. imperialism becomes disguised as fighting for equality. It also shapes the global stage for queer activism, as LGBTQ activists in some countries must not only fight homophobic policies but also shoulder the blame for military aggression from abroad.

In addition, governments and far-right activists also use similar justifications to regulate immigration, particularly against Muslim migrants, who they allege are more homophobic than the citizens of Western nations (Puar, 2007). Indeed, this same "homonational" logic has played out domestically in the U.S. in a variety of ways. For example, some conservative gay and lesbian Americans, empowered by recent legal victories (e.g., same-sex marriage, the end of "Don't Ask, Don't Tell") that grant them a sense of full citizenship, have come out to support reactionary candidates such as Trump or join racist organizations such as Gays Against Islam.

What happens next?

In the U.S., we are at a significant moment for the mainstream gay rights movement, because not only has it succeeded in legalizing same-sex marriage, but in recent years it has also accomplished two of its other main priorities: LGBTQ inclusion in federal hate crimes legislation, and ending the military's "Don't Ask, Don't Tell" policy. The mainstream movement has little left on the agenda which has dominated its work for two decades. This begs the question: What will these organizations focus on now?

Although these successes resulted in several major organizations shutting down because "their work was done," other large LGBTQ organizations in the U.S. are seeking to broaden their work and set new priorities. They continue to receive financial support for this new work. For example, the Human Rights Campaign has begun working on international issues, much to the concern of activists across the globe who worry about them ignoring the priorities and strategies of local activists (Feder, 2013). And in 2015, foundation support to U.S. LGBTQ groups increased for "new" issues: work with transgender communities (increased by 40 percent over the previous year), and reform of the criminal legal system (increased by 105 percent) (Funders for LGBTQ Issues, 2017).

However, many queer grassroots organizations have already been engaged in this work for years. As I explain in Chapter 4 of this book, "queer liberation" groups across the country, led by queer people of color, transgender people, immigrants, and low-income people, have already been doing multi-issue, intersectional work, addressing issues of racial and economic justice. Now that the equality-focused mainstream organizations are looking for a new agenda, will they support the work of these grassroots queer liberation organizations? Unfortunately, many activists have reported to me that they are already seeing, instead, the co-optation of their work and the hijacking of their resources. The Audre Lorde Project's Cara Page discusses this in her interview in this volume. She and other activists fear that the white wealthy funders and leaders of the mainstream gay rights movement will take over work that queer people of color have been doing for years.

Lisa Weiner-Mahfuz, an activist with over 20 years' experience organizing around LGBTQ issues, discussed with me how the mainstream equality movement and funders are in conversation right now about what happens beyond marriage, as they begin work on issues that have not been historically considered queer issues.

She explained how, rather than respecting the work the queer liberation groups have been doing on these "other" issues for decades, the mainstream organizations and funders are seeking to shut them down and take the work for themselves. In her words:

> The game that is at play is: "If we squash them, and it's lights out in this part of the queer justice liberation movement, if we don't have to compete with them, then that work becomes ours, we get to own it as a piece of capital. And nobody's going to call us on it because they're not going to exist long enough to say: 'wait a second, that's our work, that's our legacy'." ... So I actually think that they think they need our work. But they don't think they need us to do it. That is really the end game. "We can do it better. We can bring it to scale. And these justice and liberation groups, they are too process-oriented, and can't bring it to scale, and as a result we need to take over that work because we can do it better." I really think that's the ballgame we're in. And I think it's a really serious ball game.

In my interviews with them, many other activists of color voiced similar concerns about white organizations taking away their resources and co-opting their work.

The question of what the mainstream gay rights movement does next, and how other queer organizations navigate this new landscape, is an important one for anyone concerned with social movements. And it is one of the central questions of this book.

Overview of the book

Drawing from critical and intersectional perspectives, *Queer Activism After Marriage* explores the questions and issues facing the next chapter of LGBTQ activism and social movement work, while also examining the recent years of activism that brought us to this new chapter. This book explores the high-profile work of national and state-wide equality organizations, taking a critical look at their work, with a specific focus on the campaigns for marriage equality. In addition, it also examines other forms of queer activism that have existed for years in the shadow of the marriage equality movement, as well as new social movements that have developed more recently. It also explores LGBTQ activism taking place in other countries, highlighting important examples in European and Muslim countries.

As described in the Preface, this book is part of a three-volume collection, inspired by the 2016 *After Marriage* conference. This volume provides an overview of LGBTQ activism through a variety of pieces accessible to readers with different interests and learning styles. The book is designed for multiple audiences: scholars, activists, and students. Each chapter begins with a brief introduction, helping orient students and others who may be new to the study of social movements and/or LGBTQ politics. Just as the three books are designed to be read individually or collectively, the same is true of the chapters in this book; each chapter can stand alone, but they also work together to paint a fuller picture of the state of LGBTQ activism. *Queer Activism After Marriage* is divided into three parts, each of which examines different aspects of LGBTQ activism and social movement organizations.

The first part, titled "Examining the mainstream LGBT movement," concentrates on the types of national and state-wide equality organizations that have led the fight for marriage equality in the United States. The chapters look both backwards and forward. They reflect on the marriage campaigns, and their impacts on LGBTQ activism broadly. They also wrestle with the future of these organizations, examining their infrastructures and agendas as they move forward in a new post-marriage U.S.A. The first chapter, "LGBTQ politics after marriage" is a transcript of the opening plenary at the *After Marriage* conference. Four seasoned activists (Gabriel Foster, Paulina Helm-Hernandez, Robyn Ochs, and Urvashi Vaid) and two prominent journalists (Steven William Thrasher and Hari Ziyad) discuss the state of LGBTQ activism, looking at the strengths and limitations of its agenda, strategies and structures. The next two chapters, by Chriss Sneed and Myrl Beam, focus on specific case studies, looking at strategies (framing, language, etc.) of different LGBTQ activist campaigns. They examine how those strategies preclude identities and goals that do not match palatable, dominant, mainstream ideals and identities.

The second part, "New social movements," presents five chapters focused on new forms of activism emerging in recent years. Specifically, these chapters examine grassroots LGBTQ groups led by queer people of color, immigrants, low-income people, and/or transgender activists. The various contributors examine how their agendas, tactics, and constituents are markedly different from those of the equality-based organizations that made marriage the primary issue. The section begins with my own "A new queer liberation movement," which argues that these grassroots groups actually compose a social movement of their own, with constituents, priorities, values, and tactics that are distinct from those of the dominant mainstream gay rights movement. Two such organizations are then profiled in the following two chapters, which are transcripts of interviews with activists, Cara Page from the Audre Lorde Project, and Jennicet Gutierrez and Jorge Gutierrez from Familia: Trans Queer Liberation Movement. These interviews with leaders of two radical grassroots organizations describe the work that those important groups are doing, and how that work is different from, and sometimes in tension with, the mainstream gay rights movement. Finally, the last two chapters in this section examine LGBTQ activism on two different issues: Courtenay W. Daum examines the state of transgender rights, while Siobhán McGuirk, Jara M. Carrington, Claudia Cojocaru, Jamila Hammami, and Marzena Zukowska focus on immigration. Although focused on different issues, both chapters share a critical lens as they appraise that work and offer prescriptions for how activism on those issues can and should be different moving forward. Daum's analysis of the mainstream organizations leads her to recommend that trans activists might be better off not working with them, and focusing instead on partnerships with grassroots organizations that use intersectional and non-homonormative frameworks. McGuirk, et al. similarly call for a more critical, intersectional vision of queer migration politics and recommend centering voices excluded from mainstream narratives and campaigns.

The third and final part of this book focuses on "Transnational perspectives," examining global LGBTQ activism in examples drawn from France, Iran, Spain, and Turkey. Caner Hazar's piece focusing on Turkey and the Raha Iranian Feminist Collective's presentation on Iran both provide important information about LGBTQ work in those countries, while also demonstrating the importance of not imposing Western values and assumptions on other cultures. Hugo Bouvard's chapter about France examines the impact of marriage campaigns there, exploring the social and political costs and benefits of these efforts. Finally, Gracia Trujillo reflects on working with a feminist LGBTQ group within an anti-austerity social movement in Spain and explores the tensions of organizing around identity within a movement focused on economic redistribution. Each of these four chapters generates important knowledge, in its own right, about different approaches to LGBTQ activism in these countries, while also offering implicit or explicit lessons for U.S.-based activists and movements.

Together, the three parts in this volume will appeal to a wide range of audiences interested in the future of LGBTQ activism. They offer multiple perspectives for understanding how social movements are emerging and changing after marriage. Obviously, the contributors share a concern about what happens to LGBTQ activism now that same-sex marriage is legal in the United States. However, in addressing that central question, other related but distinct questions emerge in these chapters. These include:

- How is leadership determined, and who speaks for a social movement?
- Do the benefits of working in a non-profit structure outweigh the limitations imposed by 501(c)3 status?
- What lessons can LGBTQ activists learn from work taking place in other countries, with different histories and contexts?
- How has a focus on legal equality limited the political imagination of activists? And related to this, who gets excluded when the focus is on legal equality?
- What are the tensions between activism that pursues incremental reform and activism seeking broad transformation? Can both forms of activism be used as compatible strategies, or are they inherently contradictory?
- When using an intersectional analysis that results in a far-reaching agenda, can a social movement work on multiple issues at the same time? Can identity-based organizations work on issues of economic redistribution, or are critics correct when they claim that identity-based organizing focuses solely on issues of access and recognition?
- What does the existence of a more radical queer liberation movement mean for the future of LGBTQ activism? How can radical queer organizing be effective during the Trump administration?
- Having achieved most of their stated goals, should the equality organizations expand their agenda to work on issues that have been ignored thus far, or

should they close up shop and allow their resources to go elsewhere? Will those resources actually go elsewhere, or will they now just remain in the bank accounts of wealthy donors who only cared about marriage?

- What happens when the equality organizations, looking for something to work on post-marriage, begin to co-opt the work already being done by POC and trans groups?

These are important but difficult questions, and the contributors to this volume engage with them in thoughtful and surprising ways. I invite you to consider these questions as you read this book, and hope that they serve as a catalyst for thinking more broadly and ambitiously about the future and potential of LGBTQ activism.

Notes

1   INCITE! is a nation-wide network of radical feminists of color. For more information about their work, see www.incite-national.org.
2   For more information about these important grassroots organizations, see: the Audre Lorde Project: https://alp.org; Southerners on New Ground: http://southernersonnewground.org; and the Sylvia Rivera Law Project: https://srlp.org.
3   For more information about OutRight Action International, visit: www.outrightinternational.org.

References

Conrad, R. (Ed.). (2010). *Against Equality: Queer Critiques of Gay Marriage*. Chicago, IL: Against Equality Pub. Collective.

DeFilippis, J. N. (2016). "What about the rest of us?" An overview of LGBT poverty issues and a call to action. *Journal of Progressive Human Services*, 27(3):143–174, DOI: 10.1080/10428232.2016.1198673.

Feder, J. L. (2013). Human rights campaign's move into international work puts global LGBT advocates on edge. *Buzzfeed*. Retrieved from www.buzzfeed.com/lesterfeder/human-rights-campaigns-move-into-international-work-puts-glo?utm_term=.lijg5kZD4#.in4daMqnj.

Foreman, M. (2015). Winning marriage equality: How the marriage equality movement won the hearts and minds of the American public. *Washington Monthly*. Retrieved from https://philanthropy.washingtonmonthly.com/portfolio_page/winning-marriage-equality/.

Funders for LGBTQ Issues. (2012). Forty Years of LGBTQ Philanthropy: 1970–2010. Retrieved from www.lgbtfunders.org/resources/pub.cfm?pubID=57.

Funders for LGBTQ Issues. (2017). 2015 Tracking Report: LGBTQ Grantmaking by U.S. Foundations. Retrieved from www.lgbtfunders.org/wp-content/uploads/2017/05/2015_Tracking_Report.pdf.

Gay Men's Health Crisis. (2010). Gay Men 44 Times More Likely to Get HIV. Retrieved from www.gmhc.org/news-and-events/press-releases/gay-men-44-times-more-likely-to-get-hiv.

Jones, A., DeFilippis, J.N., & Yarbrough, M. (Eds.) (2018). *The Unfinished Queer Agenda After Marriage Equality*. Oxford: Routledge.

Lewis, D. (2015). Hearts and minds: The untold story of how philanthropy and the civil marriage collaborative helped America embrace marriage equality. *The Proteus Fund*. Retrieved from www.proteusfund.org/sites/default/files/upload/inline/29/files/CMC% 20Case%20Study%20FIN3_pages.pdf.

Movement Advancement Project. (2016). 2016 National LGBT Movement Report: A financial overview of leading advocacy organizations in the LGBT movement. Retrieved from www.lgbtmap.org/file/2016-national-lgbt-movement-report.pdf.

OutRight Action International. (n/d). The Issues We Face Today. Retrieved from www. outrightinternational.org/issues.

Puar, J. K. (2007). *Terrorist Assemblages: Homonationalism in Queer Times*. Durham, NC: Duke University Press.

U.S. Census. (2016). America's Families and Living Arrangements: 2016. Retrieved from www.census.gov/data/tables/2016/demo/families/cps-2016.html.

Vaid, U. (2012). *Irresistible Revolution: Confronting Race, Class and the Assumptions of Lesbian, Gay, Bisexual, and Transgender Politics*. New York: Magnus Books.

Yarbrough, M., Jones, A., and DeFilippis, J. N. (Eds.) (2018). *Queer Families and Relationships After Marriage Equality*. Oxford: Routledge.

PART I

Examining the mainstream LGBT movement

1

LGBTQ POLITICS AFTER MARRIAGE

A panel discussion with Gabriel Foster,
Paulina Helm-Hernandez, Robyn Ochs,
Steven William Thrasher, Urvashi Vaid,
and Hari Ziyad

Edited by Joseph Nicholas DeFilippis

Editors' introduction:

Marriage dominated the agenda of the mainstream LGBTQ movement for over a decade. What was the impact of the marriage campaigns on broader LGBTQ activism? And now that same-sex marriage has been legalized, what is next for the movement?

This chapter presents a transcript of excerpts from the 2016 After Marriage conference's opening plenary, a roundtable conversation where a group of seasoned LGBTQ activists attempt to answer those questions. The participants were Gabriel Foster (Director of the Trans Justice Funding Project), Paulina Helm-Hernandez (Co-Executive Director of Southerners on New Ground), Robyn Ochs (bisexual activist and educator), Urvashi Vaid (long-time LGBTQ movement leader), Hari Ziyad (writer), and moderator Steven William Thrasher (journalist).

Their discussion focused on identifying key issues facing LGBTQ activists after marriage, including immigration, poverty, incarceration, health care, and violence. In addition, the panel focused on larger political challenges facing queer liberation organizations and activists, such as fundraising, the limitations and strengths of identity politics, the importance of race, the challenges and potential of the non-profit structure, recruitment in the south, coalition-building, multi-racial leadership, and challenging liberal political frameworks in favor of a politics that actually challenge the state.

Readers are encouraged to consider these important issues in LGBTQ activism, and to contemplate what they mean about the future of a post-marriage equality LGBTQ social movement. What issues remain unaddressed by LGBTQ organizations? What should the agenda of the movement be? Who should decide that? How should organizations be structured?

STEVEN WILLIAM THRASHER: Thank you. Good morning everyone! Homosexuals, bisexuals, queers, friends, and even deviant straight people—we welcome you too. I'm really honored to be here. I've seen how much work Angela Jones and

Michael Yarbrough have put into planning this day, and I look at this panel and think of all the panels I have been on that did not look like this. I really appreciate the organizers for finding such a really rich, fantastic group of people to speak from different kinds of experiences about LGBTQ politics. So, we're just going to start off with each panelist talking very briefly about our work, and where we are, and then we're going to talk to each other and really make it an engaged conversation.

I want to start us off by asking: Where are LGBTQ politics right now? How do you see them in terms of the work that you do and the issues that are important to you? And was marriage central to what you're doing?

For me, HIV criminalization has been the focus of a lot of my work, which marriage was not necessarily central to. It's helped me understand why my issue was not taken up more broadly. A couple months before marriage came legal, I wrote an article about a day where I spent the morning at the Supreme Court covering the last hearing for it, and then that evening I was 40 miles away in Baltimore covering an American city burning during the second night of protests happening in response to the police killing of Freddie Gray. And so, I've sort of been interested in different levels of activism.

And there's nobody better to speak to this than Urvashi Vaid, who has been in our community for some really important challenges, related to how power and protest work.

"Our 'victories' have been limited – still partial, still incomplete"

URVASHI VAID: Thank you. Twenty years ago, in my book Virtual Equality,[1] I argued that equality could feel like appeasement. Like being bought off by the things you wanted to buy. Like living in a simulation, which feels mighty real inside its confines, but which ends in a return to life unchanged. Like declaring "Victory" and "Mission Accomplished" based on a narrow definition of what winning means.

We are living that appeasement today. Marriage embodies all that is good and insufficient about equality. It matters—because it did and does deliver meaningful rights, tangible benefits, access, recognition and social respect for those who participate in the institution. It matters—because the jurisprudence that won us the right to marry expands the 14th Amendment, concedes that we have liberty, at least a few fundamental rights, and the opportunity to challenge laws based on animus.

Marriage has worked culturally and legally because it made us legible to straight people—it turned outlaws into in-laws. And because it helped straight people to be less afraid of queer sexual desire—more of those folks could grudgingly concede our "common humanity," to quote the MA Supreme Court's 2003 decision, and started to change *some* of their attitudes.

But marriage fails for the reasons that formal legal equality as an end goal fails—it does not deliver justice, transform family or culture, nor expand queer freedom for all. It does not touch, much less end, structural racism; does not change the enforcement of compliance with the gender binary; does not deliver reproductive justice; nor end familial homophobia. It has nothing to offer about ending mass incarceration, and the systematic deployment of state violence against Black and Brown communities.

The queer movement's focus on marriage, in fact, had the effect of delaying and slowing its work on critical problems—like poverty, violence against transgender people and transgender women of color, heterosexism and bias against cis-gender women, transphobia, divestment from the public infrastructure, and investment in wealthy people's wealth.

In a sense, even the premise of this conference is a bit frustrating, because it reinforces the power of the paradigm it is trying to question. Marriage is not, and never was, the only, or the most important, or even the most worked on, issue in the LGBT movement. But if one reads the new triumphalist accounts of queer success, one would not know this. The narratives that center marriage—they reduce justice to access, liberation to liberalism, same sex to same old sex. Equality in this narrative is little more a straight people's club to which queers most willing to conform have gained admission. And I'm one of them. I'm married. Include me in the critique please. These new narratives erase or minimize the progressivism of the very queer movements that set the stage for marriage and that still work, beyond marriage, to win liberation and equity for all parts of queer communities.

Straight culture's supposed, newfound embrace of "queerness" itself, leaves me distrustful and actually irritated. I feel so perverse, and I ask myself, "Isn't this what I wanted, and what we worked for? To be able to be welcomed by heterosexual society and my family of origin?" But there are reasons to feel distrustful.

The Right has not disappeared. They have not stopped trying to contain, control or convert us. Trump and the entire Republican party platform attest to the sexist, racist, and homophobic Right-wing's power in this country.

Allies now say, "Isn't the LGBT movement remarkable?" These same allies who now want to "learn lessons from the LGBT movement on how we won marriage" actually are still doing nothing to engage with queer people's lives and movements, or to resist religious-based discrimination against us. Their new compassion reeks of yet another experience of being tokenized in a lifetime of tokenization.

When people ask, "What lessons can we learn from that movement that we can apply?" I want to say—okay, here's what you do. Start by reading the history of colonialism, indigenous people's genocide, slavery, women as chattel property. Then live as outsiders to every institution. Live being shunned and beaten and abused—by family, clergy, police, prisons, and everyone else. Try that for about a century. Then go on to dying. By the thousands. No, by the tens of thousands. No, by the hundreds of thousands. Victory required massive sacrifice—thousands of deaths from shame and stigma (AIDS, suicide, murder, alcoholism, drug use, hate violence).

Victory came because we created positive defiant queer identities (which continue to be mocked to this day as a distraction). Because we built communities and institutions (which continue to be funded at 28 cents for every $100 dollars of funding given by US foundations, and with less than 3 percent participation from our own communities).[2] Because we created community and queer cultures—we laughed, sang, wrote, danced, made family and sexual communities in defiance and in love.

Finally, I would advise those who ask how'd we do it—have a lot of people go to law school and start filing suits. Then start wearing suits, and buying political favors. Then create that mythic "safe space" so really reactionary people with power can think it's safe to join you. If you do all of this, then maybe you win.

I am irritated because so much remains unchanged—from the continued racial siloing that renders so many queer organizations still not *fully* engaged in the fight to end mass incarceration and end police violence, to the misogyny that renders lesbians, bi, queer and trans women irrelevant to decisions made in this movement.

The bottom line is we can put on the rainbow lip gloss, and celebrate diversity day at the corporate and university tables, but our "victories" have been limited, still partial, still incomplete. Formal legal equality—which has still not been won—is indeed necessary, but it is insufficient.

Where I find home and hope, where I live today, is not the queer movement but a stateless place where the intersectional has replaced the identity. This new space of shared analysis and common purpose can be seen in each of the progressive movements that are actually *moving* today. I respect and take direction from the Movement for Black Lives, a brilliant and deeply thoughtful movement, grounded in Black feminism, and inclusive in profound ways. I respect and take direction from the immigrant rights movement, another intersectional and expansive movement in which queer and trans people are leaders; in the movements and organizing by transgender and GNC (gender non-conforming) people, and the transformation of the gender binary that is underway. In the anti-criminalization and prison abolition movements, in the workers' rights to fight for 15, in the Chicago teachers union strikes, in the reproductive justice movement which still fights for birth control access and fights against the ban on public funding for abortions and reproductive control, in the anti-poverty activism, in the global climate justice movement, the environmental justice movement, and more.

Marriage is virtual equality. We are living it now. The neoliberal movement has "won" mainstreaming for middle class LGBT people, of all colors. And it has not won the same for those queer people whose lives remain constrained by economic inequality, racism and White supremacy, a colonial US foreign policy, and a brutal economic system that cannot exist without exploitation. Real social justice, real liberation, real freedom requires a structural change, not just integration.

SWT: Thank you, Urvashi. Next is Paulina Helm-Hernandez. I'm really honored you've traveled here all the way from Atlanta. And tell us, coming from part of the country that often gets overlooked, compared to the coasts regarding gay politics, tell us where we are politically after marriage.

"The power of love and kinship"

PAULINA HELM-HERNANDEZ: Well, thank you for having me. I feel like Urvashi just dropped the mic. I really agree with a lot of Urvashi's reflections, about all the political compromises that we've had to make to get here.

SONG has been around for 23 years, now. And we were started by six incredible feminist-dyke organizers, who were involved in organizing fighting against the Klan, fighting against really harsh White supremacy and the way it manifests in the south, and fighting against all of the dyke-baiting, the lesbian-baiting, that was happening inside of the anti-violence movement, inside of feminist organizations, multiracial organizations, and civil rights organizations. So, a lot of their mission and vision was to challenge homophobia and transphobia inside of those civil organizations. And also, to really push the gay and lesbian organizations around race and class. So that was all part of their strategy.

For us, we have been thinking about how much same-sex marriage should be a marker of progress, and asking how much it represents a culture shift. What have we seen shift? What hasn't shifted? We have to reflect on this now.

For a long time now, since same-sex marriage was first being debated, SONG recognized that we were in a fight for the soul of the LGBTQ movement. There were a lot of questions on the table about it. And we questioned what we were willing to do so that some of us could get married and so some of us could walk down the aisles and to go, as Urvashi said, from being outlaws to having in-laws.

One of the things that we've been reflecting on deeply is the power of love and kinship. *The power of love and kinship.* Because what often drew our southern people into the same-sex marriage conversation had very little to do with marriage itself. Very little. Instead, it had to do with the need for our people to have access to more support. Like, for instance, dyke moms, who were the foster parents to ten kids, who were saying "We're taking in more and more queer kids by the day. We need help. Something has to happen. Something has to break. Like, we have to be able to do more for our people." And so, in some ways, some of the compromises that people made to get on board with this issue—it was really about that. It was trying to figure out the answer to this question: "What are all the formulaic ways that we can have as much of a safety net as we can?" That's what it was about for some of us.

And I think some of us got lost in that conversation. And it became about the metrics of marriage and about the metrics of federal reform. It became about who was on our side and who wasn't. And I think we left a lot of people out of that conversation and I think we're paying the cost of that. We're paying the cost of that.

And I know in the south it's been so profound, because ultimately people turn out for each other in so many different ways. They support each other in complicated ways. People don't just build their lives around being couples. But marriage only supports couples, and not these other ways that people turn out for each other.

And, you know, I actually really understand and have a lot of empathy and sympathy for people wanting to be married, and wanting to be in loving relationships that they feel are validated and supported in a collective sort of way. But I think that when we have explicitly, more deliberately, focused on the framework of liberation is when we have said "That is actually not good enough." It is when we recognize that one individual family, one individual couple, really can't transform the conditions of our community that are at the core of our survival. It can't just be about individual couples.

And so much of what the law is telling us in the south, and what so much of the policy conversations that we have are about, are our *individual* fears. It's like: "What is the one protection that's going to inoculate against me being discriminated against and fired?" Which is absolutely the thing to ask if that's the thing that's politicizing you. But I think we often allow our people to remain in that place. In that place of individual-ness, in that place of, "What can you do for me? What can the movement do for me?"

Versus when I came into the movement, when SONG adopted me (and that's what I say because they adopted me, and they literally saved me from myself in so many ways), it was one of those things where they said "No, you have to be committed to the movement. And you have to be where people can see you." In so many ways, I was taught to really humble myself to the queer south. And to go all over the place and talk to small town folks, asking them: "What are your dreams?" And that's literally what our folks have been wanting and asking for. And what they want is love and kinship. And all the things that come with it: safety, not being so isolated, not being fragmented, not being pitted against each other, not using the fact that some of us can't be out—not using that against each other.

There are so many people that have contributed so much to SONG's livelihood, and to our strategies, to our winning strategies, who are not out of the closet yet, because they live in small towns. But they do what they can do. And what they can do is they can help strategize. And they can mentor people. To be out. Even when they can't be out themselves. They support young people who want to come out.

For us, we're in that moment where we just have to ask, "How do we actually get more LGBTQ people to join liberation movements?" But I feel like so many of our people are getting burnt out by these limited identity politics that they're actually leaving. I've had people from all around the country say, "I don't know if I can keep doing this, y'all. I don't really want to keep doing this."

And maybe that's actually the moment that we're at. Are we going to be involved in a much broader liberation movement, or are we going to be happy with just this? Happy just that my identity matches a letter in somebody else's alphabet? Is that what we want? I don't think that's what we want.

"A de-racialized queer movement can be weaponized for anti-blackness"

SWT: Thank you, Paulina. Next is Hari Ziyad. So, tell me, where do you think we are with LGBTQ politics? How has marriage changed it? And, particularly since you are quite tied into the Black Lives Matter movement, how does marriage fit into the kind of politics you write about and the work that you had been doing and are doing?

HARI ZIYAD: Yes, thank you. I think it was last year, a month before the Supreme Court decision, that I reached out to you about an incident. If any of you were in New York around that time, you might have heard about this.[3] It was a fight that happened at Dallas Barbeque in Chelsea, NY, and it was between a White gay man and a Black guy, and we did not know about the Black man's sexuality at the time. And the narrative that was created around this incident was really interesting. Immediately, politicians came out and said the Black man committed a hate crime, and people began organizing in the streets as if it was. We eventually found out that the Black person involved was a queer man as well. And we also found out that he was attacked first. But, by this point, this was probably months later, and the public narrative had already been established that it was a hate crime by a Black (straight) man against a White gay man. And then we had just also had the gay marriage ruling, and so that was pretty much the topic of conversation in the queer political movement. So, by that point, the truth about this story was kind of buried. And I kept up with it up until this year when the court date was set. And I reported on it through the whole process, up until about two weeks ago when the Black queer man was sentenced to nine years in prison.

And so this was really interesting for my work, because I am also really interested in how the queer movement, when it's de-racialized, can be weaponized for anti-Blackness. This is what happened here.

And I think that's really important in the conversation around marriage because, as Urvashi said, marriage delayed and slowed some of the work around more serious problems. I think that's really important and overlooked. It's not just that gay marriage left some people out, and it's not just that it has a limit, but centralizing this marriage conversation can also work *against* certain racialized queer people.

So, I'm thinking about this in the context of Calvin Warren's critique of queer theory, where he points out that there's an assumption of human subjectivity that can be recognized by the state, that happens in some of the queer movement work we do, and some of us do not have that subjectivity. Some of us are not recognized as human under the state, so how can laws apply to us? And in the context of Black Lives Matter, this shows up in conversations about prison reform versus prison abolition. And whether or not the movement can come out and be anti-state or work through the state, and what that means for Black people especially but especially Black Lives Matter as a queer movement. Where do queerness and Blackness meet, and how can they meet to liberate all of us? So, I definitely think we need to work through questions of what the state can do for certain bodies and what it cannot and will not.

"Building your own damn table"

SWT: Thank you. Next is Gabriel Foster. Gabriel, where is marriage, what does it have to do with gay politics? Was it central to the work that you are doing?

GABRIEL FOSTER: I'm going to try to answer this question to the best of my ability but, first, I've got to give you a little background about myself and where I come from, and what I'm doing, what I'm engaged in right now.

I grew up in the Pacific Northwest, I'm Black, trans and queer. I didn't graduate from high school and most certainly never thought I would be working in the field of philanthropy. In fact, I don't even think I knew what philanthropy meant for a long time. So, it's always a surprise to be in an Executive Director role, talking about philanthropy. But, I think those experiences and who I am are a good fit for the way that the Trans Justice Funding Project exists.

We've been in existence since 2012. My friend Karen Pittelman and I met in a coffee shop in Brooklyn and were discussing our frustrations. Karen is not trans, she's a White cis-gender woman who comes from wealth and is an ally to trans people and communities. And she had been at a lot of funder meetings as a donor, and been pretty frustrated and disheartened seeing the amount of money that goes to some things. And contracts are very important. Reports are very important. And at the same time, watching money not move quickly and directly is really hard for her to watch, like on a soul-level. I myself, having been involved in community organizing in different states and cities, have seen first-hand the effect of what it means to sit and write grants, or to do your song and dance and to hope with all your heart that you might get a little bit of money, and then not get it. And what that ripple effect looks like to the youth I've worked with or to the homeless folks I've worked with – the long-term effects of that.

So, we weren't really sure what to do with those frustrations, but we knew we wanted to do something that we hadn't quite seen before. And so, we're a community-led funding initiative, and we raise money all throughout the year, mostly through individual donors, and we pull those funds together. And then we bring six trans and gender nonconforming activists together each year, from different locations and experiences, and those are the folks, the people that are most effected, who read grant applications and determine who the grantees will be and how much they'll receive. And that felt really important to us for several reasons, but particularly about what it means to not wait for someone else to create something that you desperately need, but to build your own damn table.

So, we support the urgent needs of grassroots groups. And it just amazes me somewhat that we're still in existence after five years. But it doesn't amaze me because there's so little funding to support trans justice work, and at the same time I've just been doing work in community organizing for so long that I don't think I've ever been blown away in the same kind of way. Watching people literally contribute a dollar, 25 dollars, or whatever it takes to make sure that we can pull our funds together. To make sure these communities survive.

So, the marriage thing, I don't really talk about it much, ever. And I understand that for a lot of folks it means access to things like health care, immigration status, and there's some really important and relevant things. *And*. And, it's like all the energy and soul got sucked out of so many things and resources. I get to talk to a lot of activists and organizers around the country, and more than once someone has said: "Oh yes, when the marriage thing was happening, there were lots of people who came into town and were doing all this work, and then it passed, and then they were just gone." And I think, "okay what is the real impact for communities when it's just gone? Now what—we won?" And so, I wonder who won, what did we win, and at what cost?

So, for a lot of the grantees and people I've been in community with, marriage may or may not have been something that they were been excited about, but at the end of the day a lot of these people have still never had their most basic needs met. They're incarcerated, contained by ICE (U.S. Immigration and Customs Enforcement), they can't access housing shelters, they can't get health care. There's a lot that's missing. And I think it is an oversimplification to say that we missed an opportunity. We missed people. We missed a movement. We missed each other.

On the evening when the marriage ruling came down from the Supreme Court, I was walking in the Village in New York, and I walked past the Stonewall Bar, and there were tons of people who were outside feeling very celebratory, and it definitely felt like a significant moment in history. And I remember walking by, and there was lots of hugging and celebrating, and someone that I kind of knew shouted my name out of the crowd, saying "Isn't this so exciting!" And I think I put a mask on and said "yes." I think I didn't want to take away from their excitement. And then I went home, and I wondered why I felt this way, because this is big— should I be more excited about this? And then I thought about my work at that point with the Sylvia Rivera Law Project, and all the faces of people I work with that are incarcerated, and thought that I don't actually know what this means for them. And I don't know that this means freedom for them. I don't know that this means they can live their lives with dignity and access any more than they could the day before it passed.

So, I don't think that it brought a lot of joy for everybody. And I believe it's because of pain and grief from being erased. From leaving people behind, from divisiveness inside and outside of the community. And I believe it's because I've witnessed how this was driven by the loudest voices. The voices that are actually listened to and validated because they have the dollar amounts and the checkbooks to back up what they're saying.

And so, for all those reasons it was really hard for me. And I was sad that I couldn't celebrate with them because I knew too much.

I've worked alongside communities with legacies of resistance, and I believe some of the best organizing and life-changing moments haven't always come out of trying to assimilate or trying to fit into narrow structures that we were never meant to truly thrive within. And maybe I shouldn't say this, but I also include nonprofits, and the 501(c)3 structure, and philanthropy too. I think it's important to bring them into the conversation. And I think it's important that we continue to find ways to break the mold, always knowing that we deserve better, and we deserve so much more than we've ever been told to settle for. Thank you.

"We can do more than one thing at a time"

SWT: Thank you, Gabriel. And Robyn, tell us about where you've seen marriage fitting into your life's work and where it takes us politically.

ROBYN OCHS: Hi everybody! I want to celebrate today because it marks 40 years of my identifying as bisexual. And some still say that bisexuality is just a phase...

In addition to my bi+ activism and work with LGBTQ+ youth, I've also served for 12 years on the Board of Directors of MassEquality, Massachusetts' statewide LGBTQ+ advocacy organization. We worked on marriage equality for several years, and when Massachusetts finally pushed back the proposed constitutional amendment, we actually had a Board retreat to ask the question: "What's next? Are we done?" Luckily, a majority of us said "Hell no! There is so much work left to be done." And so, we turned our attention to other work. And I want to announce that today, October 1, the Transgender Public Accommodations Bill went into effect in Massachusetts, and for me this is a huge thing. We've been working toward this for more than ten years, and it will be tremendously impactful on many people's lives.

That said, I just want to recognize that this room is filled with amazing people who are doing all sorts of amazing activism on all sorts of amazing issues and using all sorts of amazing strategies. And if we were to sit down here in this room and ask: "Okay, so what's next? What should we all be doing now?", we could sit here forever and we would not come to consensus because there is no single answer to that question. There is so much work that needs to be done. There is so much work remaining. And what you think is most important will depend very much on what you've had the opportunity to learn, who've you'd have access to, what conversations you've had the privilege of engaging in. And it would depend also on your personal beliefs, your personal perspective, what is most salient to your lived experience. *All of our work is important*—I don't think there's one single issue.

I also don't think there's a single strategy. There are so many ways to get from here to better. Do we work in the courts? Do we work in the legislatures? Do we raise funds to make sure movements have the resources they need? Do we provide direct service to individual people? Do we try to change the entire system? Do we go out on the streets and protest? Do we focus on inter-movement work? Do we build it up? Do we burn it down? What do we do? I don't think there is a single answer. One thing I've learned in my 40 or so years of being an activist is that any successful movement requires multiple simultaneous strategies. And you can't just have one issue in your focus because there are all these other issues that also require our attention.

And I see a lot of frustration, a lot of hurt, a lot of pain in our community. We don't have what we need, and we are not treated with respect. And often, when we are frustrated, we turn our frustration laterally on each other. There's an expression: "hurt people hurt people." For me, the people who are engaged in social change work are not the problem. We are a part of the solution, and I'd rather we turn our energy toward multiplying ourselves. Instead of saying "How come you're working on that issue and not on my issue?" I want to figure out how we can get a lot more people engaged. Urvashi mentioned that less than 3 percent of LGBTQ+ people are actually donors to the LGBTQ+ movement. We need to reach out to the 97 percent of people inside this community who are not doing anything yet and call them in and try to figure out how to get them involved. Because if we just stay small and fight over the crumbs, we're not going to get anywhere, we're all going to get burned out, and tired, and sick, and dead. So, I want to figure out how, instead of just fighting over slices of the small pie we have, we can get our own ovens and bake a really big pie. Let's make more pie. Instead of operating within a model of scarcity, how can we increase the resources that we actually have?

Along with that comes the issue of sustainability. To be sustainable over the long haul, we must commit to be in it for the long haul because we're not going to be able to solve all of these problems any time soon. As for me: I'm in it for the duration. I hope that when I die, I'm 106 years old and out on a picket line somewhere. I want to be able to stay in movement work for my entire life, and so I've had to learn how to engage in self-care, in self-love, and in caring for the people around me.

There's a lot of horizontal hostility in our community, and I believe we'll be stronger and healthier if we can figure out how to support each other across different strategies, across different issues, and take care of ourselves and each other, so that we can stay engaged for the long haul and move from issue to issue. If we fix one thing, then we should jump right into the next thing. And we can do more than one thing at a time. We must.

So, I just want to say to people in this room: thank you for everything you're teaching me. Thank you for everything you're doing. Thank you for everything that you've given so far, and thank you for everything you will give in the future.

"Inventing things that had never existed"

SWT: Alright, there's a lot on the table. So, let's talk about the benefits and challenges of working within a formal organization. Urvashi, in your book *Virtual Equality*, you write about the decision to leave the Task Force when you were Director there. And I was wondering if you could talk a little bit about the reality of leaving a formal organization. What did that align you to do politically?

UV: Nonprofitization and the formalization of social movements is something that Paulina and Gabriel mentioned, and I think that's a really key challenge. On one hand, you need structures through which you organize. Whether it's a collective or nonprofit, you need a group or something. And the nonprofit form has been the model. It just doesn't need to be the only model. What's cool is that the movements today have distributed leadership, in Black Lives Matter, in the ways the immigrant rights movement has been organizing. There's creative adaptations going on inside social change organizations and inside movements. But for me, I came up in a different moment when the idea of creating LGBT infrastructure was really necessary. It didn't exist. We didn't have community centers. We didn't have paid staff.

I got involved in the late 1970s in Boston, and I started by volunteering at a newspaper called *Gay Community News*, which was a weekly, community-based newspaper, put out by a collective that started in 1973 and which was published for about 20 years. It was extraordinarily influential in the 1970s and 1980s, because it was really radical. There were some people who were paid and most of us worked as volunteers. And that was one of the only infrastructures that existed in Boston. The Fenway Community Center (now Fenway Health) was a bunch of volunteers providing social services. The AIDS Action Committee was formed with volunteers in 1981. Hardly anything we see today existed back then. And so, part of our excitement as activists was building that new infrastructure—inventing things that had never existed. "We've got this crisis, let's create a group and make something happen!" There was a lot of creativity that went into building those institutions and infrastructures.

Today, I and others critique the way the nonprofit form has produced professionalization, bureaucracy, and reproduced the power dynamics we organized ourselves to change. Non-profitization has happened in every movement. Today, I am working outside of the nonprofit structure for the first time. I've always worked inside an infrastructure of some sort, an organizational form—the

law, educational institutions, civil rights institutions, philanthropic institutions. Today, it's just me. There's much more freedom and there is much more
creativity. But it's also much more difficult, because the funding runs through
501(c)3 non-profits.

"Over time, you start to see how things come to be top down"

SWT: Hari, I thought maybe you could talk about the debate within Black
Lives Matter, whether it's an organization, a formal organization, and
what politics and what questions are brought up. How are you seeing it
play out?

HZ: To clarify, I'm not a part of the Black Lives Matter organization, but I
would consider myself part of the movement for Black lives. I have close
relationships with a lot of the people who are a part of the national organization, and those relationships have created some really insightful moments
about this tension. This week, I was having discussions with some of those
organizers about where we are in talking about reform vs. revolution. And
it was a very intense conversation. And as you were saying, the building of
these corporatized structures is really accepted. And then, over time, you
start to see how things come to be top-down. And I think we're hitting
that moment right now in the movement, where we're trying to push back
against this top-down structuring of Black Lives Matter. So, there's obviously a network, and we have a lot of different perspectives within the
movement, but last week there was a more reformist perspective that was
put out there in national media outlets and it was presented as if it was on
behalf of the entire movement. And, in speaking for the movement, it
erased a lot of other perspectives.

So, I definitely agree with you that we need to have both people within
and outside of these structures. But there has to be a lot of push back to make
sure that all of those voices are recognized. If this is a movement, if we all
recognize that this is a movement, a network with various different viewpoints, then there can't be one perspective for the whole movement. Especially
when there are very strong critiques from people who were in Ferguson,
who probably have a lot more radical perspectives than what was being put
out in that moment. And I think that that is where we are now. Just figuring
out how to fight that.

Because I think it's kind of inevitable, this is how things are set up. Once
you get to a certain level of structuring, things just kind of flow better; they
go a certain way, and they don't flow as well when you're saying things like
"I'm anti-police" or something more radical like that. So, there are conversations happening about this issue, and hopefully we stay in that moment we're
speaking about, which is this beautiful moment of building where everyone
comes together, where we work with each other, without erasing all those
different viewpoints that have built this.

"We're not married to the nonprofit structure – we're more like fuck buddies"

SWT: Paulina, when I interviewed you for my story from Pulse in Orlando, you used this phrase: "The consolidation of gay White power, even in spaces that are supposed to be for people of color." How did you confront that in your organization? How do people confront these issues?

PHH: Well, we can have a whole separate panel on that. But at SONG we just think leadership matters. And we think we can't be neutral about what we mean by leadership or about what kind of leadership we're incubating.

In the south, it's just rampant White supremacy. And guess what? It also runs all throughout the LGBT movement. And so, a lot of our White allies, a lot of our White members and staff, that's part of their active role—to do that level of intervention. That level of ally ship-building. And they have been the ones to restore my faith in multiracial organizing, because they've actually shown what they're about, versus just talking about it. And that's really the commitment that we made at SONG. We could talk about multiracial organizing all day long. We could criticize the people that are doing it wrong, and we could point out the ones that keep messing up. And we can do this talking without changing structural problems. So, we wanted to be able to show versus tell. I just want to name my former Co-Director Caitlin Breedlove. We were Co-Directors of SONG for the last nine years, and she taught me a lot, and we taught each other a lot, about what it actually means to have a multiracial Co-Directorship. About the role of White people in the movement. The role of multiracial organizing shops in this time.

Part of our job was also to not allow everything to be put on the back of the nonprofit. Because, real talk: the 501(c)3 nonprofit is a structure to get capital. If someone has a better one, that we can still raise money off of, and do what we need to do, then come at me. I'll take it. But it is what is. That's been part of the challenge, you know.

We're not married to the nonprofit structure. We're more like fuck buddies, a little bit. Like, "We see you baby, it's good, there's some benefits. But you keep messing up sometimes. We got security problems." We got some things that are going on because of the C3. But when its good—when you get your money? It's one of the things that helps us get leverage and to build to scale. Unless somebody has something comparable that's going to help us build and sustain LGBTQ infrastructure in the south. Thank you for naming that Urvashi. Because people take that for granted. There are few and far between LGBTQ organizations that are helping our people that our people can find in the south. Our people are still trying to figure out who to connect with. And so, the best thing that 501(c)3s can do right now is just be incubators for leadership, incubators for strategies, incubators for actually seeing what else there is to be done to be able to become more politically autonomous movements.

That's what pains me actually about nonprofits. It's that we are not going to be able to be as politically autonomous and as brave as we need to be. If we stay as nonprofits, we are never going to do experiments and be willing to fail. And we need to be able to fail, to win in the long term. It's gotten so brutal. Even the fundraising for SONG has been so brutal. The nonprofit metrics by which people talk about progress and what's possible is part of what's killing our political imagination. So that's my challenge to us: What other capital structure do we want to become friendly with, or give the side eye to? And help this exodus from the nonprofits, to liberate some of our social justice work? To not be so confined.

But I think that some of the critiques that people have about nonprofits aren't actually about nonprofits, they're about the leadership. You don't like who you're rolling with. And that's a problem. So, for us these are two separate questions. They're related, but I feel like there's a particular part about leadership that has been incubated in order to run nonprofits. And we know now they're out there saying what our movement demands should be, when they're actually not related to our communities. So, we just need to be less neutral about that, you know? We need to be like "Good for y'all but stay in your lane. Stay in your lane." That's what we have to do, real talk.

"Is it self-interest or is it liberation?"

SWT: Thanks. So, there are two news things that absolutely fascinated me this week as we prepared for this. The first is a working paper from the Treasury,[4] looking at income of same-sex marriage tax filers. It's just a working paper, not a peer reviewed study, and is just the beginning of scholarship. And it should also include the lens of Mignon Moore, who's done fantastic work in the south and on invisible families. It's not broken down by race, but generally it finds that same-sex marriage filers make a lot more money. It's broken down by age, most couples that file are younger, so it's not including retired people. They're also very much clustered in DC, New York, and San Francisco. Married couples are averaging $275,000 a year per couple. That's more than $100,000 more than other same-sex couples. Married same-sex women couples on average earn more than straight couples. But when you look at them within geography, you look at couples in DC, in New York, the lesbian women couples earn less than straight couples. The married gay men still earn a lot more. And when the women have children they earn a little bit less and the gay men earn a lot more. So, we're only starting to get data, but these are really fascinating things.

The second news item I'd like to point out was about Edie Windsor (the lead plaintiff in the Supreme Court case that overturned the Defense of Marriage Act). Last night was her marriage announcement. She got married again, and I am thinking about: How did her story count as the civil rights debate? And it really came through her tax bill of $363,000 dollars with the federal government. So, to have that work in your favor, you have to have some change in your pocket, to have something that is applicable to you.

And the person she married is a Wells Fargo financial advisor. Which I find really funny, because they're one of these organizations that prides themselves on being part of our community. Like they're always sponsoring Pride, they put rainbow shit on everything, but they've also completely decimated Black and Brown communities. They have settled for hundreds of millions of dollars issues with the Justice Department of targeting Black and Brown people for subprime mortgages, very intentionally partnering with Black churches and Black community centers to try to put shoddy financial products in the hands of Black people. So, to see Windsor, the image of marriage equality, get married to a Wells Fargo Vice-President was something I found interesting.

Marriage is very much helping capital accumulation. One of the major things it does is help people have money, pay less tax, pass on some money, get health care through the institution, rather than taxing everyone and having it in universal health care.

PHH: I mean that's what a lot of people fought for right? For some, it was about capitalism and accumulating capital. I think that we've seen, over and over again, this belief that class trumps homophobia. Somehow, money is going to vote for us over homophobia, and that if we live in our gated communities, then that is going to be thing to stop us from getting us gay bashed, from getting our partners killed on the streets. But we know that's not true. That means safety for some people, yes, if they want to live behind the gated communities. But that doesn't mean community, and that doesn't mean collective survival. And it just keeps coming up over and over again, and it's part of the debate we're having. Is it self-interest or is it liberation? Where are we really at?

And that's part of why I talk about the consolidation of gay White power, because they're turning away from collective liberation. They're like, "we're actually good! And we're now exiting the movement." And that's not everybody. But we're actually seeing people leave social justice work because of that.

And some people are like, "We've raised all this money on the back of same-sex marriage and now that that win has been met, we're going to give it back to our donors." What? Versus giving it to the anti-violence movement? Versus talking about our trans sisters of color and what is happening in the streets, in the detention centers? Versus talking about what is happening to our undocumented communities. To me, this is the real question: Where are we really at, on our soul-level? Because our financial ramifications are just an indicator of that—the mass accumulation of wealth is a sign of an even bigger issue.

And I want economic justice for everybody. I came up working class, working poor. My family came to this country undocumented. All my people are blue collar workers. I'm the first to have this nonprofit gig and get paid for it. And my people organize. They also organize, on top of working full-time. And so, I don't romanticize being broke or having to live paycheck to paycheck. I don't want that for anyone.

But what I'm tired of seeing is people who come into movement when they need something and then they get it, and take a big chunk of our resources and infrastructure to get it, and then they run back into their little corner of safety. And that's the part that irks me. And that's the part that I do think we need to have more explicit conversations about. About the radical economic injustice.

And I just want to lift up Joseph DeFilippis and Amber Hollibaugh, who totally changed my life through their work with QEJ (Queers for Economic Justice). Thank you. Thank you so much. Because they fortified so much of SONG's economic justice work at the time, in our work with QEJ through the Roots Coalition. QEJ was constantly bringing up poverty, and bringing the poverty of poor LGBT people, homeless LGBT people, to the table. And they did it when a lot of people were really uncomfortable with it, y'all. Like visually uncomfortable sharing space with working-class people and poor people and homeless people, and just thought these poor people wanted a chunk out of them. Versus thinking that we're just all trying to make it y'all. And knowing that you elites have done what you needed to do in your upper echelon, and our people are doing what they need to do at the street level. And, instead, the level of judgement and punishment of the poor. I do feel like that is such a deeper spiritual question because the economic inequality feels like the tip of the iceberg to me. And we need to have some of the conversations about what is really happening to some of our folks.

"In a capitalist society, this doesn't make any sense"

GF: I also feel like I should mention that the Trans Justice Funding Project structure is pretty unique in a lot of ways. And I want to talk about the other Co-founder, Karen Pittelman. Like I said she's not trans, she comes from wealth, and she's White. But she has given literally millions of dollars to fund this project, of her own. And she worked for four years, unpaid, 40–60 hours a week to make sure that everything was in place and ready to go. And she was always saying to me, which I never had anyone say, I just want to be your back-up dancer. And at first I was like, "That's some weird shit," but then I was just like, "Oh, you mean I'm listening to you, I want to take direction and leadership from you. And I want to be the kind of ally that's there to support you." And she always does this thing: "I'm always on call." She's always just ready for whatever I need and whatever the Trans Justice Funding Project needs and I just don't think I'd ever seen an ally show up in a way that she had. And I think a lot of that has to do with privilege, but I think it also has to do a lot with herself too.

So, for like for a minute, we questioned whether or not we should become a 501(c)3, and then Karen got all paranoid, and concerned that it would give the government too much access and control over what we're doing. So, instead, we became a small business, an LLC (limited liability company), because then we could raise and give away money very quickly. But then the government was like, "Damn, you're the worst small business we've ever seen. Like there's all this money, and then it's all just gone?" And they were like, "Karen, are you embezzling?" Because in a capitalist society, giving away all this money doesn't make any sense. So, Bob, the IRS lawyer, he said, "Maybe you want to look at some different structures, because y'all are going to get audited and red flagged all over the place." And we didn't want that, because what does that mean for our grantees in the long run.

So, Karen was like, "What are we going to do? Well, I am rich, I could start a trust." So, now we are officially a trust. So, we write checks and we have trustees, and I manage a trust. And we call ourselves a project because we know that we still have a lot to learn. We haven't figured it out. And we also don't think that this is everything, it's just the money piece. But with that said, we've been really creative, because we don't want to mess with people's benefits, public benefits. So, when we issue a check to a group we have to be really thoughtful about how to do that. And we have been wanting to encourage other people who give, or other foundations, to find ways to lessen the barriers, to make sure our people have the most money and the most means to be able to do the work that they do. But to make it simpler, because we need equality too in that work, first and foremost.

"What happened to my queer dream?"

UV: I wanted to pick up on the study by the Treasury, the data they showed is incomplete because so little data on LGBT people exists. So, who's getting married and who's not, and who's captured in the data sets they analyzed and what is left out? That's what determines those numbers. Because there are many other data, from other data sets, that show that not all LGBTQ people are wealthy. They show a clear picture of queer poverty. From the work of Queers for Economic Justice (QEJ), which did its own research because none existed, to the work that CAP (Center for American Progress) has done on youth homelessness and general homelessness, to the research that Lee Badgett and the Williams Institute have done to document poverty in LGBTQ communities. These data show a significant part of our community living below the federal poverty line, which is itself an arbitrary number. So, there are LGBT affluent people yes, but there are many other levels of income and experience in queer communities as well.

I also wanted to say a few things about marriage. I have to add, as a married girl, that there are a couple other dimensions to it too—I meant what I said when I started: it has mattered. One of these other dimensions that gives marriage meaning to many people is that queer people come from, for many of us, deep histories of family rejection. And I think marriage and having children are ways that a lot of LGBT people I know are redeeming their relationships with their families of origin. It's the truth. We can say, "Go to therapy instead of fighting for marriage," but it is what it is. And it has made a difference. Having the legal recognition has made difference in many families. Ironically, I have to leave early today, to run to my niece's wedding. I have known her for her whole life, and she is lovely. I can't even stay at the conference on marriage because I have to go to a marriage. What I'm trying to say is that there's an emotional and material dimension around family acceptance to this issue that shouldn't be glossed over.

And here's the other thing, I'll just say it. We're all part of traditions and they are problematic. I think tradition is actually the enemy, but redefining those traditions is the work that we're doing, I think tradition is the enemy because it locks you into certain ways of normalization and certain ways of thinking about kinship.

Kinship is a great word. When I was 20, I thought I'd be living in a group, dyke, queer house with multiple partners, we'd all be raising each other's children. We talked about it passionately day in and day out, saying "This is what we're gonna be doing. We're going to be old dykes in this old commune." But, it's not happening. It didn't happen for anyone that we talked about that with. And I think, "Wow, what happened to my dream, to my queer dream?"

Notes

1   Urvashi Vaid. *Virtual Equality: The Mainstreaming of Gay and Lesbian Liberation*. Anchor Books. 2015.
2   Funders for LGBTQ Issues—2015 Tracking Report. See www.lgbtfunders.org/wp-content/uploads/2017/05/2015_Tracking_Report.pdf.

Overall $160,702 given by 334 foundations for LGBTQ work. For every $100 dollars awarded by U.S. foundations, 27 cents goes to LGBTQ issues. LGBTQ philanthropy is not focused on poor queer communities or ending poverty (2 percent of funding went to the economically disadvantaged). It does not fund criminal legal systems work or anti-violence work in meaningful ways (4 percent went for CJ work overall). It is not dealing with the realities confronting LGBT immigrants and undocumented persons (2 percent). It has stepped back from funding of organizing by PLHIV, which is funded largely by the government. It has built a new infrastructure for itself rather than building out the infrastructure of those that can get work done. It has not challenged the straight funding world to do more on LGBT issues at all (59 of the 100 largest U.S. foundations gave *no* LGBT grants; and the ones who did, barely gave anything (0.17 percent of their overall grantmaking went to LGBT organizations).

The Movement Advancement Project estimates that combined donors to the 36 national organizations it surveyed total 3.3 percent of the total LGBT population in the US. See: www.lgbtmap.org/file/2015-national-lgbt-movement-report.pdf, p. 9.

3   See https://mic.com/articles/147556/what-bayna-el-amin-s-assault-case-says-about-racism-in-the-lgbtq-community#.ptStNyZhe.
4   See www.treasury.gov/resource-center/tax-policy/tax-analysis/Documents/WP-108.pdf.

2

GA(Y)TEKEEPING IDENTITY, CITIZENSHIP, AND CLAIMS TO JUSTICE

"Freedom to serve," "freedom to marry," and the U.S. thirst for good gay subjects

Chriss V. Sneed

Editors' introduction:

In this chapter, Chriss V. Sneed looks at the language used by the Human Rights Campaign (HRC), the largest LGBTQ advocacy group in the country, and the Department of Justice (DOJ), during the campaigns for LGBT access to marriage and the military. By examining political statements and documents circulated by HRC and the DOJ, Sneed examines who was included and excluded from their ideological construction of LGBTQ identities, and analyzes the repercussions of this discourse.

Sneed shows that the discourse used by HRC and the DOJ constructed LGBTQ identity in ways that assimilate some types of LGBTQ people into mainstream culture, and exclude others. Sneed illuminates how this construction not only informs political agendas, but also social lives.

Readers are asked to consider the questions raised by this research: How might this rhetoric be detrimental to creating inclusive visions of social justice? What other organizations engage in similar tactics? How can activism deploy a different construction of LGBTQ identity? What are the challenges and benefits of doing so?

Introduction

Let us begin this story in New York City *c.*2015—where warm, mid-June weather had started to warm parks and residents across boroughs. As some folks began to plan vacations, groups of organizers anxiously awaited a ruling that would impact not just the "City that Never Sleeps", but the entire country. Days later, on June 27th—the night before the annual Pride parade was slated to take place—the Supreme Court issued a historic ruling[1] that wrote same-sex marriage into legal standing across the United States. Over the next 24 hours, crowds swelled and an air of jovial optimism hung in the air, matching the celebratory fervor experienced by those who attended New York City Pride in 2011 after Governor Cuomo legalized same-sex marriage across the state just two days before. It was, as the website of a major gay rights organization wrote, a major victory after all. Almost immediately, the Human Rights Campaign circulated flyers, stickers, Facebook posts, and other media that declared repeatedly: "WE HAVE WON".

Yet, many LGBTQ folks, were left to question who the "WE" in those declarations represented. A similar question had already been raised during other legislative measures related to LGBTQ rights, especially the repeal of "Don't Ask, Don't Tell" in 2011. During that political debate, the Human Rights Campaign (HRC) played a huge role in the political discourse surrounding military service and LGBT folks, to the extent that HRC was thanked in a speech by Senate lead sponsor Joe Lieberman for their involvement in its repeal (Hirschman, 2010). However, as Spade (2013) noted, the intense advocacy for same-sex marriage and access to military service had—and still does—generate much tension across LGBTQ communities, not merely because of differences in life choices, but in life circumstances and experiences of inequality. The intimate linkage of neoliberalism, citizenship, and sexual politics are just some of the more complicated aspects of these efforts. This work seeks to interrogate that dilemma, one that has arisen from two simple inquiries often rendered invisible within discourses on identity-based movements: who are *we* and who are *they*?

In this chapter, I look at recent LGBT activist discourses and their potential for changing social and political landscapes within the United States. First, I quickly review major advocacy efforts of the Human Rights Campaign, an LGBT organization based in the United States. Second, I focus on how advocacy efforts centered on same-sex marriage and access to the military—particularly those made by HRC—demonstrate the potential of these discourses through their appropriation by the United States Department of Justice. Through my analysis of the Department of Justice briefings, I illustrate how this appropriation highlights how certain images of "gay" identity have been used in ways that exclude other folks in the LGBTQ community. Further, I argue that the *who* that is privileged in these discourses and the *other* who is rejected reflect how neoliberal rights-based activism can be detrimental to creating inclusive visions of social justice.

Neoliberal—taken from the term neoliberalism—refers to the intertwining of democractic ideals and free market economics in the social, cultural, and political imagination of the U.S. landscape since the 1970s. When applied to ideas of human rights, neoliberal thought relegates such concepts to the level of the individual; removing structural or institutional perspectives. Like many other phenomena, racialized and sexualized ideologies are also embedded within these same neoliberal attitudes, discourses, and policies (Ferguson & Hong, 2012, p. 1057). And, as DasGupta (2012) reminded us, the implications for these types of frameworks are often felt most at the marigns. Thus, I conclude this discussion by elaborating on how contemporary and future activist organizations have and can continue to reinvent alternative forms of advocacy that move away from these types of exclusionary narratives.

Methodology

This chapter relies on the evaluation of primary documents through the qualitative analytical method known as discourse analysis. As van Dijk (2008) indicated, critical analysis of discourse has practical and theoretical relevance for understanding the structural and interpersonal aspects of the social system. The data used for this work is a collection of statements taken from the Department of Justice (DOJ) website, along with a historical and contextual review of publications and media circulated by the Human Rights Campaign found through HRC's own website. To create a data set of Department of Justice statements on this subject, I conducted many searches that included the terms "same-sex marriage," "Defense of Marriage Act" (DOMA), "gay marriage," and "Don't Ask, Don't Tell" (DADT) within the DOJ site that were dated between September 2001 and July 2015. After accounting for overlapping articles, the number of statements used for analysis within this work was reduced to 41, which includes one article that was found by hand. Of these 41 statements, 26 solely referenced same-sex marriage while the remaining statements touched on both same-sex marriage and the "Don't Ask, Don't Tell" case. Except for a September 2006 press release, all the articles were dated between May 2010 and July 2015. After engaging in a multi-level content analysis that included textual, contextual, and interpretive analytical review, several themes emerged from this data that underscore this work.

When "queer" goes national

While many organizations supported and become partners in the advocacy for same-sex marriage the United States, the nation's largest LGBT organization—the Human Rights Campaign (HRC)—became a central player in these efforts (Crowley, 2007). Aside from political endorsements, HRC has benefited from a wealth of financial and material resources that give strength to its national campaigns. This is quite evident in the "Our Victories" section on the Human Rights Campaign website (Human Rights Campaign, 2017), which boasts an estimated $20 million contribution to former President Barack Obama's 2012 re-election. With this type of fiscal access, HRC is able to sustain its advocacy campaigns and propell them into the mainstream. Thus, the images and discourses stemming from these campaigns are not only important due to their focus or perspective, but also because they are amplified by structural and institutional forces.

Indeed, we must consider this when evaluating the mounting success of the million-dollar 2004 and 2006 campaigns centered on same-sex marriage that were followed by continous media and print advocacy efforts, which heightened in 2011 until the *Obergefell v. Hodges* verdict in 2015. Two of HRC's major same-sex marriage campaigns illustrate particular constructions of "gay"/"LGBTQ" identity. The 2014 campaign, entitled "All God's Children," which meant to rally support for LGBTQ people in the state of Mississippi was also used in other Southern states. An important aspect of this project was the use of short, vingette-like portraits of

LGBT folks living in Mississippi (Guequierre, 2013). The emphasis on each of the participants' work ethic, faith, and contributions to the community was used in print and media accounts—which highlighted LGBT teachers, students, pastors, and military personnel (Miller, 2015). While these images do represent the lives of some LGBT people and may help garner ideas of respect, they reinforce the tendency to frame rights in accordance with how relatable to the norm a population is, and not necessarily because of respect for their differences. Another campaign, entitled "The People's Brief," was launched in 2015 to garner national support for same-sex marriage prior to the Supreme Court's ruling that same year. In its text, which was circulated and summarized through digital and print media, one finds several themes.

On one hand, as a legal document, it emphasizes the neutral and fair nature of law for individual American citizens—underscoring the similiarity between LGBT and heterosexual families' "aspirations to life, liberty, and the pursuit of happiness as everyone else" (Carpenter, Kaplan, & Saunders, 2015). As it continues, the brief suggests that when LGBT people engage in the courageous act of "coming out," it has helped otherwise ignorant people learn that loved ones or friends could be gay and thus challenges prejudicial fear of the unknown. Yet, while the text alludes to systematic discrimination against non-heterosexual communities, the examples focus on individualistic plights—such as a gay person's ability to make medical decisions for their partner at hospitals; access to family insurance plans; or reciprocal marriage status across states—as points for legislative change. The People's Brief concludes by invoking the imagery of two lovers scorned by a state that does not certify their love or "dignity even in death" (p. 32). In doing this, the brief and the media portrayals that anchored this campaign push the public and the national courts to look at LGBT issues not as social rights for inclusion of difference, but as the negation of everyday citizens who—despite being gay—are living normal lives.

Similar themes were prevelant in HRC's campaigns to end "Don't Ask, Don't Tell." In 2009, HRC launched a comprehensive campaign to end the ban on LGBT service in the military. One facet of this work was the "Voices of Honor" tour, which highlighted the stories of valiant, patriotic ex-military personnel through various media platforms aimed at the United States' public and congressional members (Human Rights Campaign, 2010). Shaw (2013) noted HRC's follow-up action, the "Repeal DADT NOW Campaign" used these images to apply pressure in key legislative arenas around the country; particularly through the discussion of the need for brave soldiers to protect the country. However, there is a dearth of research examining the interconnected nature of the identity constructions that have emerged from the DADT and same-sex marriage debates.

As several works indicated (Belkin, 2013; Conrad, 2014; Crocker, 2009; Frank, 2013; Scotti, 2004; Ward, 2013; Yoshino, 2010), these two legislative battles have been intimately linked. One blatant connection between the two policies comes from the material realities they promise: each legal issue related to economic benefits that *eligible* members of the LGBTQ community could and would potentially access. Another linkage stems from the heavily individualistic language of activist campaigns, such as those of HRC that I have just described. These portraits—which heavily rely on narratives of sameness, normalcy, and civic duty—have been heavily criticized as an exclusionary rendering of sexual citizenship. Weeks (1998) defined sexual citizenship as the crossing of the public and private spheres that had been popular in mainstream U.S. culture. While some liberal advocates consider these changes as a sign of progress, other scholars have argued that it marks the popular entrance of homonormativity and homonationalism into the public sphere. First coined by Lisa Duggan, homonormativity was used to describe the rise of gay rights, activism-reliant neoliberal and respectably conservative values (Duggan, 2005). Homonationalism, which was articulated later by Jasbir Puar, mixes the former term with nationalism to signal how images—such as HRC's same-sex marriage and anti-DADT campaigns—create narratives of gay normalcy through patriatism both at the expense of other nations and through biopolitical, or embodied, acts of violence against those who are not included in the framework of good sexual citizenry (Heike Schotten, 2015). In the next section, I demonstrate that the discursive imageries of advocacy and activist organization do have power to influence social change by illustrating how the Supreme Court appropriated these rhetorics over time.

Constructing the queer: discourses of the state

The leading theme one would expect from the DOJ statements on same-sex marriage and military access would be a sound focus on the LGBTQ community. As it turns out, the centering of "LGBT" is not the highest priority within these statements, as the phrase is repeated only 94 times within the 41 statements included in this analysis. Other words – like "legal," "nation," "civil," "equal," "services," and "constitutional"—are referenced many more times than any identity category associated with gender or sexual minorities. However, it is not just the quantity that counts, but the descriptive foundations that underscore these occurrences. While there were dozens of telling narratives, three were most salient: (1) discussions of citizenship through either the invocation of citizenship as a boundary of justice, the call for equality for all *committed* Americans, or the importance of individual rights or; (2) American nationalism articulated by the idea of bravery and determination, coupled with a quest for progress; and finally, (3) invisibilizing the government's involvement in perpetuating inequality by invoking the so-called "legacy of freedom" left by the Constitution and "Founding Fathers" or through the construction of oppositional or allied parties or sub-groups. In the following sections, I explore each of those three themes.

Citizenship

On August 23, 2012, former Attorney General Eric Holder stood before the audience of the Lavender Law conference (the annual conference of the National LGBT Bar Association) in Washington, DC. Predictably, among his remarks were references to recent legal victories associated with the LGBTQ community.

He stated, "As we approach the one-year anniversary of the end of Don't Ask, Don't Tell, it's worth celebrating the fact that so many brave servicemen and women can now serve their country proudly, honestly, openly, and without fear of discharge" (Department of Justice, Office of Public Affairs, 2012a).

Holder's statements are laden with constructions of freedom and the rights of everyday citizens. On the surface, such an approach is seemingly benign or even noteworthy. However, the continued use of the trope of citizenship overshadows the very subjects it is meant to highlight. Paradoxically, discussions of citizens' rights are markedly divorced from LGBTQ people throughout the press releases. Although abstract references to the legal exclusion of "LGBT" people are mentioned in relation to "Don't Ask, Don't Tell" and the "Defense of Marriage Act," the invocation of generalized American citizenship becomes the primary way that the Department of Justice theorizes about these stories. Another statement from Holder exemplifies this discursive framework. In his 2013 reflection on the Supreme Court decision in the case *United States v. Windsor*, Holder mentions sexual orientation just once and instead focuses on the promise of equality this action has brought to the American people as a collective, aggregated mass. Holder stated,

> Today's historic decision in the case of United States v. Windsor, declaring Section 3 of the Defense of Marriage Act unconstitutional, is an enormous triumph for equal protection under the law for all Americans. The Court's ruling gives real meaning to the Constitution's promise of equal protection to all members of our society, regardless of sexual orientation. . . . And, as we move forward in a manner consistent with the Court's ruling, the Department of Justice is committed to continuing this work, and using every tool and legal authority available to us to combat discrimination and to safeguard the rights of all Americans.
>
> *Department of Justice, Office of Public Affairs, 2013*

Again and again, the Department of Justice relies on homogenizing language that erases disparity and difference. Yet, erasure is not the only problematic aspect of this discursive framework. By shifting the right to marry and service to the military as categories of citizenship, the state reproduces larger frameworks of exclusion at individual, institutional, and international levels. Franz warned of this in her discussion of illegality and the rights of non-citizens, and writes,

> By barring individuals from inhabiting the rights of the citizen-subject, illegality is also a vehicle by which liberalism's exclusions manifest. Scholars have argued that like citizenship, illegality is not just a juridical status, but also a discursively constituted position of "deportability" (De Genova, 2005), "social death" (Cacho, 2012), and "impossibility" (Ngai, 2004), that is racialized as non-white and sexualized as deviant.
>
> *Franz, 2015, p. 184*

The construction of citizen—those deserving of rights due to their nation of birth and patriotism —marginalizes those who have become despised as not only "foreign" but all who are considered as *against* the nation. Liberal gay rights activism has capitalized off this chasm for decades through reformist measures like political lobbying for elite gay interests at the expense of other social programming or transnational solidarities, and, as Potter (2012) demonstrated, presidential administrations have continued to respond to them through legislative positions tied to the maintenance of governmental regimes. Thus, the added specificity of commitment—via marriage or nationalism—comes as no surprise. The mix of these two themes is evident in a 2014 statement from Holder regarding the recognition of same-sex marriage in Utah. He stated:

> This ruling marked a historic step toward equality for all American families. And since the day it was handed down, the Department of Justice has been working tirelessly to implement it in both letter and spirit—moving to extend federal benefits to married same-sex couples as swiftly and smoothly as possible.
>
> *Department of Justice, Office of Public Affairs, 2014a*

Holder made a similar statement on March 28, 2014, in response to the *United States v. Windsor* verdict and again on October 17th, 2014, stating that, "[w]ith their long-awaited unions, we are slowly drawing close to full equality for lesbian, gay, bisexual, and transgender Americans nationwide" (Department of Justice, Office of Public Affairs, 2014b). While it may have been unintended, the imagery that HRC relied on to demonstrate the respectable and patriotic nature of gay Americans is reflected in the state's discursive creation of a "calculable and manageable gay subject" (Harvey, 2011, p. 165). Pellegrini (2015) lamented that the "responsibilization" of sexuality promotes inclusion but limits freedom against those considered to be outside of the "good" structure of practices (p. 243). One of Acting Assistant Attorney General for the Civil Rights Division Stuart F. Delery's 2012 speeches reflects this formulation. He stated:

> As all of these examples make clear, the Department is working hard to protect and support LGBT families. And I want to end by sharing one more important initiative on this front: our broad-reaching efforts to protect consumers. This work isn't really particular to the LGBT community. But I mention it out of recognition that LGBT families are, really, just families. And families spend most of their day worrying about basic issues. Like mortgages, and tuition, and health.
>
> *Department of Justice, Office of Public Affairs, 2012b*

By framing these legal disputes as victories or potential wins for all Americans, the Department of Justice depoliticizes the very position of marriage and *queerness* within the political order, effectively letting the triumph of the "universality of family" usher in respectable subjects— insofar as the populations named could mirror typical Western, middle-class, and neoliberal standards. Coontz (1992) showed that this imagery has never been a mainstream or collective precedent within American (or global) societies. Despite this historical fact, the material effects of these metavisuals are seen through the production of neoliberal policies that give rights to the right subjects.

Within the DOJ statements, "Don't Ask, Don't Tell" and the repeal of DOMA are connected through the economic benefits that they offer individual citizens. Yet, there is a troubling side to this and as Maeder (2013) stated, we must "deconstruct and rethink the regimes we take for granted to identify whose needs are not being accounted for and why" (p. 276). Indeed, the commodification of individual cases to perpetuate a specific kind of rights bearing citizen is also seen with the Department of Justice's frequent citing of *Lawrence v. Texas* as a parable of both universal love and the right to privacy. However, both approaches have not been articulated in ways that grapple with the racialized conflicts found within the case. Park (2006) suggested that, although the case was hailed as a victory for marginalized groups, it is "nothing less than a watershed moment both for a renewed soundness in constitutional jurisprudence, and for the revival of the libertarian values" (p. 838). Farrow (2011) argued that, indeed, access to the military helps individual queer people attain work, it does not account for one important problem: the racialized and classist system that pushes lower income, LGBTQ folks – many of whom are people of color—to need those jobs in the first place. While the Bush-era statements yielded but one press release related to either legislation, its contents are also related to the dominance of normalized individual rights in the United States. By making citizenship central to these discussions—through the linkage of gay rights to American citizens, emphasizing commitment and respectability, and the advocacy for individual rights—the Department of Justice reproduces existing ideologies about social institutions and upholds existing socio-economic, neoliberal political formations.

Nationalism and the American imagination

Additionally, more social and political recognition of LGBTQ communities had taken place, particularly during and after the Carter administration (Potter, 2012). Even before the passage of same-sex marriage, gay and lesbian access to military service was supported by 70 percent of respondents of a 2010 Gallup poll. This number, which had been rising by over 60 percent since 2005, corresponded to the budding tolerance of LGBT families in social arenas (Gallup, 2010). Yet, despite the 1999 murder of Private First Class Barry Winchell, which made DADT come under federal review, the law continued in the face of growing social acceptance of LGBT soldiers.

The change in tide did occur; however, soon after the 9/11 attacks on the World Trade Center and the Pentagon. The *Washington Post* reports that growing dissent against DADT came after the dismissal of nine military officers, among them being six men fluent in Arabic, despite the security crisis that had unfolded just months before (Nieves & Tyson, 2005). Some scholars such as Allsep (2013) have even suggested that if the military could not change the image of its soldier ideal, not only would discrimination persist, but the "ability of the U.S. Military to fight and win future wars may hang in the balance" (p. 398).

In some ways, both the absence of discourse about gay marriage and "Don't Ask, Don't Tell" by the Bush administration and the zealous narrative of inclusion by the subsequent government party are two different responses cut from the same cloth. Each ruling party acknowledged the shifting terrain of public support—and protest—and used these realizations to build narratives that mask the constraints placed upon various communities by the state. While the pre-2009 statements failed to yield much data regarding gay marriage and "DADT," a quick examination of the budget requests throughout the 2002–2008 fiscal years articulates an extremely pro-nationalist agenda, not an overtly homophobic one. Anker (2012) noted that after the terrorist attacks on September 11, 2001, freedom was the dominant term used to describe the United States in national political discourse. It was articulated as sovereign power, unencumbered agency, and military triumph. "Freedom" eventually animated global violence, becoming a justification for the wars in Afghanistan and Iraq, as well as for substantial increases in state surveillance.

Thinking back to then-Attorney General Holder's August 2012 statements at the Lavender Law conference, one can make sense of how the Department of Justice discursively offers American Exceptionalism to its citizenry: through bravery, courageousness, and dedication to the nation. Indeed, the repeal of DADT is portrayed as the "beginning of a new era for many brave servicemen and women," letting "lesbian, gay, and bisexual Americans serve proudly, honestly, and openly—without being fired for who they love" (Department of Justice, Office of Public Affairs, 2014c). This narrative overlaps with the judicial discourse about same-sex marriage.

These descriptions are just pieces to the larger discursive framework produced in these statements which posit the United States and its subjects as always working toward moral, modern, and military progress. With the distilling of queer subjects into what Cossman (2002) theorized as the "broader matrix of familialized heteronormativity," the governmental turn towards inclusivity can be linked to nation-building discourses (p. 483). An excerpt from President Barack Obama's 2011 statements after signing the repeal of "Don't Ask, Don't Tell" is but one example of discourses that can be read through this lens.

> I was proud to sign the Repeal Act into law last December because I knew that it would enhance our national security, increase our military readiness, and bring us closer to the principles of equality and fairness that define us as Americans. Today's achievement is a tribute to all the patriots who fought and marched for change; to Members of Congress, from both parties, who voted for repeal; to our civilian and military leaders who ensured a smooth transition; and to the professionalism of our men and women in uniform who showed that they were ready to move forward together, as one team, to meet the missions we ask of them.
>
> *Department of Justice, 2011*

In President Obama's words, one finds the construction of nationalism and the reification of military force—two ideological constructions heavily connected to projects of neoliberalism— juxtaposed to discourse on freedom. However, whose freedom is posed here? Certainly, as Puar (2007) has suggested, it isn't the freedom of bodies who are labeled as threats or terrorists by virtue of geography. Yet, legal rights and protocols surrounding "marriage equality" and DADT have long failed to recognize how American queer and transgender folks, people of color, poor communities—and all intersections inbetween found in the U.S.—are not saved with such nationalism either. Time and time again, queer activists and critical scholars have challenged the assumption that nationalism serves justice to all, particularly as social programs and advocacy efforts are slashed under the guise of protecting individuality (and business). To theorize these contradictions, others have continued to focus on how sexual politics are intimately linked with the intersections of various forms of mobility, neoliberalism, and citizenship (Bacchetta & Haritaworn, 2011; Brown & Browne, 2016; Gross, 2013; Katyal, 2010; Yep & Elia, 2012). As some have suggested, the abstract notions of personal choice or lifestyle have been so connected to nationalism that arguments addressing structural oppression are often dismissed as being antithetical to the American "pull yourself up by the bootstraps and wear your stripes when you've made it" dream focused on personal achievement. Moreover, as Goldberg (2008) argued, the seemingly open market of citizenship is laced with racialized implications, especially as segments of the population are still framed as being criminal, untrustworthy, or riddled with "cultural values" against work and upward movement—and thus, deserving of the inequalities they face. Ferguson (2005) contends that whiteness and the historical and institutional domination of racist social systems intertwine with heterosexist bias to produce a narrative that ignores the larger structural issues that reflect deeply embedded inequalities. Thus, one can see how the advocacy efforts of HRC, (as seen in HRC's 2013 screening of the pro-gay marriage film *Before God: We Are All Family*), have influenced the state department to issue statements that mark gays as being "just like other families," but those "other families" are constructed in very racialized ways (Guequierre, 2013). However, this is not a recent occurrence. Sociologist Feagin (2012) suggests that processes of exclusion (such as slavery, witch hunts, and the racist criminal legal system) have always been a part of American history and are still often ignored in discussions of social "progress" or change. Moreover, these erasures allow for governmental power and structures to remain exempt from critique, thus sustaining the political and social power of mainly white, heterosexual, cisgender populations across the country.

The invisible hand of law

Although the quest for equality is mentioned time and time again within these statements, the press releases do little in challenging the structure of the U.S. political system. While DADT and same-sex marriage represent unfortunate barriers, their treatment is framed within a potential to correct or even strengthen the existing legislative or epistemological underpinnings that are integral to the reproduction of the nation-state at large. The two dominant ways this can be seen in these documents is either through either the invocation of the freedoms outlined by the "Founding Fathers" and the Constitution, or through the construction of specific opponents, allies, and stakeholders—such as the ever-present democrat vs. republican rhetoric laced in governmental discourse—as the "real" enemies within these debates.

The emphasis on the constitution and legislative justice is not wrong simply by its own accord. Many social movements have appealed to federal and state policymakers, judges, and judicial spaces. The issue with this rendering is that, throughout the statements, the state itself is left as a mere bystander—neutral and objective. A February 2014 speech by Eric Holder becomes an exemplary representation of this type of discourse:

> America's most treasured ideals were not put into action or given the full force of law in a single instant. On the contrary: our ideals are continually advanced as our justice systems – and our Union – are strengthened; and as social science, human experience, legislation, and judicial decisions expand the circle of those who are entitled to the protections and rights enumerated by the Constitution. As we gather here in Washington today, I believe that our highest ideals – realized in the form of landmark Supreme Court rulings, from *Brown* to *Zablocki*, from *Romer* to *Lawrence*, from *Loving* to *Windsor* – light a clear path forward. They have impelled us, in some instances, to extraordinary action. And the progress we've seen has been consistent with the finest traditions of our legal system, the central tenets of our Constitution, and the "fundamental truth" that, as President Obama once said, "when all Americans are treated as equal … we are all more free."
>
> *Department of Justice, Office of Public Affairs, 2014d*

In addition to the historical inaccuracies of the trope of freedom, these discursive formations allow for the state to take a back seat, while blame for inequality can be pinned on "bad apples" within Congress or unfortunate cultural clashes, along with other actors, eras, or very specific political antagonists.

While the inclusive rhetoric highlights the shifting political landscape of the United States of America throughout Democratic- and Republican-headed cabinets, I suggest that these statements weave together partisan agendas to create a fuller understanding of state-level interests. For, as the Department of Justice website indicates, the Attorney General is both the head of this department and the chief law enforcement officer of the Federal Government. Moreover, the "Attorney General represents the United States in legal matters generally" (Department of Justice, 2015). Further, this office can offer opinions and suggestions to the President, along with other executive governmental departments. Thus, this position acts as a conduit of information and ideology that captures and underlines the positions and interests of the state. However, discursive frameworks like these—ones that do not focus on the foundations of oppression—are not new, nor are they not static. They are bound to the socio-historic context in which they emerge and in being socially constructed, are not omnipotent. However, the precariousness of their success is also important, as this type of binary-laden discourse is often used to reframe social issues as palatable neoliberal matters instead of deep-rooted social conditions inherent to the political landscape.

Through the subtle portrayal of legislative matters as battles between progress-makers and unruly opponents, the DOJ statements convey the judicial system as a passive, if not ahistorical, actor on the sidelines of "culture wars" and partisan debate. No alternatives to these frameworks or doubts about the strength of this system are posed. This narrative remains unchallenged within the HRC campaigns that were referenced earlier in this work, and, instead, was perpetuated through the repeated reliance on labeling specific parties or people as individual bigots. This was particularly evident in the language of the People's Brief and the "Repeal DADT Now Campaign," which questioned Barack Obama's individual character, rather than the foundation of a system built on heteronormativity and patriarchal values (Shaw, 2013).

Until death do us part? Implications for queer activism and solidarity

The reverberation of discourses – from the Human Rights Campaign to the Department of Justice – illustrate how activism and advocacy efforts have the potential to influence cultural landscapes and institutional measures. However, as shown by a critical examination of the imageries that emerge from theses discourses, the narratives that underpin this work can also perpetuate exclusionary forms of oppression. Here, wedding rings and military medals start to those their allure. Yet, because of their usefulness, campaigns for racialized and sexualized neoliberal human rights remain, and unfortunately still stand as popular ways of garnering victories—even if these successes only help a privileged few of the LGBTQ community: white, cisgender gay men with socio-economic clout. This issue has become even more complex, considering the shifting political discourses of the near-past and now-present futures.

After a campaign filled with misogynistic, xenophobic, and classist commentary, Donald Trump was elected president. Although structural racism existed well before this time, Trump's victory upset the current social climate that privileged abstract racial boundaries—color-blind racism and other less visceral forms of dominance—instead of outright oppression. Because of this change, it has become even easier to want to blame individual people and political parties for the inequalities that marginalized groups like LGBTQ people face every day. Moreover, the impulse to prove a population's worthiness or how much they give back to the country become easy talking points when trying to rationalize against bigotry. However, in doing so, advocates reproduce the very rhetoric that assisted in creating them: neoliberal, nationalistic, and normative portrayals of who belongs and who doesn't.

Despite provoking such responses, the Trump administration has also deployed a set of discourses that rely on a collective imagination of normal. While his administration used deeply discriminatory rhetoric in policies towards migrant bodies and policing, much of the political discourse has grown out of the neoliberal past–present I have described earlier. What does this look like? Individualized health care, a quest to make great workers and to support creative, lone-wolf entrepreneurs; and on a global scale: America first. These notions have existed before; however, at this historical moment, they act as buffers for privileged classes to look out for their own interests—like same-sex marriage or military access—without having to fight for wide-scale social alternatives for others. Thus, in some ways, "Make America Great Again" is a ghostly haunting that makes explicit racist, sexist, patriarchal, transphobic, and heteronormative oppression in an era where U.S. society has tried to forget. The discursive reading presented earlier directly articulates how some social movements have attempted to address this problem in vain, reproducing the very erasures they mean to combat.

So, how *can* activists and scholars committed to queer social justice projects use this discussion to make sense of the scholarly research and organizing work they will continue to engage in during these precarious times? Cohen (1997) suggested that we "start our political work from the recognition that multiple systems of oppression are in operation and that these systems use institutionalized categories and identities to regulate and socialize" (p. 458). A call to a contentious queer agenda that includes analysis, theory, and action is an integral aspect of "critical counter-discourse and context for the emergence of counterpublics and challenging constructions of sexual citizenship" (Davies, 2008, pp. 98–99). Why queer? For as Ellis (2015) wrote, queer is that thing that tells us that what we have is not enough. Several movements, led by queer and trans young people of color, offer practical evidence of what organizing for fundamental changes to our social world can look like and sound like.

FIERCE NYC's 2008 political organizing regarding the West Village Pier, Familia Trans Queer Liberation Movement's (Familia: TQLM) work challenging deportation, and most recently, Southerners on New Ground's (SONG) co-organized initiative to raise bail for incarcerated mothers, all represent alternatives to the liberal judicial framework and thus are markers of such work. Each of these organizations has paid careful attention to how previous LGBTQ advocacy efforts have privileged (mostly white, masculine, and wealthy) groups by lobbying for individual rights on the backs of other, less socio-economically advantaged queers. By doing this, these organizations continue to reimagine how to support the diversity of experiences – not just a generalized identity "masquerading as universalism" (Stein, 2013, p. 60). Moreover, each organization demonstrates what Weiss (2016) called a place beyond the typical narratives of law and belonging and examines public issues through an embodied structural perspective (Bonilla-Silva, 1997). Thus, in identifying these shifting narratives of nationalism, normativity, and racialized neoliberalism, this work sheds light on how processes of domination can be reproduced, even in well-meaning contexts. As Browne (2015) suggested, "talking back, then, is one way of challenging surveillance and its imposition of norms" (p. 62). Thus, going forward, queer activists have an opportunity to either challenge the oppressive frameworks stemming from and connected to such projects or, as, a queen once said, put "a ring on it."

Note

1   *Obergefell v. Hodges* was the landmark case.

References

Allsep, M. L. L. (2013). The myth of the warrior: Martial masculinity and the end of don't ask, don't tell. *Journal of Homosexuality*, 60(2–3):381–400.

Anker, E. (2012). Feminist theory and the failures of post-9/11 freedom. *Politics & Gender*, 8(2):207–215.

Bacchetta, P. and Haritaworn, J. (2011). There are many transatlantics: Homonationalism, homotransnationalism, and feminist-queer-trans of color theories and practices. In K. Davis & M. Evans (Eds.), *Transatlantic Conversations*. Farnham: Ashgate, 127–144.

Belkin, A. (2013). The politics of paranoia. *Journal of Homosexuality*, 6(2–3):214–218.

Bonilla-Silva, E. (1997). Racism: Towards a structural interpretation. *American Sociological Review*, 62(3):465–480.

Brown, G. and Browne, K. (2016). Sexual politics: Section introduction. In G. Brown & K. Browne (Eds.), *The Routledge Research Companion to Geographies of Sex and Sexualities*. New York, NY: Routledge, 64–78.

Browne, S. (2015). *Dark Matters: On the Surveillance of Blackness*. Durham, NC: Duke University Press.

Carpenter, D., Kaplan, R., & Sanders, S. (2015). *Brief of the Human Rights Campaign and 207,551 Americans as Amici Curiae Supporting Petitioners*. Vol. I. Washington, DC: Wilson-Epes Printing Co., Inc.

Cohen, C. (1997). Punks, bulldaggers, and welfare queens: The radical potential of queer politics? *GLQ: Gay and Lesbian Studies Quarterly*, 3(4):437–465.

Conrad, R. (Ed.). (2014). *Against Equality: Queer Revolution, Not Mere Inclusion*. Oakland, CA: AK Press.

Coontz, S. (1992). *The Way We Never Were: American Families and the Nostalgia Trap*. New York: Basic Books.

Cossman, B. (2002). Sexing citizenship, privatizing sex. *Citizenship Studies*, 6(4):483–506.

Crocker, T. (2009). From privacy to liberty: The fourth amendment after Lawrence. *UCLA Law Review*, 57(1):1–69.

Crowley, C. (2007, August 10). Democratic Hopefuls Pressed on Gay Issues at Forum. *CNN*. Retrieved from http://edition.cnn.com/2007/POLITICS/08/10/gay.forum/.

DasGupta, D. (2012). Trans/nationally femme: Notes on neoliberal economic regimes, security states, and my life as a brown immigrant fag. In M. B. Sycamore (Ed.), *Why Are Faggots So Afraid of Faggots?* Oakland, CA: AK Press, 15–24.

Davies, C. (2008). Proliferating panic: Regulating representations of sex and gender during the culture wars. *Cultural Studies Review*, 14(2):83–102.

Department of Justice. (2011). Obama: Americans no longer have to lie to serve. *American Forces Press Service*. Retrieved from www.defense.gov/news/newsarticle.aspx?id=65381.

Department of Justice. (2015). About the Office. September 15, 2016. Retrieved from www. justice.gov/ag/about-office.

Department of Justice, Office of Public Affairs. (2012a, August 23). Attorney General Eric Holder Speaks at the 2012 Lavender Law Conference [Press release]. May 10, 2016.

Retrieved from www.justice.gov/opa/speech/attorney-general-eric-holder-speaks-2012-lavender-law-conference.

Department of Justice, Office of Public Affairs. (2012b, April 28). Acting Assistant Attorney General for the Civil Division Stuart F. Delery Speaks at the White House LGBT Conference on Families [Press release]. May 10, 2016. Retrieved from www.justice.gov/opa/speech/acting-assistant-attorney-general-civil-division-stuart-f-delery-speaks-white-house-lgbt.

Department of Justice, Office of Public Affairs. (2013, June 26). Statement by Attorney General Eric Holder on the Supreme Court Ruling on the Defense of Marriage Act [Press release]. May 10, 2016. Retrieved from www.justice.gov/opa/pr/statement-attorney-general-eric-holder-supreme-court-ruling-defense-marriage-act.

Department of Justice, Office of Public Affairs. (2014a, January 10). Statement by Attorney General Eric Holder on Federal Recognition of Same-Sex Marriages in Utah [Press release]. May 10, 2016. Retrieved from www.justice.gov/opa/pr/statement-attorney-general-eric-holder-federal-recognition-same-sex-marriages-utah.

Department of Justice, Office of Public Affairs. (2014b, March 28). Statement by Attorney General Eric Holder on Federal Recognition of Same-Sex Marriages in Michigan [Press release]. May 10, 2016. Retrieved from www.justice.gov/opa/pr/statement-attorney-general-eric-holder-federal-recognition-same-sex-marriages-michigan.

Department of Justice, Office of Public Affairs. (2014c, February 10). Attorney General Eric Holder Delivers Remarks at the Human Rights Campaign Greater New York Gala [Press release]. May 10, 2016. Retrieved from www.justice.gov/opa/speech/attorney-general-eric-holder-delivers-remarks-human-rights-campaign-greater-new-york-gala.

Department of Justice, Office of Public Affairs. (2014d, February 25). Remarks as Prepared for Delivery by Attorney General Holder at the National Association of Attorneys General Winter Meeting [Press release]. May 10, 2016. Retrieved from www.justice.gov/opa/speech/remarks-prepared-delivery-attorney-general-eric-holder-national-association-attorneys.

Duggan, L. (2005). The new homonormativity: The sexual politics of neoliberalism. In R. Castronovo and D. D. Nelson (Eds.), *Materializing Democracy: Toward a Revitalized Cultural Politics*. Durham, NC: Duke University Press, 175–194.

Ellis, N. (2015). *Territories of the Soul: Queered Belonging in the Black Diaspora*. Durham, NC: Duke University Press.

Farrow, K. (2011). A military job is not economic justice. *The Huffington Post*. July 10, 2017. Retrieved from www.huffingtonpost.com/kenyon-farrow/post_1732_b_824046.html.

Feagin, J. (2012). *White Party, White Government: Race, Class, and U.S. Politics*. Abingdon: Routledge.

Ferguson, R. (2005). Racing homonormativity: Citizenship, sociology, and gay identity. In P. Johnson and M. G. Henderson (Eds.), *Black Queer Studies: A Critical Anthology*. Durham, NC: Duke University Press.

Ferguson, R. and Hong, G. K. (2012). The sexual and racial contradictions of neoliberalism. *Journal of Homosexuality*, 59(7):1057–1064.

FIERCE. (2008). *LGBT Youth Center: Pier 40 Recommendation*. New York.

Frank, N. (2013). The president's pleasant surprise: How LGBT advocates ended Don't Ask, Don't Tell. *Journal of Homosexuality*, 60(2–3):159–213.

Franz, M. (2015). Will to love, will to fear: The emotional politics of illegality and citizenship in the campaign against birthright citizenship in the US. *Social Identities*, 21(2):184–198.

Gallup, I. (2010). Gay and Lesbian Rights. September 18, 2015. Retrieved from www.gallup.com/poll/1651/gay-lesbian-rights.aspx.

Goldberg, D. T. (2008). *The Threat of Race: Reflections on Racial Neoliberalism*. Hoboken, NJ: Wiley-Blackwell.

Gross, A. (2013). Post/colonial queer globalisation and international human rights: Images of LGBT rights. *Jindal Global Law Review*, 4(2):98–130.

Guequierre, P. (2013). "Before God: We Are All Family" to Premier at HRC. May 25, 2017. Retrieved from www.hrc.org/blog/hrc-to-premier-film-before-god-we-are-all-family.

Harvey, D. O. (2011). Calculating risk: Barebacking, the queer male subject, and the de/formation of identity politics. *Discourse*, 33(2):156–183.

Heike Schotten, C. (2015). Homonationalist futurism: "Terrorism" and (other) queer resistance to empire. *New Political Science*, 37(1):71–90.

Hirschman, L. (2010). 'Don't Ask, Don't Tell': How it was repealed. *The Daily Beast*. May 25, 2017. Retrieved from www.thedailybeast.com/articles/2010/12/18/dont-ask-dont-tell-how-it-was-repealed.html.

Human Rights Campaign. (2010). The Repeal of "Don't Ask, Don't Tell". May 25, 2017. Retrieved from www.hrc.org/resources/the-repeal-of-dont-ask-dont-tell.

Human Rights Campaign. (2017). Our Victories. Retrieved from www.hrc.org/hrc-story/our-victories.

Katyal, S. 2010. The dissident citizen. *UCLA Law Review*, 57(1):1415–1476.

Maeder, S. (2013). Divorcing marriage from its incidents: Framing Perry as a celebration of family self-determination. *NYU Review of Law & Social Change*, 37(1):275–289.

Miller, H. (2015). The Guardian: HRC's All God's Children Campaign Spreads LGBT Equality in the south. May 25, 2017. Retrieved from www.hrc.org/blog/the-guardian-hrcs-all-gods-children-campaign-spreads-lgbt-equality-in-the-s.

Nieves, E. and Tyson, S. (2005). Fewer gays being discharged since 9/11. *The Washington Post*. December 10, 2016. Retrieved from www.washingtonpost.com/wp-dyn/articles/A17522-2005Feb11.html.

Park, M. (2006). Defining one's own concept of existence and the meaning of the universe: The presumption of liberty in Lawrence v. Texas. *Brigham Young University Law Review*, 2006(3):837–887.

Pellegrini, A. 2015. Responsibilization, same-sex marriage, and the end of queer sex. *Psychoanalysis, Culture & Society*, 20(3):237–245.

Potter, C. (2012). Paths to political citizenship: Gay rights, feminism, and the Carter presidency. *Journal of Policy History*, 24(1):95–115.

Puar, J. (2007). *Terrorist Assemblages: Homonationalism in Queer Times*. Durham, NC: Duke University Press.

Scotti, G. W. (2004). Queer eye for the military guy: Will "Don't Ask, Don't Tell" survive in the wake of *Lawrence V. Texas*? *St. John's Law Review*, 78(3):897–931.

Shaw, R. (2013). *The Activist's Handbook: Winning Social Change in the 21st Century*. Berkeley, CA: University of California Press.

Spade, D. (2013). Under the cover of gay rights. *New York University Review of Law & Social Change*, 37(79):79–100.

Stein, A. (2013). What's the matter with Newark? Race, class, marriage politics, and the limits of queer liberalism. In M. Bernstein and V. Taylor (Eds.), *The Marrying Kind? Debating Same-Sex Marriage within the Lesbian and Gay Movement*. Minneapolis, MN: University of Minnesota Press, 39–66.

van Dijk, T. A. (2008). *Discourse and Power*. Basingstoke: Palgrave Macmillan.

Ward, M. (2013). The military must lead in advocating for marriage equality. *NYU Review of Law & Social Change*, 37(2):457–511.

Weeks, J. (1998). The sexual citizen. *Theory, Culture, & Society*, 15(3–4):35–52.

Weiss, M. (2016). Collaboration: Integration. Correspondences, *Cultural Anthropology*. June 16, 2017. Retrieved from https://culanth.org/fieldsights/975-collaboration-integration.

Yep, G. A. and Elia, J. P. (2012). Racialized masculintiies and the new homonormativity in LOGO's Noah's Arc. *Journal of Homosexuality*, 59(7):890–911.

Yoshino, K. (2010). The gay tipping point. *UCLA Law Review*, 57(1):1537–1544.

3

WHAT'S LOVE GOT TO DO WITH IT?

Queer politics and the "love pivot"

Myrl Beam

Editors' Introduction:

In this chapter, Myrl Beam looks at the strategies of the same-sex marriage campaigns and considers their implications for the future of LGBTQ activism. Specifically, Beam analyzes the decision made by some LGBTQ organizations to stop publicly focusing on marriage as an issue of rights or discrimination. Instead, in the final years of the same-sex marriage campaigns, these groups shifted their public messaging to focus on the question of "love". Beam examines why Minnesota marriage advocates made this decision, how they implemented it, and what results it produced.

Beam argues that although this strategy proved successful at achieving marriage rights, it was also problematic for a variety of reasons. In particular, Beam is concerned that this strategy prevents building broad-based coalitions that have the potential to make larger progressive change.

Readers are encouraged to consider the implications for future LGBTQ activism? How might the "love pivot" limit the imagination of the LGBTQ movement as it moves forward in a post-marriage America? What are the challenges and benefits of focusing on rights or discrimination, rather than focusing on love? What other frameworks should be considered? What strategies are necessary to achieve the progressive coalitions for which Beam advocates? How might they lead to larger structural changes?

Introduction

On the day of the *Obergefell v. Hodges* Supreme Court decision legalizing same sex marriage, the hashtag #lovewins reached 6.2 million tweets (Flynn, 2015). But as paradoxical as it now seems, given the ubiquity of that "lovewins" sentiment, marriage equality wasn't always about love. Prior campaigns centered issues of fairness and discrimination in their appeals for marriage equality. Though the love branding was certainly successful, in what follows I consider the implications of the turn towards love as the animating rhetoric of the marriage equality campaign on the future of queer political movements.

While the decision to appeal to so-called "American values" of love and freedom, and tie gay and lesbian couples to those values, may have been successful at winning marriage rights in the short term, I argue that it actively precludes the kind of broad-based progressive coalition that could fundamentally change the distribution of power and resources in this country. To illustrate this, I analyze a 2012 "Vote No" campaign in Minnesota opposed to a proposed constitutional amendment banning same-sex marriage. This campaign was one of four state-level campaigns that year that implemented this strategic messaging shift championed by national movement organizations. I conclude by assessing the impact of this shift on the LGBT movement post-marriage, asking how the "love pivot" disciplines the imagination of the movement even after marriage is no longer the target.

Love won?

In 2012, Minnesota made a unique kind of history: it was the first state in which a ballot initiative to ban same-sex marriage in the state constitution was defeated. It was four years after Proposition 8 in California rocked the LGBT movement and same-sex marriage was banned through an amendment to the California State constitution. Though Proposition 8 was the most highly publicized, 30 other states passed constitutional amendments banning same-sex marriage prior to 2012.

Minnesota, however, bucked the trend. It remains the only state to have successfully fought off a ballot initiative. Many activists that I spoke to credited this win, after years and years of defeats, with changing the tide of public sentiment and demonstrating to the Supreme Court that the mood of the country had changed, and was now ready to embrace marriage equality.

This was the case, they believe, due to another feature of the Minnesota campaign: strategy. After years of utilizing a strategy focused on equality that centered the unfairness of a ban against same-sex marriage, the national marriage movement went another direction, and Minnesota was the launching pad for this new strategy. Based on significant focus-group research on messaging conducted by the national organization Freedom to Marry and the centrist think tank Third Way in the four years after Proposition 8, the four marriage equality campaigns in 2012—the ballot initiative in Minnesota, and marriage referendums in Maine, Maryland, and Washington—instead chose to centralize love, freedom, responsibility, and sameness. As a result, the proposed ban on same-sex marriage in Minnesota was successfully defeated, and voters approved referenda legalizing gay marriage in Maine, Maryland, and Washington. Love, apparently, *does* win.

So instead of a mass mobilization of queer and progressive people, the "vote no" campaign became the first focus-group-tested, "data-driven" ballot initiative marriage campaign. Richard Carlbom, the Executive Director of Minnesotans United for All Families, the organization driving the "Vote No" campaign, described the messaging shift:

> A massive public education campaign that eliminates the misunderstanding between straight voters and the lived experience of the LGBT community, in that what marriage means to us is very similar, it's the same thing: it's you

meet the person you want to spend the rest of your life with, you fall in love, and then the next step is you get married. And unfortunately, the way we had been talking about it for so long, straight people thought we wanted to get married for the benefits that came from marriage.

Personal communication, June 26, 2016

According to Carlbom, the reason for the 30 previous losses was that the focus on discrimination and equality simply did not resonate with straight voters. This messaging shift would show them that, apparently, gay people get married for the "same reason" that straight people do: *love*.

Though this messaging focus-grouped well, it was, interestingly, a hard sell when it came to actual queer people. Ann Kaner-Roth, the then Executive Director of Project 515, one of the two organizations that convened the campaign, said that initially there had been "disagreement internally about the messaging. There was a pretty strong desire in the community and among many donors about how we should be talking about it from a discrimination/bigotry lens, which had been tried and failed" (personal communication, June 26, 2016). Ultimately, she said, people who cared about marriage equality needed to understand a basic principle: "You are not the target market." In other words, the past marriage campaigns' primary hindrance was that it was built by and for LGBT people, using a message that felt real to many queer people: that it was unfair to privilege one form of family and shower that form with benefits. This "love pivot" ushered in a campaign geared towards straight people, one that mobilized fantasies of the American dream where love is depoliticized and private.

This has long been a critique posed by those on the queer left of the marriage equality agenda: it has always privileged one form of sexual or romantic relationship—coupled, monogamous, private, unpaid—and participated in a sexual culture that demonizes and polices other forms of sexuality: hook-ups, multiple partners, non-monogamy, sex work, public sex (see, for example, Duggan, 2003; Cohen, 1997; Eng, 2010; Spade & Willse, 2005; Warner, 1999). The turn towards the rhetoric of love only intensified this embrace of normativity.

However, my interviews suggested that many queer people active on the campaign did *not* feel compelled by or included in this vision of the good life the campaign sought to mobilize. Instead, the campaign had to *create* the ideal gay and lesbian life narrative based on focus-group research that revealed what straight people wanted to hear—a story that would validate and re-affirm the moral rightness of straight people's own identities and life choices—and then teach that story to real live queers, so that they could repeat this story back to straight people. In fact, Carlbom described how, unlike at most campaigns where volunteers are handed the script and then head to the phones, volunteers for the "Vote No" campaign would have to sit through 45 minute training sessions prior to being allowed to work the phone banks. The training, he said,

laid out all of our messaging research. Because people really had to have an authentic conversation. . . . The best thing we could do was show people, this is the research: when you talk about equality people STOP listening. . . . They think we're getting married for rights and benefits while they're getting married for love, commitment, and to start a family. We have to reverse that.

Personal communication, June 26, 2016

People, according to Carlbom, had to have an *authentic* conversation. But before they could work the phones, volunteers had to be taught the story that they were to authentically relate.

Alfonso Wenker, the Deputy Finance Director for Minnesotans United, described how, though it was difficult for the queer staff, they were taught to target their message—and their life stories—to white suburban women. He went on:

> For real, we had a campaign psychologist! She . . . helped us think about the values-based mindset of the people we were trying to move. . . . And she said to us: "voters are scared of butt sex, and we need a message that doesn't get them to think about butt sex." . . . We just kind of need to get them to stop thinking about the kind of sex people have, and we've got to get them to think about their version of love and how our version of love isn't creepy, right? And I was like, oh! I get it: this is what people think marriage is, and let's get them to think our version is the same as their version, even if it's not.
>
> *Personal communication, June 28, 2016*

So instead of just revealing to voters the heretofore unknown similarities between gay and straight relationships, Wenker suggests that this was instead about learning how to refract the complexities of queer lives through the filter of the most stereotypical heteronormative fantasy of marriage. It was, as critics have rightly argued for two decades, a re-affirmation of the most normative version of marriage, rather than any sort of expansion or re-invention of it. Further, it went to great pains to erase the specter of gay sex from the project of marriage. Marriage was positioned for voters as a way to domesticate and control the danger posed by gay sex.

The stakes of single issue organizing

There is another interesting and unique feature of the "Vote No" campaign: at the same time voters were asked to decide on a possible ban on gay marriage, they were also asked to consider another constitutional amendment, this one requiring an ID to vote. This measure was part of a wave—that has only intensified in the ensuing years—seeking to restrict the right to vote, measures that disproportionately affect low-income, disabled, older folks, students, and folks of color. The Brennan Center reports that in 2012, 25 laws and 2 executive actions were passed in 19 states restricting voting, either through constitutional amendments, like the one proposed in Minnesota, or through legislative action limiting early voting, requiring proof of citizenship, ending same-day voter registration, and making it more difficult for people with past felony convictions to restore their voting rights (Weiser & Norden, 2012).

In Minnesota, one might imagine that the opposition to these two right-wing ballot initiatives might have joined forces, and even asserted an affirmative progressive political vision. These two types of ballot initiatives serve the same political purpose for the right—wedge issues that drive the Republican electorate to the polls—so it would make sense that a progressive political coalition counters both, crafting a message of inclusion and fairness, a message that challenges both attempts to limit the rights of marginalized communities. This was, however, not the case. Minnesotans United for All families took great pains *not* to take a stance on the Voter ID measure in the hopes of attracting some Republicans who could get behind a particular vision of marriage equality but would seek to restrict voting rights. Ann Kaner-Roth comments:

> From the progressive community there was a lot of interest in linking the campaigns. [But]... we made a promise that we weren't going to deal with any of that stuff, the point wasn't to create this broad-based group that would agree on twelve different issues, we wanted these folks to be very laser-focused on this particular issue. ... And a decision was made early on we are simply not tying these together; we're not dealing with this, this is not our fight.
>
> *Personal communication, June 24, 2016*

There is no clearer articulation of single-issue politics than this. And as Vaid (1996), Duggan (2003), Cohen (1997), and others have so ably articulated, the danger in imagining that "gay" issues can be separated from issues of racism, classism, immigration, etc., is that it centers on affluent White people. White middle-class people are the ones for whom their sexual identity is their only area of marginalization— for whom there are solely "gay" issues. For all others, the policing of sexuality is bound up in immigration status, racist policing, anti-welfare rhetoric, to name a few of the ways that sexuality and race are experienced simultaneously.

My interest, then, is in what such single-issue politics means in terms of the structure of the movement going forward. In our interview, Alfonso Wenker, the highest-ranking person of color at Minnesotans United, offered a more nuanced assessment of the refusal to take a stance on the Voter ID campaign within the context of the broader organizing landscape:

> But what we hadn't done as a movement is build the kind of a movement that in a tough moment can respond in an intersectional way. ... And so we also have to look at our own movement say ... what kind of communities and institutions can we set up to be like "No to both, and we're gonna fight both" and figure out the message.
>
> *Personal communication, June 28, 2016*

What Wenker wisely points to is that the infrastructure of the movement itself was not prepared to deploy one message that understands race and sexuality together.

But marriage itself is both a symptom and an engine of this failure. Marriage was able to emerge as an issue *because* of the infrastructure of movement organizations, and their reliance on the wealthiest members of the community for funding—wealthy donors that largely benefit from the current system of racialized capitalism, and thus have no critique of it to offer.

Immediate aftermath

I think it's important to dwell on the terms of this "victory" for a moment. To reiterate, many activists I spoke with credit this messaging shift away from equality and towards love to be the catalyst for the sea change to which the Supreme Court responded in the *Obergefell* decision. For 40 years there were aspects of the movement that challenged the primacy of one vision of the "family," challenged the idea that any particular relationship or household structure was more ethical, more sanctified, more worthy of personhood than any other. It wasn't until the movement shifted away from claims based on discrimination that "the country was ready" for marriage equality. And the movement infrastructure, the donors, the staff, the volunteers had to be—and were—trained to articulate queer lives through the lens of love, where love stands in for a whole host of ideas about which kinds of people and relationship structures are valuable, moral, and ultimately worthy of citizenship, and which are not.

For Maria De La Cruz, who had been the fundraising director at OutFront Minnesota, the statewide LGBT organization, "it feels like people moved on" (personal communication, September 12, 2016). De La Cruz recounted for me what fundraising for a statewide LGBT organization was like immediately after marriage. I asked her about whether the massive influx of funding that supported the "Vote No" campaign continued:

> It did dry up for us. . . . One of the conversations that I had with this donor right after the governor signed the marriage bill, I went to him and said "hey listen," I said, "we are going to be fighting for safe schools, I'd really like to see you make a significant investment." And what he said to me was, "You know what, that's not my issue". . . . That played out instantly.

So, for movement organizations attempting to shift to other issues in the wake of marriage, many donors did not shift with them. And this is compounded by another unique feature of the "Vote No" campaign: it was massively appealing to straight people, which translated into a gigantic haul of cash from donors who had never given to LGBT issues. And, as it turns out, likely never will again, since they believed they hype: this was *the* issue, and #lovewon.

Conclusion

In the wake of *Obergefell v. Hodges,* it appears likely that much of this movement infrastructure will now turn its attention to transgender issues. This is especially true now that legislating transgender people's access to bathrooms and other public spaces has replaced limiting queer people's access to marriage as an effective wedge issue to drive the Republican electorate to the polls. This shift towards trans issues is an especially concerning example of the dangers of the "love pivot." When we gear our movement strategy toward what will be most palatable to dominant voters, we create movements that will trade the precarious inclusion of those most acceptable within the status quo for any dream of actually *changing* the status quo. In this age of focus-group-driven movement strategy, I fear that what we will see is this: increasing "acceptance" of some transgender people, those who most embody traditional ideas about masculinity and femininity (people who "pass," who are pretty, young, middle class or wealthy, and do not challenge the gender binary), at the expense of a movement strategy that would challenge the racialized policing of gender conformity and the ubiquity of the binary itself. In other words, those who most embody cis people's own ideas about gender will be accepted, and those of us who don't will find ourselves on the outside of our own movement. The embrace of love worked similarly, privileging gay and lesbian couples that most embodied straight people's ideas of what love should look like, and consigned other forms of queer relationality to continued policing, danger, and cultural stigma.

Though it is regarded as a win for the movement, I argue that the "love pivot"— a strategy determined by what does well with focus groups—is actually destructive to the political horizon of the movement. Though it is quite evocative, relying as it does on normative ideas about family, nation, and duty, love is not the rhetorical backbone of a progressive coalition—in large part because those normative ideas about nation, duty, and family rely on and entrench White supremacy and nationalism. And this is not simply a failure of the story that was chosen; this is a broader structural failure of the movement itself. When our ability to organize for change relies on funding from the wealthiest in the community—people for whom the status quo has largely worked—we will always prioritize a reformist, assimilationist vision, and this will not change, only intensify, I fear, in the wake of this "victory."

Ultimately, in the context of increased precarity under Trump, we cannot afford to abandon justice as a goal for the movement. In this historical moment, when visions of the good life have frayed beyond recognition and so many are locked out of a neoliberal economy, experiencing the immanence of ecological collapse, we cannot abandon the idea that there is more wrong with the status quo than simply the exclusion of LGBT people from its dominant institutions.

References

Cohen, C. (1997). Punks, bulldaggers, and welfare queens: The radical potential of queer politics. *GLQ: A Journal of Gay and Lesbian Studies*, 3(4):437–465.

Duggan, L. (2003). *The Twilight of Equality: Neoliberalism, Cultural Politics, and the Attack on Democracy*. New York: Beacon.

Eng, D. (2010). *The Feeling of Kinship: Queer Liberalism and the Feeling of Kinship*. Durham, NC: Duke University Press.

Flynn, K. (June 26, 2015). How #LoveWins on Twitter became the most viral hashtag of the same-sex marriage ruling. *International Business Times.*

Spade, D. & Willse, C. (2005). Freedom in a regulatory state? *Lawrence*, Marriage, and Biopolitics. *Widener Law Review*, 11:309–329.

Vaid, U. (1996). *Virtual Equality: The Mainstreaming of the Gay and Lesbian Movement.* New York: Anchor Books.

Warner, M. (1999). *The Trouble with Normal: Sex, Politics, and the Ethics of Queer Life.* Cambridge, MA: Harvard University Press.

Weiser, W. & Norden, L. (2012). Voting law changes in 2012. *Brennan Center for Justice at New York University School of Law.* Retrieved from www.brennancenter.org/sites/default/files/legacy/Democracy/VRE/Brennan_Voting_Law_V10.pdf.

PART II
New social movements

4

A NEW QUEER LIBERATION MOVEMENT

And its targets of influence, mobilization, and benefits

Joseph Nicholas DeFilippis

Editors' introduction:

This chapter makes the argument that a separate queer social movement has emerged, led by LGBTQ organizations that are run by people of color, transgender people, immigrants, and/or low-income people. DeFilippis analyzes staff interviews, mission statements and promotional videos of seven such organizations to examine the underlying values and shared agenda of this separate Queer Liberation Movement (QLM). The QLM has a common analysis of the issues impacting their communities, a shared set of principles, and similar organizing strategies. They have a more intersectional, multi-issue, and radical agenda than the mainstream "gay rights" movement that dominates the public eye.

The author uses a framework developed by social movement scholar William Gamson to demonstrate that the organizations in this movement choose targets that makes it distinct from that of the mainstream movement. The QLM offers a model of queer activism that is ultimately broader, more intersectional, and more justice-centered than the mainstream movement.

Readers are invited to consider the following questions: What is the potential of this new social movement? Given that one of the reasons the mainstream movement has been so successful is because of its narrow focus on single-issue politics, what challenges might be faced by the QLM? How might its intersectional, multi-issue agenda bring benefits to overcome those challenges? Does the passage of legal same-sex marriage make it easier or harder for the QLM to bring forward a queerer agenda?

Introduction

From 2000 to 2009, I worked as one of the co-founders and executive directors of a small organization in New York called Queers for Economic Justice (QEJ). During this period, QEJ worked closely with a number of other small, grassroots, radical queer groups, locally and across the country. Working with them was logical, because these queer liberation groups each had values, goals, constituents, and strategies that were similar to those of QEJ. These values, goals, constituents, and strategies were, however, markedly different from those of the national LGBT organizations and state-wide equality groups that dominate the mainstream gay rights movement (referred to in this chapter as the GRM).[1] It was clear to me from the beginning that there were two very different types of organizations operating alongside each other in the movement.

Over the years, I witnessed many disagreements (about priorities and strategies) between the queer liberation groups and the larger GRM organizations, leading to ongoing tensions between the two different kinds of organizations. When I later entered academia, I decided to focus my research on these queer liberation organizations, studying different aspects of their work, including those tensions with the GRM. In this chapter, I show how the queer liberation organizations have similar values and targets that situate them in two important ways: (1) outside of the GRM, and (2) as comprising their own distinct social movement: A Queer Liberation Movement. They are not merely a random set of small outlier organizations, but something more coherent, and therefore significant.

The mainstream gay rights movement

Over the past two decades, the GRM has had tremendous success moving forward its agenda. The work of the GRM organizations has principally involved advocacy and legislative lobbying, and litigation in state and federal courts; these efforts have been framed in the context of "equality" for LGBTQ people. These equality groups—ranging from national organizations such as the Human Rights Campaign to state-wide equality groups at the local level—have pursued equality primarily by increasing LGBTQ people's access to institutions previously restricted to them (i.e., marriage, military service, etc.) on the one hand, and legal remedies for discrimination (i.e., hate crimes legislation, and employment non-discrimination) on the other (DeFilippis, 2015; Rosenblum, 1994).

Conceptually, the focus on LGBTQ equality has rested on a default understanding of LGBTQ people as united under an umbrella of homophobic discrimination. The GRM has employed a laser-sharp focus on combatting homophobic discrimination, making it not merely its primary goal, but its solitary goal. Similar to second-wave feminism, this conception ignores the impacts of racism, classism, xenophobia, transphobia, and other intersectional experiences that complicate the notion of monolithic "gayness" (Cohen, 1999; Vaid, 2012). Activists and scholars have long noted that because the equality organizations have ignored the impacts of those other "isms," while myopically focusing exclusively on combatting homophobia, they have excluded LGBT people of color, low-income LGBT people, and transgender people. Nevertheless, the GRM has been largely successful at characterizing themselves in the public eye as *the* organizations representing the interests of *the* LGBTQ community.

An alternate movement

However, for as long as these GRM organizations have pursued their equality-based agenda, other local grassroots LGBTQ groups have actively organized around intersectional, multi-issue interests. Structuring their work around core principles of intersectionality and centering the interests of the most marginal among queer communities, these queer liberation organizations present a stark counterpoint to the dominance of the GRM. These organizations explicitly center the leadership and membership of queers who are people of color (POC), transgender, poor and/or immigrant. These organizations employ both a redistribution (economics-based) and recognition (identity-based) politic in their activism. They complicate narratives of who constitutes "the LGBTQ community" and consequently shift the conversation about that community's most pressing interests. While referring to themselves as LGBTQ organizations, they also position LGBTQ concerns as inextricably linked with concerns related to identities including race, class, gender, national status, and institutions like the immigration and the criminal/prison legal systems.

This chapter[2] highlights the underlying values and shared agendas of seven such organizations: Affinity Community Services in Chicago; allgo in Austin; Audre Lorde Project (ALP) in New York; National Queer Asian Pacific Islander Alliance (NQAPIA) in New York; Queers for Economic Justice (QEJ) in New York (now closed); Southerners on New Ground (SONG) in Atlanta; and Sylvia Rivera Law Project (SRLP) in New York. For each group, I conducted interviews with staff, and analyzed mission statements and promotional videos.

I argue that they not only differ from the equality-based framework of the GRM but also constitute their own Queer Liberation Movement (QLM) distinct in its own right from the mainstream movement. This QLM has a shared set of principles, and a coherent analysis of the issues impacting their communities, which informs its strategic choices, and operates with its own set of organizing strategies. They choose similar targets, engaging in work that complements each other, in pursuit of a political agenda that is decidedly different from that of the GRM. The QLM offers a model of queer activism that is ultimately broader, more intersectional, and more justice-centered than the mainstream movement.

Gamson's framework of three targets

To understand how the QLM groups are outside of the GRM but aligned with each other, I use the ideas of influential social movement scholar William Gamson. Gamson (1975) presented a framework useful for understanding what he called "the nature of a challenging group" (p. 14), or any organization concerned principally with challenging a political, social, or economic system.

He suggested that challenging groups organize their efforts around three distinct, though often related, targets: targets of influence, of mobilization, and of benefits. These characteristics of challenging groups can differentiate the QLM from the GRM, while also illustrating points of alignment among the QLOs.

A challenging group's *targets of influence* are the set of individuals, policies, or institutions they identify as problematic and seek to influence in order to achieve their desired social change. In some cases, the targets of influence are individuals (e.g., an elected official), while in others, they may be significantly broader (e.g., the public education system).

The *targets of mobilization*, meanwhile, are those people the challenging group needs to activate in order to impact the targets of influence. Often conceptualized as the challenging group's constituency or base, these targets are those people whose direct effort can be harnessed to apply pressure to the targets needing to change.

Finally, *the targets of benefits* are the people most likely to benefit from the changed condition, once the target of influence has shifted its conduct. In short, they are the people who are helped if the challenging group is successful in its efforts.

Targets of the mainstream gay rights movement

Much has been written about the agenda and strategies of the mainstream gay rights movement. Nevertheless, in seeking to understand the contrasting agenda of the queer liberation organizations, it is useful to summarize the GRM's efforts in the context of Gamson's three targets.

First, the GRM organizations' primary targets of influence are elected officials and the judicial system. The GRM attempts to influence elected officials through lobbying efforts, and they target the judicial system in the form of litigation (Carpenter, 2014; D'Emilio, 2000; Farrow, 2012; Funders for LGBTQ Issues, 2016; MAP, 2012, 2016; Rosenblum, 1994; Vaid, 1995, 2012).

The GRM has attempted to influence these targets by focusing on single-issue policy issues, lacking an intersectional perspective (Carter, 1999; Cohen, 1997, 1999; DeFilippis, 2016; Duggan, 2003; Jones-Yelvington, 2008; Mahfuz & Farrow, 2012; Shepard, 2001). These organizations seek to address the exclusion of LGBTQ people from existing legal and social structures; consequently, their agenda has focused primarily on gaining inclusion into those structures. Specifically, GRMs have focused on access to family protections (e.g., marriage and adoption), inclusion of sexual orientation in hate crime and civil rights/ anti-discrimination laws (e.g., employment protection and access to the military), and support for youth, specifically in the context of the education system (e.g., safe schools, GSAs (Gay-Straight Alliance)). The majority of their resources have been spent on those issues (Bowen, 2012; Funders for LGBTQ Issues, 2012, 2016; MAP, 2007, 2011, 2016; Proteus Fund, 2015). Consequently, when equality organizations target elected officials and courts, they focus on those well positioned to influence these concerns.

Gamson (1975) has suggested that the targets of mobilization and the targets of benefits are sometimes closely aligned. This stands to reason; after all, the people most likely to benefit directly are also often those most likely to be motivated to take part in activism towards that change. In the context of the mainstream gay rights movement, this has certainly been the case. The GRM has structured its work around the pursuit of equality for gay and lesbian people. Based on an understanding of homophobia as the prime cause of inequality between LGBTQ and straight people, the movement has effectively argued that homophobia can be remedied through the inclusion of LGBTQ people in institutions and laws formerly closed to them. In this context, the movement has naively articulated that its agenda is in the best interest of all LGBTQ people (given that homophobia, which all LGBTQ people must navigate, is the central barrier to equality). Consequently, the GRM's stated constituency is all LGBTQ people.

In practice, however, the constituency is predominantly the White, middle-class gay and lesbian citizens who are most motivated by an equality rhetoric that centers homophobia so prominently among "the community's" interests. This applies to the leadership mobilizing the movement as well as the constituency being mobilized; the GRM's leadership has been overwhelmingly White, middle-class cisgender people (Boykin, 2000; Carter, 1999; D'Emilio, 2000; TransGriot, 2007; Vaid, 1995, 2012). Similarly, the beneficiaries of the GRM are rhetorically all LGBTQ people, but in practice consist of mostly White, middle-class gays and lesbians who most directly stand to benefit from the narrow range of policy and legal interests advanced by the movement (Carter, 1999; Conrad, 2010; Duggan, 2003; Hermosillo, 2013, Hutchinson, 1999, 2001; TransGriot, 2007; Vaid, 2012).

Queer liberation movement: three shared principles

The QLM groups approach their work from an entirely different orientation. These organizations have shared a commitment to approaching their work with an intersectional analysis, and to centering the interests of the most marginal among queer people from their very inception.

Intersectionality

For decades, the construction of "gay rights" as the domain of White, middle-class people has allowed single-issue theories of homophobia to drive the LGBTQ political agenda (Cohen, 1997; Conrad, 2010; D'Emilio, 2012; DeFilippis, Anderson-Nathe & Panichelli, 2015; Duggan, 2003; Hutchinson, 1999; Richardson, 1999; Vaid, 2012). An intersectional analysis, however, makes clear that homophobia alone is an incomplete explanation for the multiple marginalizations experienced by queer POC, poor queer people, queer people who are immigrants or incarcerated, trans people, and more. Instead, these organizations approach their work from a fundamentally intersectional perspective, attending directly to the multiple intersections of oppression affecting queer communities.

Intersectionality is one of the most important theories to come out of feminist studies. Black feminists, such as The Combahee River Collective (1981), Lorde (1983), and Crenshaw (1991), theorized that gender, race, class, and sexuality constitute intersecting systems that shape each person's experiences. Intersectionality posits, among other things, that it is impossible to understand any one form of oppression without understanding how it is impacted by all other systems. They argue that people have both advantages and disadvantages due to their locations in multiple systems (capitalism, racism, sexism, heterosexism), and could receive privilege from their position in one system (e.g., racism), but be disadvantaged because of their position in another overlapping system (e.g., homophobia).

QLM organizations operate from this intersectional analysis. In their origin stories, most QLOs describe their founders' frustration with other organizations' lack of an intersectional approach in their work. These organizations were born out of a desire to create a place that centers the intersections of their communities' identities. For example, in my interview with Ben de Guzman, former NQAPIA (National Queer Asian Pacific Islander Alliance) Co-Director, he explained, "All of those (GRM) groups are predominantly White. Their perspectives don't appropriately include communities of color perspectives. . . . We look at ourselves as providing a more intersectional analysis and lifting up queer POC and immigrants." These queer liberation groups bring theorizing about intersectionality into practice, in why they do their work, who does the work, and how they do the work. And by operating from a shared value of intersectionality, they have developed a very different platform from the GRM's focus on White, affluent gays and lesbians.

Trickle up social justice

This focus on intersectionality has led the QLM organizations, both independently and in their collaborative work, to additional shared principles. I have written elsewhere (DeFilippis & Anderson-Nathe, 2017) about the missions and values of the QLM organizations, and the significance of their commitment to the interests of the most marginal. The GRM has frequently been accused of inaccurately assuming that policies which help middle-class White people will "trickle down" and also benefit LGBT people of color or poor people. The QLM groups do the reverse. They choose their priorities by engaging in what SRLP's Dean Spade has called "Trickle Up Social Justice" (DeFilippis & Anderson-Nathe, 2017). Informed by hooks' (2000) concept of organizing from margin-to-center, this approach stresses that until the needs of the most vulnerable members of a community are addressed, progress toward other goals simply reinforces the dominance of those people most advantaged. Put differently, as long as organizing priorities remain targeted on the interests of White affluent gays and lesbians, "victories" will benefit those people over queers of color or poor queer people—and often at their expense. The reverse, however, is not true. When the interests of the most marginal are centered, justice will "trickle up" —the benefits of activism will be shared even by those who hold positions of greater privilege. Organizing in this way, by identifying first the interests of the most vulnerable among queer communities, the QLM organizations employ a version of trickle up social justice, in which benefit is conferred first to those in most need of it.

Transformation, not reform

Because of the QLM's intersectional analysis and margin-to-center orientation, they view many social institutions as broken and in need of complete overhaul. They seek not access and reform but, rather, transformation and redistribution. By contrast, the GRM does not, overall, question the fairness of the institutions into which it has sought equal access. It does not seek to overhaul or dismantle institutions; rather, it merely seeks LGBTQ admission into them.

While QLM groups do often advocate for access into the systems they target, this is usually a short-term goal; their long-term goals are much bigger. Regardless of which institutions these groups are trying to influence, they are clear that they are trying to change the institutions as a whole. Almost all the interview participants explain that their concerns extend far beyond merely gaining access for LGBTQ people to social institutions. In their views, access to a system that treats people poorly is no victory. The queer liberation groups are critical of the larger systems in which they are working, whether it is capitalism, immigration policies, or the criminal legal system. For these groups, the context for any of their specific day-to-day work is their larger vision of social justice, best articulated in the Sylvia Rivera Law Project's (SRLP) mission statement: "We can't just work to reform the system. The system itself is the problem." In the following sections, I describe the QLM's agenda and examine how the QLM has focused its efforts on the complete transformation of specific institutions.

Queer liberation organizations: three shared targets

Those three shared values among the QLM organizations (trickle up social justice, intersectionality, and broad social transformation) come together to constitute the foundation of an activism agenda that differs from the GRM in many ways. These values are instrumental in shaping how the organizations prioritize their targets of influence, mobilization, and benefit. Table 4.1 shows a comparison of the targets of the QLM and the GRM.

Perhaps the most important difference is how the QLM begins with the targets of benefits. Put differently, all the QLM groups began with a recognition that a segment of the queer community was not being served by the agendas of mainstream organizations. Most began with an explicit commitment, for instance, to centering the interests of queer people of color, among others. Recognizing that these LGBTQ people were largely ignored by the mainstream movement, QLM groups articulated early on that all their activities must benefit, first and foremost, these communities. Targets of mobilization and of influence were identified subsequently. Critically, and distinct from the methods of the GRM, the constituents and antagonists were defined with the leadership of the beneficiaries, to ensure the margin-to-center orientation of the organizations.

The QLM organizations demonstrate significant alignment between their targets of benefits and targets of mobilization. When the people setting the agenda are

TABLE 4.1 Comparison of primary targets

	Queer liberation movement	*Mainstream gay rights movement*
Primary targets of influence	Community members, elected officials, and social justice organizations positioned to transform: • The criminal legal systems • Healthcare systems • The immigration system • Social services and welfare	Elected officials and courts that are well positioned to affect policies relevant to: • Anti-discrimination laws • Hate crime legislation • Marriage • Military • Youth/education
Primary targets of mobilization	• LGBT immigrants • Low-Income LGBT people • LGBT People of color • Transgender people	• All LGBT people* • White, middle-class, cisgender citizens*
Primary targets of benefits	• LGBT immigrants • Low-income LGBT People • LGBT People of color • Transgender people • All LGBT people	• All LGBT people* • White, middle-class, cisgender citizens*

* There is disagreement about these claims. GRM leaders maintain they mobilize and benefit all LGBT people, while critics have long argued that they primarily mobilize and benefit White, middle-class, cisgender citizens.

benefiting from the work, it stands to reason that they also are motivated to do the work required to actualize that agenda. For example, the SLRP mission statement attests to how the organization provides services for transgender POC and low-income people (their targets of benefits) specifically by engaging them in SRLP's work and developing leadership from within these communities:

> We work through a collective structure built on the idea that our work should be by and for our community. ... It is critical that transgender, intersex, and gender variant people and people of color, especially low-income people, youth, and people with disabilities, take leadership in our work.
>
> *Sylvia Rivera Law Project, n/d*

Each of SRLP's projects concentrates on a different issue, so each project mobilizes corresponding community members to guide the work, such as the Medicaid users who lead their efforts around Medicaid, or the Prison Advisory Committee, comprised of 70 people who are currently incarcerated. Like SRLP, the other organizations are clear that their beneficiaries and constituents are the same.

Based on the guidance of their beneficiaries, the QLM organizations tend to focus their activism efforts in three principal areas: (1) health and health care, social service delivery, and anti-poverty efforts; (2) immigration justice; and (3) the criminal legal system. While some of the organizations may also work on additional issues, these three issues are prioritized by most of the groups in my study. I turn now to a brief examination of each of those three areas.

Health and healthcare, social service delivery, and anti-poverty efforts

Despite mainstream public imagination, which depicts the LGBTQ community as White, affluent, and stylish, poverty rates are higher among queer communities than in the general population, compared along lines of race, gender, and sexual orientation (DeFilippis, 2016; Gates, 2014). Like their heterosexual peers, queer POC generally earn lower incomes than White men and women (Albelda et al., 2009; Bond et al., 2009; Dunn & Moodie-Mills, 2012; Human Rights Campaign, 2009). African American LGBTQ people have higher poverty rates than their White or heterosexual counterparts (Albelda et al., 2009; Badgett, Durso, and Schneebaum, 2013; Dang & Frazer, 2005; Ramos & Gates, 2008). Latino LGBTQ people also have higher poverty than heterosexual Latinos (Albelda et al., 2009), as do Two-Spirit or LGBTQ Native Americans (Albelda et al., 2009; Badgett, Durso, & Schneebaum, 2013), and LGBTQ Asian-Americans (Asian American Federation of New York, 2004; Dang & Hu, 2004). Transgender people have much higher unemployment rates, poverty rates, and homelessness rates than the general population (Badgett et al., 2007; Grant, Mottet, & Tanis, 2011; National Black Justice Coalition, the National Gay and Lesbian Task Force, and the National Center for Transgender Equality, 2011).

LGBTQ individuals and families often lack health care and are more likely than their heterosexual counterparts to be without health insurance (Dallas Voice, 2008; Redman, 2010; The Rainbow Health Initiative, 2004). LGBTQ people of color are even more likely to have their healthcare needs gone unmet (Charles & Conron, 2002; Kreheley, 2009). The high rates of joblessness and poverty among transgender populations means that they are particularly likely to live with a lack of health care or health insurance. (Human Rights Campaign, 2013; National Center for Lesbian Rights and the Transgender Law Center, 2003; National Coalition for LGBTQ Health, 2004; Transgender Law Center, 2013).

In response to these issues of poverty and lack of access to social services and health care, the QLM groups often focus their work on influencing government programs that provide public benefits and health services. Six QLM organizations work explicitly on issues such as poverty, welfare, homelessness, health care, Medicaid, and HIV, and four have devoted substantial resources towards influencing public policies about public benefits and health care systems. Other QLM groups target other health and human services providers, and/or try to influence the GRM groups (to get them to focus on health care and social services).

To this end, QLM organizations have employed a variety of strategies to effect change in those systems they have named as antagonistic. For instance, until it closed in 2014, Queers for Economic Justice (QEJ) targeted New York City's

Department of Homeless Services, successfully influencing their policies. According to Kenyon Farrow, former QEJ executive director:

> [QEJ focused on] organizing and advocacy in the shelter systems and with the welfare system. . . . [Staff] spent two years leading a successful campaign to get the City to change its policy around transgender homeless shelter residents, and now people can self-select which shelters they want to be in. This was a real victory. And staff worked for three years to get the city's shelter system to allow domestic partners access to the shelters for homeless families. And we won. Before that, you needed to be married. So, the shelter project has accomplished a lot.
>
> *Personal communication, 2014*

By focusing their work on the shelter system in this way, QEJ prioritized the needs of people at the bottom of the economic ladder and made the shelter system their target of influence.

Similarly, three New York-based queer liberation organizations (ALP, QEJ, and SRLP) collaborated to influence the NYC welfare system, striving to eliminate barriers to TANF (Temporary Assistance for Needy Families) for transgender people by targeting the Human Resource Administration (HRA). Guided by beneficiaries, themselves affected by these systems, these organizations also targeted Medicaid, and other health care systems, around discrimination against transgender people in health care. SRLP filed a class action lawsuit and worked with ALP to organize a related grassroots organizing campaign, against New York State Medicaid policy that denied health care to transgender people. They have also worked together to change NYC's birth certificate policy, which required transgender people who need health care to have surgery, although many could not afford it or did not want it.

On its website, the queer POC organization allgo claims that oppression and inadequate health care results in queer POC succumbing to preventable or treatable illness and disease. As a result, allgo has selected non-queer-specific health providers in Texas as a primary target of influence. For example, they worked with Austin's health department on a project for Black women of childbearing age, helping them develop a plan for the inclusion of queer POC. In addition, allgo has always focused on HIV (including offering HIV/AIDS prevention training, and providing safer sex education and supplies to community members), and its recent work has expanded to include other sexual health issues and reproductive justice. It also runs an extensive wellness program, offering breast care education and information (and access to free mammograms and breast exams once a year), and wellness workshops/discussions and support programs, with a focus on queer men of color. By making the connections between HIV rates among communities of color and queer people (and also recognizing that these are not mutually exclusive categories), and by making connections between health care, HIV, and reproductive justice, allgo demonstrates an example of work grounded in an intersectional analysis.

Similarly, Affinity works in Chicago on health and wellness issues facing Black LGBTQ people. Their work started in part as a response to the disparate health outcomes they see among Black queer women. Executive director Kim L. Hunt explains that Affinity views health broadly, with their work ranging from overall physical well-being, to reproductive health and STIs, to physical safety (hate crimes and intimate partner violence), to mental health issues (such as depression and suicide prevention). Hunt states that Affinity does this work "on a range of things because we are approaching this from an intersectional lens rather than an LGBTQ-silo lens. And because of that we also work with a lot of organizations that are outside of the LGBTQ community." She explains that Affinity often finds it more useful to partner with non-LGBTQ racial and economic justice organizations than with the gay equality groups:

> Because the larger LGBTQ organizations are not ready to examine race and poverty, our members are really more anxious to work with organizations who are tackling those issues. They may not have the LGBTQ component down, but that might be something we bring to those movements that makes them more inclusive.

It is significant that Affinity, like other QLM groups, would sooner work with progressive non-queer organizations than with the GRM. Many of the QLM activists explained to me that this was because progressive POC organizations or economic justice groups were more willing to expand their work to include LGBTQ people than the gay and lesbian equality groups were to address racial justice or poverty.

These examples illustrate how the QLM groups employ their values of intersectionality and centering the interests of their beneficiaries as they work on poverty and health care. However, as they do this work they also enact the value of social transformation rather than simply reform. Many of the organizations ground their anti-poverty work not merely in the context of bringing greater opportunity to queer people but to questioning capitalism itself. For instance, QEJ's Kenyon Farrow states, "I don't think it is possible to be politically or legally equal under capitalism." And SRLP founder Dean Spade, while insisting that activists focus on the actual material conditions of people's lives, claims that hardships in the community "are being exploited and increased by neoliberal austerity measures" (Flanders, 2012). By connecting their day-to-day work to a larger critique of capitalism and neoliberalism, the queer liberation groups work toward a larger vision of social change than mere reform.

Immigration justice

An intersectional analysis must go beyond race, class, and gender to incorporate issues such as nationality and migration (Mehrotra, 2010). Aligned with this value, QLM groups explicitly target the U.S. immigration system and its effects at the intersections of citizenship status, race, gender, sexual orientation, and class. At least 904,000 LGBTQ immigrants live in the United States, almost a third of whose documentation status is precarious (Gates, 2013). Immigration laws in the United States are largely centered around two concepts: "merit" and the reunification of the "family," which is most often defined in nuclear and heteronormative terms. Consequently, the advocacy of the mainstream immigrant movement often emphasizes heteronormative relationships (marriage and biological family) and conceptions of normality (e.g., hard-working immigrants) to gain basic citizenship rights. At the same time, the mainstream GRM has focused its (minimal) immigration efforts on seeking protection for LGBTQ refugees and citizenship status exclusively for those immigrants who are partners of U.S. citizens (Nair, 2008).

As a result, most LGBTQ immigrants have been marginalized within both the immigrant rights movement (because of the heteronormative nature of immigration policies), and the mainstream GRM (because of its focus on romantic couples or refugees). These queer immigrants lack support as they contend with homophobia and transphobia within their communities of origin, and xenophobia and racism within the LGBTQ movement. This, coupled with restrictions upon immigrants' access to public benefits, has contributed to heightened poverty within LGBTQ immigrant communities, and therefore LGBTQ immigrant communities are left to fend for themselves. At this time, most LGBTQ organizations do not assist queer immigrants who are already in the country and struggling to make a living. LGBTQ immigrants face economic hardship, food insecurity, and lack of health care (Gates, 2013; Tanev, 2007).

Given this context and the queer liberation organizations' values of intersectional activism and organizing for social transformation rather than single-issue policy reform, these groups have selected three primary targets of influence around immigration justice: (1) the mainstream immigration rights movement; (2) the mainstream gay rights movement and LGBTQ communities in general; and ultimately (3) U.S. immigration policy broadly.

Mainstream immigration rights movement

Many queer liberation organizations in particular have structured at least part of their work around challenging the mainstream immigration rights movement. Part of this commitment has grown from these organizations' own analysis of the shifting demographics in their local (queer) communities. In the South, for instance, increased immigration has highlighted the compounded marginalization experienced by queer immigrants, who, due to intersections of heterosexism, transphobia, and xenophobia, often enjoy even less of a social safety net than their heterosexual peers. In response, SONG is not merely targeting the government to gain more access for LGBTQ immigrants; they are also targeting the immigrant rights movement, attempting to complicate the analyses of groups within this movement. SONG and other queer liberation organizations work in active partnership with existing immigrant rights coalitions. Some of SONG's immigration-related work has focused specifically on the issues facing LGBTQ people, such as their 2014 protests against Immigration and Customs Enforcement's (ICE) treatment of transgender detainees in immigration detention. However, the majority of SONG's immigration efforts are not specifically LGBTQ-focused. Examples of this include their campaigns in 2015, organizing against North Carolina's HB318 (a bill which prohibited local officials from using their cities as "Sanctuary Zones" for immigrants) and participating in protests against plans to provide ICE agents with increased access to jails. SONG has continued to focus on non-LGBTQ-specific immigration work, such as their 2016 protests outside of the Etowah Detention Center in Gadsden, Alabama, and their organizing work, that same year, against Georgia's anti-immigrant "felony driving law."

By working in sustained partnership with non-queer immigrant justice groups, SONG and other QLM groups make the immigrant rights movement more inclusive of queer people, while pushing it to expand its analysis. ALP, for instance, has sought to radicalize the existing immigrant justice movement along the dimensions of gender and sexuality. According to ALP's former executive director Cara Page:

> The understanding of how queer and trans POC are centrally located inside of immigrant justice has really elevated to a different level, especially in the global south ... it's a movement we've always been inside of but we are now radicalizing ... We are transforming that movement by bringing that queer and trans lens. By looking at gender violence, and sexuality, and politicalizing what that means in terms of body, and sovereignty, and state. And taking the immigrant justice movement to another level.

By targeting the immigrant justice movement, and bringing a queer analysis to it, groups like ALP and SONG broaden the work of that movement, while simultaneously expanding the definition of what constitutes a "gay issue."

Mainstream LGBTQ communities and organizations

In 2007, QEJ organized the drafting of a vision statement, outlining the political priorities of LGBTQ immigrants, which was signed by 50 organizations (DasGupta, 2012). Their concerns were varied, including the policing of the border, the HIV ban, the process of applying for asylum, the guest worker program, the provisions for harboring, an end of immigrant detentions, eliminating the high-income requirements for immigrant sponsors, broader definitions of family (beyond marriage) and kinship patterns for sponsorship. The aforementioned issue of bi-national couples[3] (the primary immigration focus of the national gay rights organizations for over two decades) was included but was not centralized as a high priority.

While 50 LGBTQ groups signed on (most small, local organizations, including community centers closely connected to the needs of community members), most of the national LGBTQ organizations did not. Indeed, they often claimed that the vision statement was "too broad" and not sufficiently focused on LGBTQ-specific issues (DasGupta, 2012). This indicates a narrow understanding of immigration reform as well as what constitutes a "gay issue." This is a stark contrast from the queer liberation organizations, many of which have chosen as their targets of influence the mainstream organizations and mainstream LGBTQ communities that have not considered immigration a gay issue.

QLM organizations work inside and alongside the GRM to influence the conversation about immigration policy. They push the GRM to expand its work beyond the issue of American citizens' right to keep their foreign-born partner in the country. Ben de Guzman, former co-director of the National Queer Asian Pacific Islander Alliance (NQAPIA), argues:

> We really spent a lot of time engaging [GRM groups] to make sure that the LGBTQ movement knew that immigration was not just about bi-national couples, that there are all these other ways in which LGBTQ folks who have immigrants in their families or who are immigrants themselves are affected and have a stake.

Now that the legalization of same-sex marriage has made moot this issue of bi-national couples, the GRM has very little on its immigration agenda. However, the QLM continues to push the GRM to recognize the needs of LGBT immigrants.

NQAPIA engages in policy efforts prioritizing the needs of LGBTQ immigrants. They organize community forums on LGBTQ immigrants' rights, publish documents telling the stories of undocumented LGBTQ AAPI (Asian American and Pacific Islander) immigrants, provide legal analysis of the impact of immigration reform legislation on AAPI LGBTQ communities, organize Asian American communities to support LGBTQ rights, and provide training for LGBTQ AAPI activists.

In addition to influencing LGBTQ organizations to take a broader view of which LGBTQ people are impacted by immigration policies, groups like NQAPIA also help the equality organizations develop an understanding of immigration policy that is more thoroughly grounded in their intersectional analysis. As stated earlier, the organizations in the GRM movement have historically offered no real critique of their own about immigration policy beyond the issue of bi-national couples (DasGupta, 2012). The GRM, therefore, does not share the analysis of SONG's Helm-Hernandez:

> Part of our work has been to do political education with the LGBTQ community about understanding what does immigration even mean? What are actually the root causes of immigration? The United States is one of the major players of driving people out of their own countries by destroying their economies. . . . We want the community to examine how citizenship, historically, has always been used to define our proximity to privilege. It's been really important to do that level of political education with our communities.

In this quote, it is clear that SONG targets the LGBT community as part of their immigration work by providing political education to their membership and other LGBTQ organizations. And by interrogating the role the U.S. plays in causing global migration, they offer an analysis of immigration that is more complicated than the single-issue analysis offered by the GRM when it focused almost exclusively on the plight of bi-national couples.

US immigration policy

While NQAPIA and many other queer liberation organizations focus on the needs of LGBTQ immigrants, their work is not limited merely to LGBTQ access to the immigration system; it is situated in a larger vision of comprehensive immigration transformation. Their ongoing immigrants' rights campaign advocates for, among other things, legalization of undocumented immigrants, expanded visa programs for students and workers (both low-wage and professional), and legal protections to guard against racial profiling, detentions, and deportations. These are not merely "gay issues"—they are issues of concern to all immigrants.

NQAPIA incorporates these larger issues in much of its programming, such as when it works with mainstream, ethnic, and LGBTQ media (via press conferences, op-eds, etc.) to promote immigrants' rights and discuss comprehensive immigration reform. For example, in 2016 NQAPIA members engaged in advocacy and public education about two significant immigrant programs initiated by the Obama administration: the Deferred Action for Childhood Arrivals (DACA) and Deferred Action for Parental Accountability (DAPA) programs.

SONG, QEJ, and ALP take these larger issues around immigration one step further, arguing for a wholesale transformation in how immigration and citizenship are conceptualized in the United States, and addressing how immigration and citizenship debates are laden with raced and classed implications. SONG's Helm-Hernandez articulates their commitment in this way:

> We see (comprehensive immigration reform) as a step in our longer goal to actually transform the idea of citizenship, to talk about indigenous sovereignty and the role of indigenous communities in defining that conversation. We push back on the White nativist movement that assumes that only White people have claim to the US, only White people have claim to legitimate citizenship in this country. . . . Our people have demanded citizenship as one of the main ways to honor the reality that most undocumented communities are reduced only to labor. This assumption that we're disposable, and as long as you can stand up and work and produce, then you can be here. In the shadows, but you can be here. And as long as you don't become a person with disabilities, as long as you're not queer, as long as all of these other things, because then it's thank you for your labor and good day.

This analysis makes connections between immigration policy with issues of race, labor, capitalism, disability, and sexuality. This is typical of the intersectional analysis that unites the QLM, and which the GRM has been so noteworthy for lacking. It is one of the hallmarks that distinguish these two movements from each other.

Between 2006 and 2008, ALP and QEJ each issued various policy papers about immigration, using an intersectional lens to address numerous aspects of immigration policy. ALP and QEJ each argued that guest worker programs result in the exploitation of temporary workers while simultaneously undercutting the U.S. labor movement. Such an analysis explicitly draws connections between immigration policy and economic policy. Additionally, it situates all workers (LGBTQ people and heterosexual cisgender people, citizen and noncitizen) in solidarity with each other. This argument is clearly rooted in an intersectional framework.

Similarly, while some of ALP's work is specific to LGBTQ communities (such as the homophobia and transphobia trainings they run in immigrant communities and organizations), they also situate their work in a larger vision for comprehensive immigration reform. For instance, ALP advocates for legalization for all people within the United States, and for all residents of the U.S. to have access to the same rights and benefits regardless of immigration/migration status.

These organizations take an approach to USA immigration policy that avoids single-issue analysis and, instead, looks for solutions that address the complexities of immigration policy. They work to influence the entire immigration system and expand the current parameters of the immigration debate set by the GRM, the immigrant rights movement, and immigration opponents. The following excerpts from a speech given by Trishala Deb, ALP's former immigration rights program coordinator, illustrates these multi-faceted targets:

> We are in a critical moment within the broader struggle for the rights of migrants in the United States and in the world. I am speaking of the mounting costs of a very small sector of wealthy people accumulating unimaginable resources off the backs of the majority of the world. Every year, over 175 million people migrate around the world in search of a sustainable existence. . . . We must accept that the transnational economy that some people benefit from is completely dependent on the suppression of economic autonomy throughout the global south.

Here Deb identifies the criminal legal system, ICE, and the military as linked. She challenges her audience to make these structural connections too, and to expand the focus of their work to address all of these systems. Her assessment is meant to serve as a call to action:

> We can build local coalitions and national strategies which will consolidate our collective understanding and power to say to anyone in Washington: we will not go through another mass registration program which results in the loss of the most vulnerable among us, we will not accept . . . another guest-worker policy, we will not consent to billions of our money spent to incarcerate entire families, including children, on top of the trillions of dollars in profit being used to kill our families abroad. . . . We will not consent to

surveillance drones used on our southern borders, the way they are used to patrol the wall in Palestine; we are not temporary, disposable, or alien.

These QLM organizations are consistent in their selection of antagonists (the GRM, the mainstream immigration movement, and the US immigration system as a whole). Similarly, they share targets of benefits and mobilization—immigrants generally, and in some cases queer immigrants more specifically.

Criminal legal system

Police harassment of the LGBTQ community remains rampant. Queer POC, youth, and transgender people are particularly targeted by law enforcement, and regularly face police brutality (Cammett, 2009; Center for American Progress and Movement Advancement Project, 2016; Donahue, 2011; Mogul, Ritchie, & Whitlock, 2011; Stern, 2012). LGBTQ people of color face distinct obstacles accessing legal counsel, getting pre-trial release, and receiving a fair sentence. Once on trial, LGBTQ people's sexual orientation or gender identity is often used to bias juries (Center for American Progress and Movement Advancement Project, 2016). They are more likely to suffer violence and sexual assault in prison and to be placed in solitary confinement (Center for American Progress and Movement Advancement Project, 2016; Stern, 2012). Indeed, they face problems with the criminal legal system as a whole. It has "a toxic effect on queer communities at every conceivable level: the marginalization and subsequent criminalization of queer youth; bias in the judicial system; trauma during incarceration in prisons and jails; and in disproportionate sentencing, particularly death penalty cases" (Cammett, 2009, p. 11).

Transgender people are particularly impacted. The rate of incarceration for transgender people is three times as high as the rate of the general population (Grant, Mottet, & Tanis, 2011). Once in prison, transgender people continue to be targeted. They are subject to excessive punishment and overuse of segregation, and must contend with transphobic health care, including denial of hormones and discrimination in even routine medical attention (Center for American Progress and Movement Advancement Project, 2016; Lydon et al., 2015; Rosenblum, 1999; Stern, 2012). They are housed in men's or women's prisons based on their assigned sex, regardless of how they may identify (National Center for Lesbian Rights, 2006). Once there, they face rampant physical and sexual abuse (Jenness et al., 2007).

The GRM has largely ignored these issues. Instead, its work on the criminal legal system has focused on expanding hate crime legislation, a priority supported by many of its White, middle-class constituents, but one which has been widely criticized by communities of color for lacking an intersectional analysis about the racist and classist nature of the criminal legal system. The QLM, on the other hand, has taken those issues seriously, and many of the groups have made criminal justice work a central part of their work.

Part of the QLM's work responds to the surveillance and harassment of low-income neighborhoods and communities of color by police. They work to challenge police targeting of their communities. Dean Spade, founding director of SRLP, highlights the ways in which criminalization in the lives of poor people is "highly ritualized, highly gendered; both in terms of who gets arrested and what the police think looks unusual and which neighborhoods they spend time patrolling" (Flanders, 2012). Cara Page, of ALP, expands on this point, pointing to her organization's participation in coalition work on police reform, characterized by efforts to resist "a right-wing agenda that further marginalized our communities and policed our bodies." She explains that ALP and their coalition allies have been "struggling with city government on *where* policing is, and how the increase of policing is certainly connected to the racial and economic injustices of our communities." These quotes reflect an intersectional understanding of queer people's lives and their interactions with the criminal legal system. In the analysis put forward by these organizations, sexual orientation and gender identity are factors in the policing of these organizations' communities, but so too are race and class.

In addition to working on the issue of police surveillance and targeting, QLM organizations focus on how LGBTQ people are treated when they are incarcerated. Several organizations engage in advocacy work that targets policies within prisons. Some also provide direct services to incarcerated or formerly incarcerated people. For instance, allgo has provided trainings for staff in the Juvenile Justice System, explaining how to better serve LGBT people, with a particular focus on trans-sensitivity and education. In addition, they have also worked to change policies for LGBT people in Texas jails – both the adult and juvenile prison systems. By not limiting their work to improving services for people within the prisons (by simultaneously working to change larger policies that guide the prison system as a whole), allgo illustrates the commitment shared by the larger QLM to not settle for mere access to existing (and problematic) institutions, but to also fight for broader transformation.

Given the structural limitations inhibiting mobilization of many people who stand to benefit most from their efforts (incarcerated and criminalized people), QLM groups often mobilize other populations, including those most likely to be targeted by the police, family members of incarcerated people, and/or in neighborhoods that are most heavily surveilled by the police. However, QLM groups also find ways to incorporate the incarcerated people most directly impacted by the criminal legal system. For instance, Reina Gossett described how SRLP works with a Prison Advisory Committee comprised of 70 people incarcerated in NY state who "really help SRLP decide what to advocate for, what to press for, what issues are the most important facing people who are currently incarcerated." Gossett explained this is because,

> We believe that the people who are navigating these issues are the experts on these issues and are really powerful and capable of changing these issues . . . people who are currently incarcerated are going to know what are the most pressing issues to advocate for and organize around when it comes to the

prison system. And often those are the very people, whether they are incarcerated or whether they are low income; the very people who are navigating an issue are historically pushed out of social movements.

This commitment to centering the people at the bottom, and recognizing their expertise and ability to guide the movement, is another marked difference between the QLM and the GRM, which is predominantly led by White, middle-class, college-educated people.[4]

An important unifying feature of the QLM's work on the criminal legal system is their resistance to expanding the prison industrial complex.[5] Kenyon Farrow, former director of QEJ articulates this as a point of distinction between the QLM and the GRM: "You have [GRM organizations] advocating for stronger hate crime legislation at the same time that we see other social movements, and communities of color, in particular, really rejecting the use of criminalization as a strategy for solving a whole range of problems." Across organizations, these activists believe that queer communities experience more violence at the hands of the criminal legal system than they do from homophobic strangers on the street. Consequently, they argue that hate crime legislation helps to strengthen a system that should instead be disempowered, if not completely abolished. SRLP's Spade associates hate crime legislation with "enhancing the punishing power of the system that is actually the main perpetrator of violence in the lives of SRLP clients," claiming that the most common perpetrators of physical violence against LGBTQ communities are police, corrections officers, or immigration officers and asking, "so, what does it mean to add power to that system, providing no relief to us?" (Flanders, 2012).

Further, several queer liberation groups talk openly with their members about what it means to be safe, when you cannot count on the police to protect you. SONG's Helm-Hernandez discusses this further: "A huge, splintering issue in our community is policing, and how people are also framing safety. For some people, safety is just not getting harassed by the police every time you walk out of the gay club." For the queer liberation organizations, these questions of safety, coupled with the role of policing and prisons, are central to their work on criminal justice and foundational to a goal of diminishing rather than reinforcing the criminal legal system.

So, while the GRM targets the criminal legal system for the creation of more laws (hate crime legislation), the QLM has, instead, targeted other entities as sites in which to create safety, while simultaneously targeting the criminal legal system to decrease its power. According to QEJ's Kenyon Farrow, the QLM is "moving to stop prisons or policing strategies." In fact, prison abolition lurks in the background of much of the queer liberation organizations' work. Although the day-to-day work of some QLM organizations involves providing direct legal services for individual prisoners, class action suits, or sensitivity training for prison staff, their long-term goals appear to be creating safety outside of the criminal legal system while also pursuing prison abolition. This commitment is shared among queer liberation organizations and is perhaps best articulated by SRLP's Reina Gossett: "A lot of my energy goes into a movement to abolish the prison industrial complex."

In addition, some of the QLM groups are working to build alternatives to the current criminal system. For example, the "Safe Neighborhood Campaign" (a project of ALP's "Safe Outside the System" Collective) challenges hate and police violence by using community-based strategies rather than relying on the police. This campaign builds numerous safe spaces in Brooklyn that publicly identify as willing to open their doors to community members fleeing from violence, and whose staff have been trained on homophobia, transphobia, and how to prevent violence without relying on law enforcement. ALP's Cara Page says, ". . . our strategy is about saying, yes, there are hate crimes, so what are we doing inside of our communities with allies, with families, with other queer and trans POC?" In ALP's approach to criminal justice, the targets of mobilization are community members themselves. ALP is working to transform relationships in local communities, and build safety by training neighbors to take care of each other, rather than to fear each other. Page adds:

> Instead of assuming that the state or criminal system or military is defining safety and will save us from each other, we are looking (at our neighbors) eye to eye, in the words of Audre Lorde, and asking of ourselves and each other "Who am I willing to be for your safety? Who are you willing to be for mine?"

This strategy of building alternatives to, rather than seeking access into, problematic institutions illustrates how the QLM rejects the GRM's reformist equality-based approach, seeking instead to transform society in pursuit of justice.

Conclusion

This chapter has highlighted the existence and agenda of a group of a queer liberation movement. While they stand in stark contrast from the mainstream movement, the QLM groups are closely aligned with one another in three primary ways. First, they adhere to a set of shared principles which guide their work—both individually and collectively. Second, they work from an intersectional lens to address the different ways queer POC, poor people, transgender people, and others face discrimination and structural barriers. Consequently, the organizations' analyses address capitalism, racism, militarism, and transphobia at least as frequently as homophobia. Building off of that commitment to intersectionality, these is also a commitment to "trickle-up justice" and a margin-to-center orientation in which the organizations center the interests of the most marginal and where benefit is passed most immediately to those most in need. Finally, third, the QLM approaches issue-specific work from a foundational principle that minor modifications to dysfunctional and destructive systems are not enough achieve their desired outcomes. Put differently, reform is only useful as a step towards both redistributive and recognition-based justice and transformation.

In addition, QLM organizations also share a focus on three significant issues that guide their activism work. While individual organizations structure this work differently (and some also work on additional issues), the queer liberation groups share an agenda characterized by activism on poverty and health care, immigration justice, and criminal justice. Given their shared values, work on these issue areas unfolds intersectionally, such that none is solely a queer issue, or solely an issue of the poor. Rather, the organizations center the points of commonality between the multiple communities impacted by these systems.

These shared principles and shared agendas result in an activism that fits cohesively within Gamson's (1975) three targets framework. They share commitments to work that benefit the most marginal in their communities, to mobilizing those constituencies in their own interest, and to influencing antagonists capable of broad social transformation—including questioning the very existence of the social institutions themselves.

These factors situate the queer liberation organizations as a social movement of their own, distinct from the GRM. In addition, the seven organizations included in this study are hardly alone. They work in partnership with numerous other similar groups across the country, which, I argue, are also part of the QLM. These groups include the Disability Justice Collective (national); the Esperanza Peace and Justice Center (San Antonio, TX); Familia: Trans Queer Liberation Movement (Santa Ana, CA); FIERCE (New York, NY); The Transgender, Gender Variant and Intersex Justice Project (San Francisco, CA); and The Transgender Law Center (San Francisco, CA), to name just a few. In addition, there are numerous other organizations that share similar values, constituents, and priorities, with whom future collaboration is possible. Just a few examples include Black and Pink (national), BreakOUT! (New Orleans, LA); Buried Seedz of Resistance (Denver, CO); Detroit REPRESENT! (Detroit, MI); the Freedom Center for Social Justice (Charlotte, NC); Get Equal, (national); and Trans Women of Color Collective (Washington, DC).

This existence of the QLM is significant because, as Duggan (2003) has documented, the GRM has successfully depicted LGBT people as mainstream, and itself as the centrist movement that represents them. However, the QLM shows this to be false. There is a large undervalued constituency pursing a much queerer set of politics. While there have always been radical outlier organizations in the GRM, my research shows that there is now a level of coherence and connection among the QLM organizations, indicating that the possibilities for queer liberation (rather than gay equality) may be stronger than is usually recognized. This queer liberation movement presents new possibilities for intersectional, multi-issue political and social organizing extending well beyond single-issue identity politics.

This post-marriage moment raises important questions about the future of LGBT activism. While the mainstream movement is struggling to identify its next post-marriage goals and justify its continued existence, how will that impact this queer liberation movement in its pursuit of vastly different and more radical goals? One possibility is that the successful campaign for marriage equality may further entrench a centrist vision of politics among mainstream society. The legalization of same-sex marriage may be viewed as evidence that moderate reform can work. If so, this has the potential to further marginalize the QLM, situating their radical, transformative politics as hopelessly naive when compared to the reformist tactics of the GRM.

However, another possibility is that because marriage is not dominating the agenda (and the majority of resources), there may be more political space to pursue a different set of goals. Now may be the time for expanding the LGBT agenda beyond single-issue politics. Indeed, the GRM has already begun to turn its attention to a number of issues that it once ignored, such as trans rights and LGBT poverty.

The concern with this is that the GRM will attempt to co-opt the work of the QLM. In an interview with ALP's Cara Page that can be found elsewhere in this volume, she discussed how this is already happening. She and several other QLM activists spoke to me about how the GRM is co-opting their work, watering down the radical politics, and producing liberal reformist versions of that work. For example, the QLM's vision for racial justice work is already being diluted by the GRM and repackaged towards "diversity" efforts. If this continues, if the GRM is allowed to take leadership on the issues of concern to the QLM, then we can expect more minor reforms that do not fundamentally transform the systems that are destructive to so many queer communities.

Furthermore, the need to totally transform these systems is even greater now during a Trump administration that is working to make them even more threatening to marginalized populations. Interestingly, as the left scrambles to resist the Trump administration, many activists are starting to turn to an intersectional framework. This is the very framework that the QLM organizations have been using for years, making them well-equipped to lead in this political moment. In addition, the QLM represents exactly the communities that are most under siege by Trump and the right wing, making it an especially relevant movement. In short, the movement we need for this political moment already exists. Now is the time to recognize it and to join it.

Notes

1 Rather than terms like "LGBTQ" or "queer", I use "mainstream gay rights movement" very deliberately, to indicate whose issues I believe have dominated their agenda.
2 This chapter has been informed by the generous input and feedback provided by Ben Anderson-Nathe, Paul Beshire, Angela Jones, Gita Mehrotra, and Michael Yarbrough.
3 Prior to the 2015 Supreme Court decision making same-sex marriage legal, gay and lesbian American citizens who were in romantic relationships with foreign-born partners were unable to sponsor them for citizenship through marriage, the way heterosexual couples could.
4 To read more about the QLM's commitment to leadership "from the bottom up", see DeFilippis & Anderson-Nathe, 2017.
5 The organization Critical Resistance defines the Prison Industrial Complex as "the overlapping interests of government and industry that use surveillance, policing, and imprisonment as solutions to economic, social and political problems." See http://criticalresistance.org/about/not-so-common-language/.

References

Albelda, R., Badgett, M.V. L., Schneebaum, A., & Gates, G. (2009). Poverty in the lesbian, gay and bisexual community. *University of California Los Angeles School of Law, Williams Institute.* Retrieved from www.law.ucla.edu/williamsinstitute/pdf/LGBPovertyReport. pdf.

Asian American Federation of New York. (2004, March). Asian pacific American same-sex households: A census report on New York, San Francisco and Los Angeles. Retrieved from www.aafny.org/cic/report/GLReport.pdf.

Badgett, M.V. L., Durso, L. E., & Schneebaum A. (2013). New patterns of poverty in the lesbian, gay, and bisexual community. *University of California Los Angeles School of Law, Williams Institute.* Retrieved from http://williamsinstitute.law.ucla.edu/wp-content/uploads/LGB-Poverty-Update-Jun-2013.pdf.

Badgett, M.V. L., Lau, H., Sears, B., & Ho, D. (2007). Bias in the workplace: Consistent evidence of sexual orientation and gender identity discrimination. *University of California Los Angeles School of Law, Williams Institute.* Retrieved from http://williamsinstitute.law. ucla.edu/wp-content/uploads/Badgett-Sears-Lau-Ho-Bias-in-the-Workplace-Jun-2007.pdf.

Bond, L., Wheeler, D. P., Millett, G. A., LaPollo, A. B., Carson, L. F., & Liau, A. (2009). Black men who have sex with men and the association of Down-Low identity with HIV risk behavior. *American Journal of Public Health*, 99(Suppl. 1):92–95.

Bowen, A. (2012). Forty Years of LGBTQ Philanthropy: 1970–2010. Retrieved from www. lgbtfunders.org/files/40years_lgbtqphilanthrophy.pdf.

Boykin, K. (2000). Where rhetoric meets reality: The role of black lesbians and gays in "queer" politics. In C. A. Rimmerman, K. D. Wald, & C. Wilcox (Eds.), *The Politics of Gay Rights.* Chicago, IL: The University of Chicago Press, 79–96.

Cammett, A. (2009). Queer lockdown: Coming to terms with the ongoing criminalization of LGBTQ communities. *The University of Nevada Las Vegas, William S. Boyd School of Law.* Retrieved from http://scholars.law.unlv.edu/cgi/viewcontent.cgi?article=1626&context=facpub.

Carpenter, L. (2014). Getting queer priorities straight: How direct legal services can democratize issue prioritization in the LGBT rights movement. *University of Pennsylvania Journal of Law and Social Change*, 17(2):106–136. Retrieved from http://scholarship.law.upenn. edu/cgi/viewcontent.cgi?article=1166&context=jlasc.

Carter, M. (1999). The emperor's new clothes, or how not to run a movement. In K. Kleindienst (Ed.), *This is What Lesbian Looks Like.* Ithaca, NY: Firebrand Books, 62–69.

Center for American Progress and Movement Advancement Project. (2016). Unjust: How the broken criminal justice system fails LGBT people of color. Retrieved from: www. lgbtmap.org/file/lgbt-criminal-justice-poc.pdf.

Charles, V. & Conron, K. (2002). Double jeopardy: How racism and homophobia impact the health of black and Latino lesbian, gay, bisexual, and transgender (LGBT) communities. *Boston Public Health Commission, LGBT Health.* Retrieved from http://lgbthealth.web olutionary.com/downloads/research/BPHCLGBTLatinoBlackHealthDispar.doc.

Cohen, C. (1999). What is this movement doing to my politics? *Social Text, No. 61, Out Front: Lesbians, Gays, and the Struggle for Workplace Rights*, 111–118.

Cohen, C. J. (1997). Punks, bulldaggers, and welfare queens: The radical potential of queer politics? *GLQ: A Journal of Lesbian and Gay Studies*, 3(4):437–465.

Combahee River Collective. (1981). A black feminist statement. In C. Moraga & G. Anzaldua (Eds.), *This Bridge called My Back: Writings by Radical Women of Color.* New York, NY: Kitchen Table Press, 210–219.

Conrad, R. (Ed.). (2010). *Against Equality: Queer Critiques of Gay Marriage*. Chicago, IL: Against Equality Press.

Crenshaw, K. (1991). Mapping the margins: Intersectionality, identity politics, and violence against women of color. *Stanford Law Review*, 43(6):1241–1299.

D'Emilio, J. (2000). Cycles of change, questions of strategy: The gay and lesbian movement after fifty years. In C. A. Rimmerman, K. D. Wald, & C. Wilcox (Eds.), *The Politics of Gay Rights*. Chicago, IL: The University of Chicago Press, 31–53.

D'Emilio, J. (2012). Creating change. *A New Queer Agenda: The Scholar and the Feminist Online*. 10(1–2). Retrieved from http://sfonline.barnard.edu/a-new-queer-agenda/creating-change/.

Dang, A. & Frazer, S. (2005). *Black Same-Sex Households in the United States: A Report from the 2000 Census*. (2nd ed.). National Gay and Lesbian Task Force Policy Institute & National Black Justice Coalition. Retrieved from www.thetaskforce.org/downloads/reports/repo rts/2000BlackSameSexHouseholds.pdf.

Dang. A. & Hu, M. (2004). Asian Pacific American lesbian, gay, bisexual and transgender people: A community portrait—A report from New York's queer Asian Pacific Legacy Conference. *National Gay and Lesbian Task Force Policy Institute*. Retrieved from www. thetaskforce.org/docroot/downloads/reports/reports/APAstudy.pdf.

Dallas Voice. (2008, May 22). 25 percent of gay, lesbian Americans lack insurance. *Dallas Voice*. www.dallasvoice.com/25-percent-of-gay-lesbian-americans-lack-insurance-1024542.html.

DasGupta, D. (2012). Queering immigration: Perspectives on cross-movement organizing. *A New Queer Agenda: The Scholar and the Feminist Online*. 10(1–2). Retrieved from http:// sfonline.barnard.edu/a-new-queer-agenda/queering-immigration-perspectives-on-cross-movement-organizing/.

DeFilippis, J. N. (2015). *A Queer Liberation Movement? A Qualitative Content Analysis of Queer Liberation Organizations, Investigating Whether they are Building a Separate Social Movement*. Doctoral Dissertation, Portland State University.

DeFilippis, J. N. (2016). "What about the rest of us?" An overview of LGBT poverty issues and a call to action. *Journal of Progressive Human Services*, 27(3):143–174.

DeFilippis, J. N. & Anderson-Nathe, B. (2017). Embodying margin to center: Intersectional activism among queer liberation organizations. In M. Brettschneider, S. Burgess, & C. Keating (Eds.), *LGBTQ Politics: A Critical Reader. A New Collection of Essays*. New York: NYU Press.

DeFilippis, J. N., Anderson-Nathe, B., & Panichelli, M. (2015). Notes on same-sex marriage: Concerns for feminist social workers. *Affilia*, 30(4):461–475.

Donahue, J. (2011). Making it happen, mama: A conversation with Miss Major. In E. A. Stanley & N. Smith (Eds.), *Captive Genders: Trans Embodiment and the Prison Industrial Complex*. Edinburgh: AK Press, 267–280.

Duggan, L. (2003). *The Twilight of Equality: Neoliberalism, Cultural Politics and the Attack on Democracy*. Boston, MA: Beacon Press.

Dunn, M. & Moodie-Mills, A. (2012). The state of gay and transgender communities of color in 2012: The economic, educational, and health insecurities these communities are struggling with and how we can help them. *The Center for American Progress*. Retrieved from www.americanprogress.org/issues/2012/04/lgbt_comm_of_color.html.

Farrow, K. (2012). Afterword: A future beyond equality. *A New Queer Agenda: The Scholar and The Feminist Online*. 10(1–2). Retrieved from http://sfonline.barnard.edu/a-new-queer-agenda/afterword-a-future-beyond-equality/.

Flanders, L. (2012). Dean Spade: The most imprisoning nation in the world [Part 1 of 2]. *The Laura Flanders Show*. Retrieved from: www.youtube.com/watch?v=fcYxqD1aElk.

Funders for LGBTQ Issues. (2012). Forty Years of LGBTQ Philanthropy: 1970–2010. Retrieved from www.lgbtfunders.org/resources/pub.cfm?pubID=57.

Funders for LGBTQ Issues. (2016). 2014 Tracking Report: LGBTQ Grantmaking by U.S. Foundations. Retrieved from www.lgbtfunders.org/wp-content/uploads/2016/05/2014_Tracking_Report.pdf.

Gamson, W. A. (1975). *The Strategy of Social Protest*. Homewood, IL: Dorsey Press.

Gates, G. J. (2013). LGBT adult immigrants in the United States. *University of California Los Angeles School of Law the Williams Institute*. Retrieved from http://williamsinstitute.law.ucla.edu/wp-content/uploads/LGBTImmigrants-Gates-Mar-2013.pdf.

Gates, G. J. (2014). Food insecurity and SNAP (food stamps) participation in LGBT communities. *University of California Los Angeles School of Law the Williams Institute*. Retrieved from http://williamsinstitute.law.ucla.edu/wp-content/uploads/Food-Insecurity-in-LGBT-Communities.pdf.

Grant, J. M., Mottet, L. A., & Tanis, J. (2011). Injustice at every turn: A report of the national transgender discrimination survey. *The National Gay and Lesbian Task Force*. Retrieved from www.thetaskforce.org/downloads/reports/reports/ntds_full.pdf.

Hermosillo, M. (2013, March 29). Human Rights Campaign fails to advocate for minorities. *Policy.Mic*. Retrieved from www.policymic.com/articles/31563/human-rights-campaign-fails-to-advocate-for-minorities/424007.

hooks, b. (2000). *Feminist Theory: From Margin to Center*. Chicago, IL: Pluto Press.

Human Rights Campaign. (2009). At the Intersection: Race, Sexual Orientation and Gender. Retrieved from www.hrc.org/files/documents/HRC_Equality_Forward_2009.pdf.

Human Rights Campaign. (2013). Health Insurance Discrimination for Transgender People. Retrieved from www.hrc.org/resources/entry/health-insurance-discrimination-for-transgender-people.

Hutchinson, D. L. (1999). Gay rights for gay whites: Race, sexual identity, and equal protection discourse. *Cornell Law Review*, 85(5):1358–1391.

Hutchinson, D. L. (2001). Identity crisis: "Intersectionality," "multidimensionality" and the development of an adequate theory of subordination. *Michigan Journal of Race & Law*, 6(2):285–317.

Jenness, V., Maxson, C. L., Matsuda, K. N., & Sumner, J. M. (2007). Violence in California correctional facilities: An empirical examination of sexual assault. *National PREA Resource Center*. Retrieved from www.prearesourcecenter.org/sites/default/files/library/55-prea presentationpreareportucijennessetal.pdf.

Jones-Yelvington, T. (2008). A half-dozen things that we are: Collective identity in intersectional LGBT/Queer social movement organizations. Part 2. *Theory in Action*, 1(2):83–105.

Kreheley, J. (2009). How to close the LGBT health disparities gap: Disparities by race and ethnicity. *Center for American Progress*. Retrieved from www.americanprogress.org/issues/2009/12/pdf/lgbt_health_disparities_race.pdf.

Lorde, A. (1983). There is no hierarchy of oppressions. *Bulletin: Homophobia and education*, 14(3/4):9.

Lydon, J., Carrington, K., Low, H., Miller, R., & Yazdy, M. (2015). Coming out of concrete closets: A report on Black & Pink's national LGBTQ prisoner survey. Retrieved from www.blackandpink.org/wp-content/upLoads/Coming-Out-of-Concrete-Closets.-Black-and-Pink.-October-16-2015.-Executive-Summary-and-Recommendations.pdf.

Mahfuz, L. W. & Farrow, K. (2012). Movement building. In P. Chamberlain (Ed.), *Resisting the Rainbow* (Section 5). 8–15. Retrieved from www.politicalresearch.org/wp-content/uploads/downloads/2012/12/Resisting-the-Rainbow-Full-Report.pdf.

MAP: LGBT Movement Advancement Project. (2007). The Momentum Report—2007 Edition. *An Analysis of Key Indicators of LGBT Equality in the US*. Retrieved from www.lgbtmap.org/file/2007-momentum-report.pdf.

MAP: LGBT Movement Advancement Project. (2011). 2010 National LGBT Movement Report: A Financial Overview of Leading Advocacy Organizations in the LGBT Movement. Retrieved from www.lgbtmap.org/file/2010-national-lgbt-movement-report.pdf.

MAP: LGBT Movement Advancement Project. (2012). 2012 National LGBT Movement Report. Retrieved from www.lgbtmap.org/file/2012-national-lgbt-movement-report.pdf.

MAP: LGBT Movement Advancement Project. (2016). 2016 National LGBT Movement Report: A Financial Overview of Leading Advocacy Organizations in the LGBT Movement. Retrieved from www.lgbtmap.org/file/2016-national-lgbt-movement-report.pdf.

Mehrotra, G. (2010). Toward a continuum of intersectionality theorizing for feminist social work scholarship. *Affilia*, 25(4):417–430.

Mogul, J. L., Ritchie, A. J., & Whitlock, K. (2011). *Queer (in)Justice: The Criminalization of LGBT People in the United States*. Boston, MA: Beacon Press.

Nair, Y. (2008, January 9). Queer immigration: Change the paradigms. *Windy City Times*. Retrieved from windycitymediagroup.com/gay/lesbian/news/ARTICLE.php?AID=17177.

National Black Justice Coalition, the National Gay and Lesbian Task Force, and the National Center for Transgender Equality. (2011). Injustice at Every Turn: A Look at Black Respondents in the National Transgender Discrimination Survey. Retrieved from www.thetaskforce.org/downloads/reports/reports/ntds_full.pdf.

National Center for Lesbian Rights. (2006). *Rights of Transgender Prisoners*. San Francisco. Retrieved from www.nclrights.org/site/DocServer/RightsofTransgenderPrisoners.pdf?docID=6381.

National Center for Lesbian Rights (NCLR) and the Transgender Law Center. (2003). Trans realities: A legal needs assessment of San Francisco's transgender communities. Retrieved from www.nclrights.org/site/DocServer/transrealities0803.pdf.

National Coalition for LGBTQ Health. (2004). An overview of U.S. trans health priorities: A Report by the Eliminating Disparities Working Group. Retrieved from www.transgenderlaw.org/resources/transhealthaug04.pdf.

Proteus Fund. (2015). Hearts and minds: The untold story of how philanthropy and the civil marriage collaborative helped America embrace marriage equality. Retrieved from www.proteusfund.org/sites/default/files/upload/inline/29/files/heartsandmindsnov5.pdf.

Ramos, C. & Gates, G. J. (2008). Census snapshot: California's black LGB population. *University of California Los Angeles School of Law, The Williams Institute*. Retrieved from http://escholarship.org/uc/item/98p6s7h0.

Redman, L. F. (2010). Outing the invisible poor: Why economic justice and access to health care is an LGBT issue. *Georgetown Journal on Poverty Law & Policy*, 17(3):451–459.

Richardson, M. (1999). What you see is what you get: Building a movement toward liberation in the twenty-first century. In K. Kleindienst (Ed.), *This is What Lesbian Looks Like*. Ithaca, NY: Firebrand Books, 210–219.

Rosenblum, D. (1994). Queer intersectionality and the failure of recent lesbian and gay victories. *Law & Sexuality: Review of Lesbian & Gay Legal Issues*, 4:83–122.

Rosenblum, D. (1999). Trapped in Sing Sing: Transgendered prisoners caught in the gender binarism. *Michigan Journal of Gender & Law*, 6(2):499–573.

Shepard, B. (2001). The queer/gay assimilationist split: The suits vs. the sluts. *Monthly Review-New York*, 53(1):49–62.

Stern, J. (2012). This is what pride looks like: Miss Major and the violence, poverty, and incarceration of low-income transgender women. *A New Queer Agenda: The Scholar and The Feminist Online*. 10(1–2). Retrieved from http://sfonline.barnard.edu/a-new-queer-agenda/

this-is-what-pride-looks-like-miss-major-and-the-violence-poverty-and-incarceration-of-low-income-transgender-women/.

Sylvia Rivera Law Project. (n/d). Our Approach and Principles. Retrieved from https://srlp.org/about/principles.

Tanev, A. (2007). *Community Health Survey, New York City Department of Health and Mental Hygiene*. Unpublished raw data.

The Rainbow Health Initiative. (2004). Minnesota Health Access Survey. Retrieved from www.rainbowhealth.org/resources-for-you/research-and-publications/.

Transgender Law Center. (2013). Recommendations for transgender health care. Retrieved from http://www.transgenderlaw.org/resources/tlchealth.htm.

TransGriot. (2007). Why the transgender community hates HRC. Retrieved from http://transgriot.blogspot.com/2007/10/why-transgender-community-hates-hrc.html.

Vaid, U. (1995). *Virtual Equality: The Mainstreaming of Gay & Lesbian Liberation*. New York, NY: Anchor Books/Doubleday.

Vaid, U. (2012). *Irresistible Revolution: Confronting Race, Class and the Assumptions of LGBT Politics*. New York, NY: Magnus Books.

5

"THIS IS THE FREEDOM RIDE WE ARE TAKING"

An interview with the Audre Lorde Project's Cara Page

Joseph Nicholas DeFilippis

Editors' introduction:

This chapter is a transcript of excerpts from a series of interviews with Cara Page, discussing her work as the Executive Director of the Audre Lorde Project from 2012 to 2017. The interviews were conducted over the course of several years, with the final one being conducted after Cara presented at the 2016 After Marriage conference.

The Audre Lorde Project (ALP) is a lesbian, gay, bisexual, two-spirit, trans and gender non-conforming people of color center for community organizing, focusing on the New York City area. The organization focuses on mobilization, education and capacity-building, working for community wellness and progressive social and economic justice.

The interview provides examples of important work that is largely ignored by the mainstream equality organizations. It also raises a number of questions for readers to consider: What is the difference between equality and justice, and how does LGBTQ activism look differently when it prioritizes one or the other? How did marriage come to dominate the agenda of the mainstream gay rights movement, over other issues of concern? Now that marriage has been won, should the mainstream movement work on these other issues that have already been the focus of groups like ALP, and if so, how? What are the challenges and benefits that come from the non-profit structure?

ALP's history and work

JOSEPH NICHOLAS DEFILIPPIS: Let's start with you telling me about the work that the Audre Lorde Project does, and how it got started.

CARA PAGE: The Audre Lorde Project (ALP) opened in 1996. We are an organizing center for lesbian, gay, bisexual, two-spirit, trans, and gender nonconforming people of color (LGBTNC). Our staff has always been led by women and people who are transgender or gender nonconforming. We started out of a collaboration between predominantly gay and lesbian and trans people of color who wanted to create a space that really identified the critical needs of their communities at that time.

We started out really wanting to identify our lives outside of an HIV/AIDS reality because, certainly in the 1990s, NYC government—you know as a larger city in the midst of an AIDS epidemic—was both isolating our communities and also only perceiving us solely in relationship to disease. Which I say cautiously, because of course it was a huge issue, and it continues to be a critical concern for our communities, but we are also more than this disease and this epidemic.

And we were also focused on resisting against increased policing in the 1990s which was targeting, in particular, queer and trans people of color. It was really about organizing against a right-wing agenda that further marginalized our communities and policed our bodies.

And then we work on identifying safety—safety in relationship to policing, in relationship to health care, in relationship to homelessness. What does safety look like?

And, while we were being told that we are less than human, we were looking at wellness and defining how our community creates an infrastructure for well-being, be that physical, economic, emotional, spiritual, psychic, well-being.

I am amidst a long legacy of leaders within the ALP, that are member led, and I want to lift up the role of members that have always guided us in the justice work that we do and that we've done for a long time.

ALP evolved into an organizing center. It didn't start like that. But it definitely decided to really politicize the role and legacy of our communities in NY and move away from a direct service model because we inherently felt that until we are organizing and changing the systems, we can't rely on the systems to provide for our communities. And since the early 2000s, we have been a member-led organizing center that really centered on anti-policing, building community-led safety strategies, examining what safety looks like, defined by our communities in NYC.

When we refer to ourselves as an organizing center—what we mean by that is we're always looking at structures of collective power that are for, by, and about LGBTNC people of color. Including immigrant communities; including two-spirit communities. We have two organizing programs: TransJustice and the SOS (Safe Outside the System) Collective. So, certainly, the work that has evolved for the Audre Lorde Project has been to center voice, our voices, in political spaces—in larger movement spaces we are building with, other radical and transformative organizers in the larger movement—not just necessarily queer but certainly racial justice movements, immigrant rights movements, economic justice movements that are really looking to make systemic changes.

JND: Can you tell me more about your two organizing programs?

CP: TransJustice is a political group created by and for trans and gender nonconforming people of color, and it mobilizes trans communities and allies into action on pressing political issues. One of its largest campaigns was against the Human Resource Administration, challenging their policy around non-trans-inclusive health care and services, and really pushing against their idea that we are not a part of community and shouldn't be taken care of. So, we are always advocating for our communities and struggling with state.

And the SOS Collective is devoted to challenging hate violence and police violence by using community-based strategies, rather than relying on the police. Certainly, struggling with city government on where policing is and how the increase of policing is certainly connected to the racial and economic injustices of our communities. And the SOS collective has really informed national strategy on community defense and security, in terms of looking at transformative practices in how we take care of each other. That goes at rallies, at public venues where we're gathering as our community. So, we're not doing national programs, but the SOS Collective has been really called upon to strategize with other community organizers across the country, helping them respond to increased violence targeting our communities, especially state violence but also community hate violence.

And certainly, in the vein of Audre Lorde, we're always centering our cultural and political identities and our survival as what motivates us to follow our desire and follow our liberations towards how we are collectively building power and livelihood for and with each other.

JND: So, tell me more about that. What would you characterize as the core values that drive the work of ALP?

CP: The Audre Lorde Project is about centering intersections. We are holding the nexus—economic, racial, disability justice, language justice—different elements that define who we are both politically and culturally.

In honor of Audre Lorde, we have a core principal around cultural work. Anything from re-telling the narrative of our experiences as queer, trans people of color and two-spirit, and also centering the cultural legacy of our existence. In NYC, it could be easily wiped in a history that only focuses on the Stonewall resistance; but we've done work prior to the Stonewall resistance and certainly since then, to both change our history of this city but then more broadly in our movements. We are queering analysis around economic justice, racial justice, immigrant rights. So that's critical—cultural work.

What is always at the center of our work is the fact that people are dying in our communities. But we work inside of a powerful legacy of resistance and we have been tremendously resilient, wanting to exist. So, this work is not a question. It is a necessity. We will be completely dismissed and removed from memory, and that is a political danger. I mean, certainly, in the words of Audre Lorde, "we were never meant to survive." We take that as a principal, as an objective of what we are charged to do here inside of our movements: to more than survive, but to take what we've learned and to push our survival into existence and into powerful organizing that transforms our work on a daily basis.

But our central core values are justice and liberation. It's about how we are liberating our experiences and our livelihood as queer and trans people of color.

Justice versus equality

JND: Why justice and liberation, but not equality?

CP: I can't stress enough that the equality lens doesn't center people of color. At all. It does not identify the links to economic and racial identities, which define our experience of being policed and targeted and marginalized. And the equality frame creates this false idea that we are going to be equal, or that it's the ultimate goal. We are not concerned with gay equality—we are concerned about how we are *well*, including having housing, having employment, having safety.

To use marriage as one example, this is not a strategy for our movement work. Marriage is not the goal. Certainly, we want to culturally and politically love ourselves and each other, but we don't need the state to define that for us. We are doing a lot of damage control since the marriage equality movement because it framed our lives in relationship to the state, and in a heteronormative way of being. And it's complicated, because I believe in love, I believe in families, but all sorts, all kinds, and I don't believe in the state defining that for us.

In the same way, our strategies around safety don't rely on the state or policing to tell us what is safe and who is safe. We are creating safety that's defined by ourselves.

JND: This reminds me of one of the main markers of equality that have been used by the national equality groups: LGBT inclusion in hate crime legislation. ALP was one of the first LGBT organizations to be critical of this goal. Can you talk to me about that?

CP: Hate crime legislation is an example of how our strategies don't align with state-defined equality. We do not believe the prison industrial complex is a place of safety, or even that criminalization and punishment are what we should be relying on to take care of our communities. Instead, our strategy is about saying, yes there are hate crimes, so what are we doing inside of our communities with allies, with families, with other queer and trans people of color? What are the strategies that define safety for us, and help us re-imagine how oppression has divided us and created a narrative of hatred between us?

And for ten years we have been organizing in Central Brooklyn, a space of predominantly Caribbean and African immigrant communities and African American communities—people the media tells us are a threat to queer and trans people—and we are working with them as allies. We are saying, as people of color, can we build safety that's not defined by police? And we are thinking about hatred and oppression and violence and how we are going to transform that amongst ourselves.

So, we are building relationships to each other that are not defined by the state, but are instead defined by our livelihood, our survival, our cultural and political existence. And we are building with allies. So instead of assuming that the state or the criminal system or the military is defining safety and will save us from each other, we are looking eye to eye, in the words of Audre Lorde, and asking of ourselves and each other "Who am I willing to be for your safety? Who are you willing to be for mine?" And so, hate crimes legislation, even though it is viewed as equality, is problematic. Because beyond relying on racist police and prison systems, they also define safety by creating an "us" and "them." And we reject that.

And for 20 years, we have always been talking about how our organizing work has always been centered around resistance to the state, and based in particular movements that are using a justice framework, not an equality framework.

Organizing, coalitions, and movement building

JND: Can you tell me more about how you organize?

CP: We have always believed in doing long-term campaign work to change the culture. Not to just do policy pushing. I spent years battling with funders, saying that we're not gonna do policy. And there was an insistence from them that policy is where we need to go. And I was like "There's always two steps to organizing. Yes, policy and legislation. But, also, culture change around violence, and around systems of oppression."

And the value of on-the-ground political organizing that's not policy-led or -driven has come full circle, to where now we're actually getting honored for the work we're doing. We're doing safety and wellness and racial justice that doesn't have a policy lens. But just three years ago, that was much harder to find financial support for.

And over the last three years, the level of direct action has been very important to the visibility of immigrant justice, racial justice, and police brutality. It has positioned ALP in a particular way, since we're 20 years old, having done work like this for so long. So, people are doing phenomenal direct action, but then also turning to ask us: "How do you do it long term?" And in some cases, having to look at our base and say, direct actions are invaluable but we're still about doing long-term organizing, so that involves building relationships and changing systems, and working locally, and building that out. This is still critical. We can't always just lean into a national policy direct action, we still have to value and understand our connections to what's happening down the street. And it's great to see that some funders are finally understanding that.

JND: Wow. Yes, that is a great change.

CP: But actually our organizing has changed in recent years—we've gotten a little more digital on the organizing. We looked at Black Lives Matter, which partially came out of a meme, right? We've looked at #Not1More deportation, and we saw this national call to a very digital social media strategy. And we hired a communications person to get more visual on how we were telling the story of our work and how we were engaging online. Now, I'm an old school door-to-door knocker but I would say our organizers have at least 50 percent social media organizing in their practice.

And we are still training people on the door-to-door, some would say, old-fashioned organizing, because we are always committed as a grassroots social justice organization to do that on the ground, know-your-neighbor work. But there's been a cultural shift in the culture and the movement, where we really have to spend time to convince people that door-to-door work is organizing. That's been weird.

JND: As you do your organizing, are there some groups that you work closely with and, if so, what kinds of organizations are they?

CP: So, ALP has always worked with our allies, mainly in racial justice and economic justice movements and networks particular to NYC. Right now, we are working predominantly with other queer and trans people of color organizations that also follow the principal of liberation and work inside of economic and racial justice and how we queer those politics together.

In New York, that means groups like the Sylvia Rivera Law Project, FIERCE, Queers for Economic Justice (QEJ), and Streetwise and Safe. We have worked very closely with those organizations over the years. And then we also work across the country in larger movement spaces with organizations like Southerners on New Ground (SONG), The Transgender Law Center, Familia, the Young Women's Empowerment Project in Chicago, and other organizations that we know share a political, liberatory framework, that is way "beyond marriage," to use QEJ's term, but really centering our political, cultural, lives from our own experiences.

JND: So, I notice that you did not mention the national LGBT organizations or the state-wide equality organizations.

CP: Well, we are distinctly different from the mainstream LGBT organizations. Because we center people of color and two-spirit people. And because legal equality isn't even part of our conversation, when we are already seen as less than human. And we're not seen as leaders in the LGBT movement, because we're not seen as critical to their framework, and our survival is not centered at those mainstream organizations.

JND: Great. Thank you. Alright so now, talk to me more about ALP's involvement in social movements.

CP: Okay, so ALP has always centered itself inside of economic and racial justice work in NYC, and then nationally and internationally. Where we are heading, or what we have been inside of recently with other social justice movements— be they people of color, be they queer and trans led, or the disability rights movement, the immigrant rights movement, the prison abolition movement, the sovereignty movement led by Indigenous and especially two-spirit folks. We are looking at a liberation movement that is centering people of color and trans and queer leadership, and young folks – taking the most marginalized, and centering our relationship to systems of state that are controlling our bodies and lives. So, I would say the ALP is queering movements that have existed, but essentially, we are a left-wing, radical social justice movement in relationship to all other movements.

And I want to say, I feel like groups like ALP, SONG, the Sylvia Rivera Law Project, Esperanza, and QEJ's legacy—they continue to radicalize, if you will. And I use that term cautiously, because I don't know always what radicalism means, but what I do know is that our existence and our being is radical *[laughs]*. You know, that we have even gotten this far.

I use the term re-memory. We are a part of a political legacy and memory that is so far and wide and deep inside of these movements, but it has been forgotten. So, we are pushing back on memory saying, this is not it, we are not heading for status quo, we are not heading for "equality." We are going for something much deeper and much wider, because this is what we deserve and what we are a part of. And our collective liberation, our collective power, and our collective love for one another, they have to re-imagine our movements at a much deeper and wider level. And that it is our role—to really widen and deepen the movements we are inside of.

The impact of marriage

JND: From your perspective, how did the marriage equality movement impact organizations such as ALP?

CP: So first, did I tell you about New York on the day of the Supreme Court ruling? Have you heard this story yet?

JND: No. What happened?

CP: Oh my God! Well, people were in the streets for marriage equality, and it was the same day as our Trans Day of Action here in New York. And we were on our route, marching from the piers back around to the piers, when, off of Christopher Street, we bumped into a huge faction of pro-marriage equality people. And their group was celebrating marriage. And our group was demanding economic justice, racial justice, gender justice, holding signs about how we need to center trans and gender nonconforming people. Saying: look at the lives of trans women of color being murdered.

And it became a contentious interaction. And the cops were holding a barrier between these two factions. It was so intense.

It was so indicative of a political moment, and we understood that this change from the Supreme Court had nothing to do with us. And that what we were fighting for is *waaaay* beyond marriage. With the institution of marriage, we're not talking about trans inclusive health care, we're not talking about access to housing, or getting out of poverty. We're still structurally oppressed. Marriage is not going to change poverty. It is not going to change racism. It was about an equality agenda that we were just not a part of. And I was amazed at how that day really and physically showed the division that marriage had created in the movement.

JND: Wow. That is kind of amazing.

CP: I know, right?

And now we are doing a lot of damage control in this movement. The marriage equality movement created this massive misunderstanding of what queer and trans liberation is. And unfortunately, those of us that were talking about poverty, homelessness, the medical industrial complex, state control, we got rolled in this tidal wave. And marriage became the priority. That became what was funded. And it completely de-funded our resources and diffused our movement in a very dangerous way. Because now I feel that we are left to pick up the pieces and re-guide and re-direct people and re-remind them where we were heading. It's like we lost, what ten years, maybe more?

So, we are accelerating our work around immigrant rights and justice because we're behind. But we had to pull people back onto the train and say, "This is the freedom ride we are taking." Marriage took us way off course. Because, okay, some of us can now get married, but what does that mean for our livelihoods? Because many of us are still getting murdered as trans women of color, from Harlem to Baltimore to the global south. Many of us are homeless. Many of us are unemployed.

And we are still dealing with the fragments of what we have lost. We watched Queers for Economic Justice close, because the marriage equality movement took us in a different direction and completely de-funded and diffused the impact that many of us cumulatively were building. So, we are trying to re-build the brick and mortar, while we know the foundation was already laid. We are just trying to re-build it quickly so that we can keep going.

JND: So once those marriage equality campaigns were successful, and same-sex marriage become legal and done, how did that victory change the work of the mainstream movement?

CP: Ugh, don't get me started with this! The level of co-optation by the mainstream LGBT movement after they got marriage equality has been shocking. When they all turned and said: "Oh, now we're all gonna talk about diversity. We're gonna talk about racism. Look at all the immigrants that are undocumented and can't access the marriage equality law." It was just a bunch of co-optation where people started using a racial justice frame, and they were completely white-led board members for white-led mainstream organizations, that have no concept of how to speak to poverty, incarceration, detention centers, they were just ad-libbing onto a social justice frame that we had all been carrying as grassroots movement.

Oh, my favorite was the funders talking about poverty and economic justice. Queers for Economic Justice had closed because they could not get funding, and then I experienced big rooms of funders that wanted to talk about economic justice, because now we have marriage equality that people cannot access because they're in poverty. I was beside myself. And to watch funders, the LGBT funders, look at a frame of poverty and economic injustice, and for them to talk as if it had just been created, that analysis of economic justice, and to not give any credit to QEJ and all the other people that had been working on economic justice forever—it was disgusting. I could not believe that. And that, today, continues to leave such a bad taste in my mouth.

JND: This raises a question I have been thinking about. When I was at QEJ, the common complaint made by all my peers, by me, by folks at ALP and other organizations, by all of us, was that the mainstream movement was not addressing issues of racial justice and economic justice. And then in 2010, I go off to graduate school for a while, and come back a few years later as a researcher to conduct interviews with all of you, and now everybody's complaining that the movement does want to focus on the exactly same issues that we were once complaining that they didn't focus on. I understand why, but I find it so interesting.

CP: But it's just a liberal frame! It's a white-led, cis-led liberal frame. They're not using a justice frame, or when they claim to use a justice lens, they are just co-opting modern language. We're watching mainstream organizations say they are using a social justice frame, but they are only about equality and they are only about diversity, not about systemic racism or changing oppression and power.

I have a good example. In 2015, at the National Gay and Lesbian Task Force's annual "Creating Change" conference, they had all these workshops on migrant justice. And then they invited one of the worst, racist, anti-immigrant people as a speaker. That is the dichotomy right there. And then the next year, they did it in Chicago. They had all these migrant justice organizers coming and then they invited ICE (Immigration and Customs Enforcement) to do a training, a workshop on how to intervene on safety. They had ICE come to do a workshop on fucking safety! That's what I'm talking about. Mainstream groups, taking this, co-opting, to bring about "safety," but relying on the state to find it. Completely co-opting our language of finding safety outside of the state and being community-led by survivors of state violence.

JND: Some people have argued that the equality groups can do their own work, and the justice groups can do their work, and the equality groups don't have to do the same work, as long as they just support the groups doing justice work. Do you feel like the equality groups support the radical queer groups or the groups of color?

CP: Hell no. No. ALP has been inside of collaborations, many collaborations. I can say that some of those collaborations were about hoping that we could leverage resources and that the larger more mainstream organizations understood what it meant to be accountable to the community-based organizations. If they could move money, resources, time, or people, then that that was their role. And in some of those collaborations, it is apparent what is really happening in this movement right now: the larger equality organizations are coveting the work of queer and trans people of color groups—because we have never prioritized marriage, and so now that marriage is won we do not have to worry about becoming obsolete the way some of these equality groups are. So as these larger centrist organizations struggle to redefine themselves and justify their continued existence, we are seeing them co-opt our work, and then re-package it differently, so it is less radical (you know, focusing on "diversity" instead of "racial justice"). Seeing larger organizations that have the resources to take our concepts and package them in a watered down, liberal version has been very much a disheartening experience.

Whether they meant to do it intentionally or not, I don't know. The fact is that we all leaned in to share political ideology, political education (and ALP centers our political education work as our strategy) and then to have mainstream organizations ask us for our resources and our thinking as thought partners, and to then not be responsible in how they uprooted that information, took it out of our context of liberation and justice, and put it back out, watered down. It's about a lack of accountability; but then also, how do we maintain transparency and truth-telling in our work if we can't even share our thoughts? So . . . it really implies a dangerous road that we are walking.

Resources, funding, and the non-profit industrial complex

JND: I want to go back to the issue of funding that you brought up earlier when you said that the emphasis on marriage had de-funded work on other issues.

CP: At ALP, we are also trying to challenge a narrative around how funding creates value. So, we have a politic around how we are working with folks who are not seeking to co-opt or consume political thinking. And, thinking about ideology and practice, our concern at ALP is making sure we do not become this large enormous machine that is not informed by lived experience. And ALP is a membership-led organization, we are moved by what our communities are telling us, not by the dollar or by a donor that is not reflective of our community.

I believe very strongly that we have the capacity as queer and trans, gender non-conforming people of color and two-spirit people to move resources in our movement, and I feel that ALP is trying to shift a little bit on how we think about giving. That 5 dollars is as important as 5,000. And getting past this mythology that we can't give back to our work.

That being said, I do hold a particular lens on allies, or people with wealth—people of color included, queer and trans, POC included—people with wealth have a role in our movement—beyond writing a check, but really to cross the wealth divide and re-imagine/re-stimulate an economic flow of how we are giving to each other's work.

Because in the same ways we have created these non-profit industrial complex borders, the funding world has de-funded political work that challenges the state. And ALP and the movement are directly impacted by that. Anyone that has a particular lens against the prison industrial complex, against . . . well against the state, they have a high, high risk of being de-funded or targeted for our work. And that is a danger in and of itself. And not surprising. We know where the funding comes from. I spent a long time in the reproductive justice movement. Population control money funds the reproductive rights movement, and hence the reproductive justice movement. So, these are hard ties that we bind.

And even progressive, political, small funders that try to exist to resist a wealth divide and re-stimulate economic work that could fund our movements—they are now being targeted and de-funded.

And so, there is a moment here to politicize the role of donors who are allies and members who are organizers. You know, how are we going to work together? And again, get past these false borders when, clearly, we have some powerful relationships to build.

JND: It is difficult having our politics and navigating the non-profit industrial complex.

CP: Our movement needs to develop a real understanding of positions and power, and talk about power. Because unfortunately we haven't had real lengthy conversations about power, so that now this sort of anti-NPIC (non-profit industrial complex) critique has shifted everyone into being anti-power, and it's seen as somehow abusive and harmful, as coming from the state. And I'm like, "Are you serious? Let's understand power at its best and power at its worst instances. Let's not make assumptions that all non-profits will steal our work and exploit us, and instead let's think about how is this organizing center available for us to do work and use it as a space to generate change?"

It's a fine line, because it comes through an anti-NPIC lens, and I'm like, okay, bring that critique, but bring that with an understanding of power, because HRC (Human Rights Campaign) with millions of dollars and corporate power is not the same as ALP with thousands of dollars and grassroots power. We have missed the boat in talking about economies and understanding power in relation to political economies and financial economies, sexual economies, really. It's good to be talking to you now, because QEJ's work is more useful than ever, because it breaks down power in ways that other institutions have not done very well.

The Trump administration

JND: Ok, let me shift gears for a minute, and ask you what does the election of Trump mean for ALP specifically, and for LGBT activism more broadly?

CP: For ALP, it means that all the work we've already been doing on economic, racial, and gender justice, on safety and wellness is accelerated. It just went from 0 to 100 because, even with all the work we had done to get us here, we just can't keep up with the way that he's operating, the situation that's operating, which is on a level of hate and fascism. We can't always keep up fast enough with the level of community violence that we're experiencing because of the way his administration generates hate, but also then the laws and the executive order shit things that are also coming down the pipe. It accelerates our work on a whole other level.

JND: And how does that actually translate? For example, what does it do for your strategy?

CP: We were already looking at imprisonment and detention, detainment for immigrants. Now we are also looking at safe houses or other methodologies that we weren't creating as much before because, well, we didn't think we were there yet. Now it's like we have to look at all levels of safety. Whereas before we were concerned about changing gender markers, now we're concerned about not only changing gender markers but how will we be able to move you across borders if your life is at risk, or if you are losing your housing because the ICE raids have multiplied. Just everything is catapulting at a whole other level. We now have to do a multi-tier strategy instead of looking at one thing at a time.

I think for ALP there's been some extraordinary creativity and adaptation to being on the ground and being available for our members one-on-one. And I would say we've been doing a lot of movement building, of course. We have campaigns that move people, move communities. But there's a lot more individual asks from queer and trans families because they are being targeted simultaneously. It's increased a great deal.

JND: And what do you think Trump means for the movement more broadly?

CP: I want to talk about the positives first. The Trump administration has really asked of us, across regions across the country, to lean in and rely on each other. Immediately, when Trump was elected, several of us got on calls and talked about what does safety look like for people on the ground. What tools can we compile? Literally. We made a digital toolkit.

So, we have a history at ALP of working with allies, especially immigrant and people of color community leaders, who are a cis-ally or straight-ally that are against the police, against the state. So, we really had to sit down and ask, how are we going to build across resources and leverage resources toward each other? So, for instance, we are looking at how violence targeting immigrants heightens detainment, but also looking at how trans women, and Latinx and other immigrants alongside trans women, are being detained. I wouldn't say we were slacking, but it really pushed us to reinvest in working with allies, and they had to reinvest in working with us, in ways that I think we were doing in the past; but there was a lull, perhaps, during Obama that we couldn't afford anymore.

And in that same way, I would say some of the justice organizations that we're working with in movements had to put out the same questions. How are we building with allies? Who can leverage what resources? How can we get to a community that maybe we can't get to yet?

And I do think as a grassroots movement in this country there was a collective grief. And we're thinking about how we're holding grief and wellness in the movement, which was less centrally located in the past, but now it's much more apparent, especially mental health. How are we really holding the mental health of our community leaders and community members? There's much more discussion about that right now in grassroots organizing. Because we have people just in emotional distress. You have a new generation of organizers that don't know how to relate to that. They grew up during Obama, which wasn't the endtimes, but it wasn't all beautiful under him either, right?

But in many ways, folks just didn't understand what this means, what this means politically in our country to have a fascist regime come back into office. And so, more than anything, we've been leaning on each other for political study, to understand what it means to survive dictatorship as queer and trans people. To look at other countries, and push ourselves beyond the US borders.

How have other countries gone through fascist regimes? To really learn about and understand grassroots movements—that's become critical to organizing now in this country.

JND: And what does Trump mean for the equality organizations?

CP: The mainstreamers? I don't know and I don't care. I mean, they're out there doing these big marches, and I'm like, okay, that brings visibility to the issue. I guess I could say that the National LGBTQ Task Force, and you know the larger machines, HRC and groups like them, they're putting a ton of money on the counter-narrative to Trump, and the only benefit I see in that is that people are feeling so torn apart by this current administration that they go to a big march. We're also getting the people that are saying that's not enough anymore, just to be gay or just to be equal, so we're getting people running out of those mainstream spaces, coming to us saying: "Whoops! I went there to be out, but now I'm coming to ALP, or SRLP or SONG, because I want to be politicized." So that's a plus.

And then the negative side of it is all the money. All the money going to all that mainstream organizing work. All the direct action and still having funders say: you're not doing enough fast enough. And having us have to say continually it takes times to change culture and it takes time to change minds. I still see funders who only go for policy, instead of long-term movement building, so they're only going to fund the mainstreamers who do policy work, but not real organizing.

Looking forward

JND: So, you're in this interesting moment where you're transitioning out of ALP leadership at the same time the country has a new president. From your perspective, what needs to happen now? What are your concerns about the next few years for the LGBT movement?

CP: Well there's definitely a split right now that's very painful, between trans women of color and the rest of the movement. We are holding, in our own base, tension between trans and gender nonconforming people.

Here's what we need: we need to readjust our frame on gender justice to really understand the gender spectrum; that it is political and it isn't based only on people's individual identities, but actually thinking about gender as a political movement. Because I think it got synthesized into only looking at individual identity, and not a political framework of gender. And that has been very harmful to our base and to our organizing. The call-out culture has resulted in a lot of time tearing individuals down, because they identify as gender-nonconforming versus as a trans woman of color. It has been very murky and painful for our base. So, I would say gender justice—we need like a re-up on what that political framing is.

I would also say we need to study. I'm gonna go back to what I said five minutes ago: people have no idea what we've done, people have forgotten what we know how to do as political liberatory traditions of survival and rising up. How are we studying and understanding movements across the world, especially against dictatorships and political regimes? And are how we applying those lessons learned to this political moment? I think study is going to be key.

And I think getting off of social media is also going to be necessary, so that organizing doesn't become just a digital battle, and so that we're really understanding long-term political strategy. And a strategy that doesn't rely on people running out onto the street after the first year and then being exhausted for the next two. We have to go long and steady on this.

I think our strategies have to be with a passion and desire to know who your neighbor is, to know who you're working with. To understand relationships is really going to be critical for us building a base and building our survival together.

At the risk of sounding free-loving, I do think we have to talk about love and desire. ALP just celebrated its twentieth year, and we used erotic power as a way to say how are we working from a place of desire and not fear. SONG's been speaking to that in creating their "Free from Fear" campaign. Where we're not only moving and working from scarcity but, seriously, where we are moving from love and desire, and from valuing our worth. It sounds so simple but I mean it from the bottom of my heart.

There's a level of internal hatred that I think has always been in movements but it's at a whole other level because it's on social media with the call-out culture. As I shift my role, I'm like, how am I contributing to the love and desire of movements? And how am I bringing in study as a black queer feminist? We cannot erase black queer feminism, disregard it as something negative, simply because it didn't always center trans leadership. These things are splitting hairs. We don't have time for this; we have to be able to value what we can get from those who have given it to us, and then keep moving.

And then on a political level, the lens on safety is critical. I'm excited about people talking about transformative justice models, about building safety outside of the state, outside of police and prisons. I do think there is a powerful resurgence of prison abolitionism, and against the detention centers, and I'm all about it. I think it's a moment for us to understand what resources we have to build community, be it food, be it health care. How can we create our own thing that doesn't rely on state models or institutions that are not going to be about us? They never have, but now we really can't depend on that. There will be thousands of places to deport us and imprison us.

JND: So, my last question is this: What signs do you see that give you hope for queer liberation?

CP: Honesty, I think the level of creation has been powerful. I mean our base is talking about food justice, and how do we interrupt food deserts and do more working with the land—going back to our traditions of survival and resiliency. There's constant generative conversations around survival and resiliency. I think it's been moving people to go door-to-door. They're like, "Oh wait,

I don't even know who's in my block or in my community," so I'm all about people really rising up in their neighborhoods more. And it has to do with how we're going take care of each other. And I love it.

And cultural work, can I just say there's also a view towards cultural work? And the role of healers and cultural workers in movement has exploded and I just love it for myself as a cultural worker and someone who does healing work, and how those things and those elements are showing up as integral to movement. It's powerful.

There's also more discussion about the economy, in ways that I just haven't heard before. People are wanting to ask this question of "Okay, how did we get here? What do we need to know about the economy moving forward? What are the tricks of our economies that we still need to hold in the forefront and value? And how will we not be criminalized for the economies in which we need to survive?" And so, anti-criminalization is still big work that ALP does and we will continue with that. But we have a next generation of young leadership that understands, or is willing to understand, how the economy is impacting the organizing work. And that feels, it feels vibrant! I'm like, "Yes! There's something happening!" And to have them come and say, "I believe we can shut down prisons!" It's beautiful. Even within how we give in grassroots fundraising. Having members give 5 dollars and having them believe they're a part of something. Five years ago, we weren't there. There's been a shift in whatever little part you can do, do it. And people are ready. And I'm hopeful.

I've been so hopeful that as I depart I honestly think there will be people that will apply that and say, "Okay I've never been an Executive Director, but I sure as shit want to be a part of change, and I'm sure I have enough to bring to an organizing center in New York City to know that we have to be able to move for our people."

I just think the questions being asked are much more critical and community-based. I feel like people have pulled away from individualism and leaned back into a collective analysis. And I'm thrilled for it. I'm tired of individual politics. I'm hopeful, Joseph. I really am hopeful.

6

"BUILDING THE WORLD THAT WE WANT TO LIVE IN"

An interview with Jennicet Gutiérrez and Jorge Gutierrez from Familia: TQLM

Joseph Nicholas DeFilippis

Editors' introduction:

This chapter is an interview with Jennicet Gutiérrez and Jorge Gutierrez, two staff members of the organization Familia: Trans Queer Liberation Movement (Familia: TQLM). Familia: TQLM was founded at the beginning of 2014 by trans and queer immigrants, undocumented and allies, youth leaders and parents. It is the only national organization that addresses, organizes, educates, and advocates for the issues most important to lesbian, gay, bisexual, transgender, and queer (LGBTQ) and Latino communities.

In this interview, conducted after Jennicet and Jorge presented at the After Marriage conference, they discuss their work with trans and queer immigrants. They focus on their campaigns to end the detention and abuse of trans and gender nonconforming people being held in detention centers run by ICE (Immigration and Customs Enforcement). They discuss the importance of doing both local organizing and national advocacy, and building coalitions. They also address a controversial incident where Jennicet interrupted President Obama at his Pride Reception (calling for "not one more deportation" and an end to trans detention), as well as the challenges of organizing under a Trump administration.

Readers are invited to consider the following questions: How does the work of Familia: TQLM serve as a model for future organizing in post-marriage activism? Why are issues like immigration moving people to action under Trump's presidency when, as Jennicet and Jorge explain, many of these issues were similar under Obama? How can different social movements find connections to work together?

The work and history of Familia: TQLM

JOSEPH: Can you to start by describing in your own words the work that your organization does?

JORGE: We're a national political organization for the LGBTQ Latinx community, formed in 2014. Our areas of work are LGBTQ rights, immigrants' rights, and racial justice. And in the broader sense we try to change immigration law and the criminal justice system. We also try to influence the media in terms of the stories that get told and the mainstream media.

We do the work through community organizing, direct action, political education, and leadership development, as a way to create a national base. So, we're trying to really build an LGBTQ Latinx movement nationally—one that is visible, coordinated, and organized to take action to be able to respond to immediate needs. And the long-term vision that we're trying to build is justice, freedom, and equity for all people of color in the US, and in some ways across the world.

JOSEPH: Can you tell me a little bit more about what your day-to-day activities look like?

JORGE: Our first focus was immigrants' right work through participating in the national Not One More Deportation campaign. Through that we've been able to lead fights for anti-trans detention nationally. We have been lifting up the stories of how immigration policies are impacting trans undocumented women, both in the detention centers and outside in our community. And to do that, we've been engaging in a lot of direct action, a lot of civil disobedience and disruptions. We've done hunger strikes and taking over public offices as a way to bring attention to the fact that detention centers are not a safe place for anyone, especially for trans undocumented women. We focused a lot of that work locally, here in California. Specifically, we targeted the Santa Ana City Jail Detention Center, which was created as the first detention center especially for trans people. We've been on a local campaign since 2012 to close down that detention center. And we've actually just had a big victory a couple of weeks ago, when ICE closed down that detention center.

JOSEPH: That's amazing. Congratulations!

JORGE: Thank you! We still can't believe it's actually happening, and are just celebrating that, reminding ourselves that community organizing does work. So, we've been through that campaign work, where we organized with folks for direct action and civil disobedience. And we have been training people on all of the different reasons of "Why community organizing?" And we see that we can do the local organizing and also the national advocacy work to be able to create a pretty effective model of how you can do both.

And the other part of our work is leadership development. We want to train people across the country to have the tools to do community organizing for whatever issue folks want to pick up locally, on the ground. We want to have and develop a network of community organizers, advocates, activists, and artists across the country that have tools and are connected to each other to make the change they want to see in their community.

JENNICET: I've just become active in the last few years, and I'm still doing a lot of learning, but Familia appealed to me because they were uplifting an issue that really impacted me personally—the detention of trans immigrant women. I started to organize and I was able, with their support, to travel to different parts of the U.S. to meet up with local, Latinx leaders. They are not only working on immigration, but also on local issues, whether it's gentrification or policing, or other issues that impact their local community. And I follow up with these leaders and do community-building with them.

One of the concerns that I see in some circles is how we concentrate so much on only one specific issue, but there are so many multiple issues, impacting so many people in the community, that are not really centered. We supported marriage equality, but it wasn't the priority for many in the community. We are being left out of conversations and critical decision-making about how we move forward. So, we are supporting the voices of people in our communities.

JOSEPH: How are decisions made at your organization?

JORGE: It's a mixture of many things. We have a steering committee, an official decision-making body of 10–13 folks from all over the country that identify as LGBTQ Latinx folk. It is pretty diverse—we have trans women, both with legal status and no legal status, we have gender nonconforming people, we have queer women, queer cismen. Their main purpose is to help us think through strategic planning, strategies, programmatic work, and fundraising. So that's one place where some decisions get made. The other is with staff. Right now, we have a National Organizer, a Community Organizer, and a National Coordinator of the organization. And among the three of us, there's some decision-making that happens. And then decisions are also made by the folks on the ground, that we do organizing with every day. We engage with them to help us make the decisions we're making, to ensure that it's the right move, and that it's really coming from those most impacted. And so those three layers are where all the decisions come from.

We've been also very mindful. At some point at the beginning, the Steering Committee wanted to spend a few months to think about structure, and I really pushed back on that. I said, "Listen I'd really rather invest time getting our hands dirty on the ground, working with people, and let that influence the structure. Because I don't want to spend six months creating a sexy, beautiful structure that doesn't work for anybody." And doing that has really allowed for the work to move a lot faster, for the decisions to come from different places rather than just one place, and I think that's been really effective.

JENNICET: Jorge made a good point about us being flexible. We don't, at this moment, have everything concrete, regarding the structure of the organization, because we want to give opportunities for new leaders to emerge and bring ideas that they have been exposed to. And we should not be dictating what that should be, right? It's essential for us to let the newer people come in and broaden our issues, to work on things that perhaps we weren't dealing with before, and guide the direction of the movement. And we want them to keep pushing mainstream LGBT rights groups and the mainstream immigrant rights community, to say yes, there is so much more happening, so many more issues. We should not just invest in one issue that is benefiting some people and not all of us. We want to hear from new leaders about the issues that they care about.

JORGE: We're definitely growing. Folks in all kind of spaces are reaching out to us saying they want to bring local groups, or engage in coalition work, or launch their own campaign. So, as we grow, we're starting to really think about what have we learned in the last three years about decision-making. What has worked for us, and what hasn't worked for us? And can we find some sort of structure that is both flexible but effective at the same time? So, the work just continues to grow and grow, and we don't get stuck in what I have experienced in other spaces and other organizations with structures where they often want to hold all the decision-making in one place. That feels so rigid and not realistic to the everyday work that has to happen.

JOSEPH: Are you a 501c3 (nonprofit)?

JORGE: We have a fiscal sponsor. Because that causes a whole monster on its own, that we don't want to get into just yet. There are so many restrictions that come with that 501(c)3 status as an organization. And just being able to spend time and invest energy making it happen is one of them. Also, we're still new, and though our political work has been robust, we still have a lot of internal development that we need to do as an organization. So, we don't want to take that step because we're not there just yet. And our budget is still pretty small too, and so we don't want for our political work to be limited, especially in this political moment. And our current fiscal sponsor is a several million-dollar entity, so our political work is not limited at all in this moment, and that relationship has worked just fine for now. There's some more internal development that we have to do, and we also need to look at other models.

JOSEPH: Could you tell me about your organization's values or vision? Why does your organization do the work that it does?

JORGE: There's been a gap in movement work that has been open for many years. When you look at the history of the LGBTQ Latinx movement in this country, you understand that there was a path before social media existed that tried to put together some sort of national entity for our community. And many didn't last for the long run. So, we're trying to fill that gap.

Centering the work of those who are most impacted is a central value we have. We want to support the ones most impacted and hold them up as the experts of the work. They are the ones that need to be at all layers, both in the community organizing, in the advocacy, in the decision-making, in the strategies, in the fundraising, making sure all of our people are part of all those spaces.

Leadership development is another of our central values. We understand that we have to share the knowledge and skills that we have, to grow and be a more organized and skillful organization and movement.

Coalition work is another big value that we have as an organization, understanding that not one organization or one person can be the leader because our communities of color are facing so much violence and oppression and there's so much that needs to be done. In the next few months we're launching an "LGBT Latinx Network," which will be composed of LGBT Latinx organizations doing local work that also want to be able to connect to a national vehicle so they are able to influence national policies and agendas.

Doing both organizing and advocacy

JOSEPH: Could I ask you to say more about how you balance local organizing and national advocacy? In some ways, I think they perfectly complement each other, and in other ways they pull an organization in different competing directions. So, I'm wondering if you could share any thoughts you have around how you do both of those things.

JORGE: For us, the way that was effective was being part of the Not One More Deportation campaign and utilizing that visibility and that political leverage to be able to say we actually want to be part of their agenda.

We did it because we didn't want to silo our work. We didn't want an insular campaign where we're just saying that we need to end the detention and deportation of trans women, and then we'll be good. No, we wanted to make the connection and say this could be a starting point for ending *all* deportation. And so being able to make that connection was really strategic and really effective and allowed us to create all kinds of coalitions. And through anti-detention work, we were able to work with SONG, Not One More, Transgender Law Center, and other groups, and we were able to also use that space to create national-level advocacy and organizing work.

And then locally, Santa Ana became an epicenter for national work. We hear stories of trans women being detained, caged, and being deported, so we took a national model and brought it to Santa Ana, and created a local coalition of both LGBT rights organizations and immigrant rights organizations that came together to say, "We want to end trans detention and we want it out of our community completely." And that is how we were able to come together locally and push for the campaign for the last three years. We have been doing direct action locally, and doing sit-ins in congressional offices, and we had an action at the White House. We have found that using these strategies are really effective for us.

We're the smaller fish in a lot of these advocacy spaces. We were not being invited to these advocacy circles where folks were having these conversations on immigration, and we actually don't have the resources to have a staff in DC. But we do know how to do direct action, so that's how we demanded a place at the table, and we know that's how we're going to be heard.

So, for us, the strategies have been: not silo-ing our work, creating both national and local coalitions, and really using direct action as a main tactic. We're starting to see that this combination has really worked for us, we're starting to see the fruits of that work.

JENNICET: Organizing is so important. Many people saw Obama as this "progressive" leader that was helping the community and making progress in the right direction. But people forget that his administration made those policy changes because of pressure from activists and organizers on the ground, pushing for these changes to happen. So, it is disappointing when politicians get all the credit, when the change really comes from the bottom up.

Even though Familia has been around for a short time, by taking risks through civil disobedience (shutting down city hall, hunger strikes, etc.), we have been able to highlight and uplift this community which hasn't been a priority. Direct action works. For example, I think the interruption at the White House was a main turning point with the work and the stability of our organization.

JOSEPH: Can you say more about the White House incident?

JENNICET: On June 24, 2015, many leaders from the LGBT community were gathered at the White House for a reception with Obama. These were leaders from many big LGBT organizations: Human Rights Campaign, the National Task Force, you name it, all these big-league organizations who have a lot of funds. Obama invited them to come in and he was going to give a speech to the community, because June is Pride month, right? And there was also a lot of anticipation by these organizations in the room because the Supreme Court was about to make a landmark decision. (Two days later, the Supreme Court declared marriage equality would be a law of the land.)

The organization Get Equal was invited, and they had a "plus-one" invitation. So, they reached out to us, because they knew the work that we were doing, and they wanted to bring an undocumented trans woman who would do direct action at the White House. They wanted someone who would say something to the President to challenge his immigration policies and ask why his administration is allowing torture and human rights violations in detention facilities throughout the country, to be committed against one of the most vulnerable populations in the country.

So, within one minute of his speech, I interrupted him and said, "President Obama, I'm a trans woman, I'm undocumented, release all LGBT people in detention centers, release trans women from these centers." And he just completely shamed me. And the leaders in that room, who are supposed to be from my own community, they turned their backs on me, and told me to be quiet. And that example shows how this disconnect has persisted. How, for years, the community has prioritized a specific group of folks with issues that benefit some, not all. And they don't care about the rest of the community.

So, Familia is going to take risks, and we know that there are so many other communities being impacted by so many issues, and so many injustices. And we cannot just turn our backs on them, like my own community, including the President, did at the time.

Post-Trump

JOSEPH: Can you talk to me about how Trump's presidency has shifted your work?

JORGE: One of the messages we have been trying to share with our communities is that everything happening with Trump and his Executive Orders is just a continuation of what was already happening. I think it's just manifesting now in such a blunt way that people who didn't necessarily see it in front of them every day are starting to see it now. We've been committed to this type of work before Trump's election, and continue to be committed to it now.

JENNICET: If we look at the Democratic administration that was in place prior to Trump, our communities were impacted deeply by deportations, detentions, and issues that mainstream LGBTQ organizations were not prioritizing. So, that's why it was essential for us to get behind the Not One More Campaign and create the End Trans Detention Campaign.

For many communities, it's not dealing with anything new. It's just more visible. But for other people, they're experiencing this sense of urgency. At times they leave messages: "What can we do in this part of the country? I see raids taking place—people are being rounded up and kicked out. So, what do we do?" Responding to all of these calls—that's one of the challenges that we are facing.

JORGE: It has shifted our work. For example, if you look at Latinx deportation work before, we would have launched public campaigns, and tried to tell the story about someone, and make the connection on why deportation needs to stop, and it was the sort of campaign that would take a couple months. And often we were successful in getting people out. But now, people are being picked up in court, in front of their children's school, in their workplace, in their own homes. These things are happening so quickly that is difficult to respond. So, we really have to think beyond this moment right now. I think that's how it has changed for us.

We were doing specific campaign work in the past. Now we're moving this broader leadership development work, coalition-building work, base-building work, which we know is the work that we need to do to reach the long-term vision we have of the communities that we're trying to build and create.

To be quite honest, we were doing leadership development during the campaign work, but we weren't necessarily making it a priority. But I think now, with this sense of urgency that has happened since Trump became president, we are really looking at two things: (1) How do we respond in this moment, and (2) how do we also build the things that we need to put in place for the long-term fight? For us, direct action and coalition building are the immediate work, and leadership development and base-building are the long-term work.

JENNICET: We're building coalitions with the Black community, with the labor community, with women's issues. And trying to build this coalition, because for some of us, these things had already been happening. We've been hit hard by deportation, by lack of access to employment and things like that, right? Some people thought we had it easier before, but now a lot of people are waking up. So, there's a lot of effort, and a major sense of urgency, and a wake-up call for many people. That's why it's important for Familia to reach out to other organizations, locally and at the national level, and we've been trying to connect, in these times.

Looking forward

JOSEPH: How has marriage equality changed things? Now that marriage equality is legal, and funders are not spending so much money on that issue, are you seeing that there's now more resources for groups that were working on other things? Is the political landscape better for your issues now that people aren't so focused on marriage?

JENNICET: Unfortunately, I don't see more resources now that marriage is the law of the land. They're still unsure if they want to support this kind of work. We don't know if it's something the mainstream LGBT community is ready to tackle, right? I don't see any of these organizations coming forward, and saying now we're going to tackle this campaign.

We have to continue to find ways to be more creative to engage the community. And it is not just Familia. Other groups that work with communities on the bottom, they're still struggling, they're still trying figure out ways to continue to push on the issues that they're connected too, and that they've been working on for years. So, I wish I could say that things are changing now, that they're being more receptive of issues, that support has been coming in, but that is not really the case.

JOSEPH: Where do you see yourself located in terms of social movements? What movement are you trying to build or be a part of?

JENNICET: Well, the issues that we're working with are immigrant justice, racial justice, and transgender justice. I think, in some sense, that we need to be true to our community and the people that we can relate to, and uplift those communities. But I don't want to just disregard any other community, any other social or racial group that also has been facing a lot of injustices.

As the organization moves forward, we want to do it in a broader, visionary way. I would like to see more multi-national, multi-generational, across-difference community between groups of people—banded together in the direction that the work needs to be moving.

Instead of just having Familia stand for just immigrant rights issues and nothing else, we become even more intersectional. And that's what I see happening. It's a lot of work, it's a big vision, and I think that it's the way that we should be moving forward as a movement.

JORGE: I think that we have not been working or functioning in the mainstream LGBT movement at all. I think that has been for obvious reasons. We really want to align ourselves with POC-led organizations, whether they're queer/trans or not, by aligning ourselves with organizations and movements that have a vision for the broader work, for the bigger picture, and that understand all the intersections of how our communities are being impacted in so many ways. We need to go deep with these organizational movements so that we're really able to build the world that we want to live in, and continue to cultivate. Maybe we won't see the fruits of this work in our lifetime, but we are making sure that we're moving in the right direction. And that direction is away from capitalism, away from White supremacy, away from patriarchy. Away from all of these systems that have really created the violence that we face every day. And if you're an organization that sees that, then we'll want to roll with you.

7

PUTTING THE T BACK IN LGBTQ?

Trans*[1] activism and interests after marriage equality

Courtenay W. Daum

Editors' introduction:

In this chapter, Courtenay W. Daum considers the question of whether transgender activist organizations should continue to work with mainstream gay rights groups or if they should organize around a specifically transgender identity and framework. On the one hand, working as part of a larger LGBTQ movement allows a smaller, marginalized population to connect with a larger group of allies who have an existing infrastructure and an established blueprint for achieving equal rights-based litigation. On the other hand, the LGBTQ movement has a long history of marginalizing transgender interests, prioritizing goals and ideals that are homonormative, and failing to work beyond legal equality. Daum concludes that trans activists would be better served by abandoning traditional equal rights-based strategies and existing "alliances" with mainstream gay rights groups in favor of grassroots movements that are centered around the needs and interests of transgender individuals.

Questions for readers to consider include: By examining the gay rights movement, what lessons can be learned about how trans issues have been addressed? What are the advantages and shortcomings of prioritizing equality and assimilation over radical queer intersectional resistance and demands for socioeconomic justice? What are the risks for trans activists if they break away from the mainstream gay rights movement?

Introduction

As a legal scholar who came to the study of the law and social movements as a result of a strong interest in and commitment to advancing LGBTQ rights, I was simultaneously thrilled and dismayed by the U.S. Supreme Court's *Obergefell v. Hodges* (574 U.S. ___ (2015)) decision. I celebrated in recognition of the fact that marriage equality extends positive benefits to gays and lesbians who want to marry and legitimates these relationships before the state. At the same time, however, I feared that the Supreme Court's decision would be recognized as the pinnacle of the gay rights movement leading to a dearth of resources and a lack of motivation around other issues that are of pressing importance to individuals within LGBTQ communities, in particular, trans* individuals who are some of the most socioeconomically marginalized individuals in the United States today and continue to suffer from ongoing workplace discrimination, lack of access to health care, systemic discrimination, violence, and criminalization (James et al., 2016, p. 239).

As Hale (2009) reminds us in his Suggested Rules for Non-Transsexuals Writing about Transsexuals, Transsexuality, Transsexualism, or Trans, "What does looking at transsexuals, transsexuality, transsexualism, or transsexual . . . tell you about *yourself*, *not* what does it tell you about trans." To that end, the discussion that follows reflects my perspective as a legal scholar and an ally of the trans* community, and it is intended to demonstrate the shortcomings of privileging the politics of rights (including a collective rights discourse and litigation strategies for rights recognition) over the diverse voices and priorities of trans* people as articulated by trans* people themselves.

As a legal scholar, I have long been interested in the utility of the politics of rights and the study of social movement mobilization, activation and litigation strategies, and how changes in the current political opportunity structure enhance or constrict prospects for the advancement of marginalized interests (Epp, 1998; McCann, 1994; Scheingold, 2004). As an ally of the trans* community, I am committed to facilitating systemic and institutional change that empowers all people, including but not limited to trans* individuals, to determine their own identities, wants and needs free from state oppression and the forces of governmentality. In this chapter, I explore whether or not the interest of trans* communities, as defined by and among trans* people themselves, are best advanced through alliances with existing liberal gay rights groups and legal advocacy organizations and strategies predicated on gaining the recognition of rights or via alternative queer and trans* community resistance strategies that advance trans* interests broadly defined.

The legal push for marriage equality and *Obergefell v. Hodges*

The LGTBQ "movement" has always consisted of diverse communities and groups with differing and competing interests, priorities, and agendas. The challenges associated with subsuming different intersecting identities under a single umbrella "movement" have been well-documented (Murib, 2015; Spade, 2004; Stryker, 2008), but in the aftermath of *Obergefell v. Hodges* (574 U.S. ___ (2015)) these challenges have taken on new resonance in some intellectual and activist communities. Assuming for the time being that *Obergefell v. Hodges* is settled law, gays and lesbians in all 50 states and U.S. territories now may be legally married. While this is a great gain for individuals who want access to state-recognized and legitimated marriage, this legal victory does not come without costs. As Ettelbrick (1992) wrote in her infamous exchange with Thomas B. Stoddard in the fall 1989 issue of *OUT/ LOOK*, "marriage will not liberate us as lesbians and gay men. In fact, it will constrain us, make us more invisible, force our assimilation into the mainstream, and undermine the goals of gay liberation" (p. 21). Ettelbrick recognized that gaining access to a heteronormative institution such as marriage works at cross purposes with "two of the primary goals of the lesbian and gay movement: the affirmation of gay identity and culture and the validation of many forms of relationships" (ibid.). Rather than fighting to contest the dominant heteronormative culture or the maintenance of the nuclear family as a primary organizing and privileging mechanism in U.S. society, prioritizing marriage equality contributed to the rise of what Duggan (2003) calls the "new homonormativity" (p. 50). As Duggan explains, this "is a politics that does not contest dominant heteronormative assumptions and institutions, but upholds and sustains them, while promising the possibility of a depoliticized gay culture anchored in domesticity and consumption" (ibid.).

While the myth of rights is pervasive and leads many to believe that the pursuit of rights recognition via the courts and legislatures is the most effective way to facilitate social change, there are other mechanisms available to those seeking to eradicate discrimination against and the marginalization of designated populations (Scheingold, 2004). For example, alternatives to the pursuit of gay rights via marriage equality include seeking to dismantle those state-sanctioned institutions (including but not limited to marriage) that are used to distribute costs and benefits as opposed to pursuing admission to them, challenging dominant discourses and norms as opposed to operating within their constraints and privileging homonormativity, pursuing economic justice as opposed to legal recognition, building community networks and support groups focused on facilitating grassroots advocacy and local change as opposed to pursuing recognition via state institutions, and so on. While these strategies may seem less viable than the pursuit of rights via the courts and legislatures, many LGBTQ individuals and organizations are committed to these alternative strategies and are affecting positive change in their communities, despite the short shrift these efforts receive from the press and public.

As such, there are both theoretical and practical implications for LGTBQ communities as a result of the liberal gay rights movement's push for marriage equality. The emphasis on conformity as the means to gaining the recognition of rights forecloses opportunities to contest the constraints of the hegemonic power structure, including the emphasis on binary identities (male–female, heterosexual–homosexual, cisgender–transgender), the privileging of monogamous sexual relationships and the nuclear family unit, and the concept that material benefits should be awarded and distributed to individuals via state recognition of relationships (see, e.g., Beyond Marriage, 2006; Butler, 1990; Daum, 2017; Polikoff, 2008; Vaid, 1995). In this way, homonormativity is especially costly for trans* and intersectionally-subjected individuals whose very existence challenges the binary operationalization of identity and makes these populations particularly vulnerable to state violence and subjection (Beauchamp, 2009; Bettcher, 2013; Currah & Moore, 2013; Currah & Mulqueen, 2011; Daum, 2015; Fogg Davis, 2014; Spade, 2011).

In addition, the fight for marriage equality prioritized marriage over other articulated and pressing needs within LGBTQ communities. As explained in the "Beyond Same-Sex Marriage" (2006) statement, "the violence of poverty" is a critical priority for many LGBTQ individuals and families (p. 2). According to the 2015 "U.S. Transgender Survey Report" conducted by the National Center for Transgender Equality, 29 percent of survey respondents live in poverty in comparison to 14 percent of the U.S. population and 30 percent have experienced homelessness (James et al., 2016, p. 3). The statistics for intersectionally-subjected trans* people are even more disturbing, with 43 percent of Latinx, 41 percent of Native Americans, 38 percent of Blacks, 40 percent of multiracial respondents, and 45 percent of disabled respondents living in poverty (p. 4). Similarly, undocumented trans* people face extreme economic hardships as well (ibid.). Marriage equality cannot begin to get at the intersecting forces of socio-economic subjection that operate on trans* people, and *Obergefell v. Hodges* may actually exacerbate these hardships by cementing marriage as the mechanism for distributing material benefits.

Regardless of one's opinion on the strategic, political, and practical consequences of prioritizing marriage equality, in the aftermath of the Court's decision in *Obergefell v. Hodges* (574 U.S. ___ (2015)) attention rapidly has shifted to transgender rights and interests. Recent media coverage of trans* people and movements suggests that the transgender "moment" is now. From *National Geographic's* January 2017 special issue on the "Gender Revolution" and the accompanying two-hour documentary to the near-constant popular media coverage of transgender celebrities such as Laverne Cox, Caitlyn Jenner, Jazz Jennings and Hari Nef, the mainstream media has recognized the existence of trans* people, and public awareness has followed. The increased attention to the socio-cultural and legal obstacles that exist for trans* people across all levels of society and government has been accompanied by a growing discourse and political mobilization around transgender rights as exemplified by the local and state legislative battles over "bathroom bills"—see, e.g., HB2 in North Carolina, which required that individuals use the restroom that correlates with the gender assigned at birth—and the dueling interpretations of Title IX's requirements for the accommodation of trans* students offered by the Obama and Trump administrations which are currently the subject of litigation in the federal courts (see *G. G. v. Gloucester County School Board*, U.S. Court of Appeals for the Fourth Circuit, No. 15-2056 (2016)).

Mobilization for and against trans* rights is taking place across all levels and branches of government. The form that this mobilization takes and the strategic calculations and articulated priorities come with consequences as exemplified by the brief preceding discussion of marriage equality. The decision to pursue rights recognition requires the articulation of specific goals and discursive, legislative, and legal strategies that inevitably engage questions of power and the distribution of costs and benefits. In much the same way that the strategic calculation to make the fight for marriage equality about the rights of gays and lesbian couples to be treated the same as heterosexual couples in the eyes of the state comes with costs and benefits and privileges, homonormative assimilation over queer resistance and pluralism, the fight for trans* rights or interests implicates questions of identity, priorities, wants and needs, and ultimately power (Daum, 2017). To that end, individual members of trans* communities and their allies are confronted with the choice to join with and support existing liberal gay rights groups to argue for a trans* politics of rights or work with or create alternative queer and trans* groups in pursuit of trans* interests broadly defined. While there are pros and cons to both strategies, the cultivation of local community queer and trans* resistance movements empowers diverse trans* communities to articulate their own identities, wants, needs, and strategies. This pluralism is more conducive to facilitating real and substantive change in the lives of trans* people than pursuing the recognition of rights in the federal courts and via congressional legislation in the current hostile national political and legal climates.

The benefits of working with existing gay rights and legal advocacy organizations

Similar to prior rights-based movements, the liberal gay rights movement has cultivated legal defense funds, political action committees, and lobbying organizations that utilize rights-based strategies and arguments to advance its interests in local, state, and national legislatures and courts (see, e.g., Barclay, Bernstein, & Marshall, 2009; Cain, 2000; Goldberg-Hiller, 2002; Rimmerman, 2002). Understanding that political mobilization is an essential component for crafting and executing rights-based movements (see, e.g., Epp, 1998; McCann, 1994; Scheingold, 2004), the existing network of liberal gay rights groups may be well positioned to harness the growing public awareness surrounding transgender rights in pursuit of legislative and legal reforms. The ability to draw on existing organizational resources provides activists with a context for effective and timely mobilization and action, and suggests that trans* rights may be advanced by working within existing liberal gay rights organizations (McCann, 1994, p. 136).

In the aftermath of *Obergefell v. Hodges*, many mainstream liberal gay rights groups stated that lobbying for transgender rights would be integral to the next phase of their agendas, thereby suggesting that these groups believe the time is right to articulate a politics of trans* rights. Freedom to Marry, the organization that played a pivotal role in devising the political and legal strategy that culminated in the U.S. Supreme Court's ruling in favor of marriage equality, spun off a new organization called Freedom for All Americans that seeks to "secure full nondiscrimination protections for LGBT people nationwide" by mobilizing at the local, state, and national level in support of legislation that that prohibits discrimination on the basis of sexual orientation, gender identity, and gender expression (Freedom for All Americans, 2017a). Consistent with its stated commitment to trans* people, Freedom for All Americans' board members include Kylar Broadus, a Black transman and the founder of the Trans People of Color Coalition, and Andy Marra, a Korean transwoman and Communication Manager at the Arcus Foundation among others (Freedom for All Americans, 2017b). Similarly, Gay and Lesbian Advocates and Defenders (GLAD), a leading advocate in the fight for marriage equality, renamed itself GLBTQ Legal Advocates & Defenders in February 2016 in order to signal its broad commitments to the GLBTQ community. In addition, groups like the Human Rights Campaign (HRC) have made transgender rights an organizational priority in recent years. At a minimum, this suggests that gay rights groups recognize that engaging in the discourse of trans* rights serves as a form of institutional maintenance now that the issue of marriage equality has been favorably resolved. Put another way, liberal gay rights groups are membership/donor-supported organizations and the attention being dedicated to trans* rights in the aftermath of *Obergefell v. Hodges* (574 U.S. ___ (2015)) suggests that for the time being this is a priority for their members and donors.

In addition, working within well-established gay rights groups enables trans* communities to capitalize on existing infrastructure, relationships, and resources to pursue their rights in legislative and legal venues. As Scheingold (2004) explains, "If they are to be taken seriously, political demands must be pressed by effective political organizations" (p. 139). Groups such as Freedom for All Americans are able to draw on the resources and experiences of those who worked on and supported the successful Freedom to Marry campaign. As previously mentioned, Freedom for All Americans specifically was created to adapt the multi-level and multi-prong strategies that proved successful in the battle for marriage equality to a push for a broader array of LGBT rights and protections (Freedom for All Americans, 2017c), and it is able to draw on its prior experiences as well as its vast networks and connections across states to coordinate and activate communities at the local and state levels as needed. For example, its Director of Development, Juan Barajas, led national fundraising for Freedom to Marry, and he has "more than 15 years of fund development and nonprofit leadership experience, he has raised more than $25 million to help advance legal protections and cultural acceptance for LGBT Americans" (Freedom for All Americans, 2017d).

Similarly, HRC's gross revenue for 2015, as reported on its IRS Form 990, was nearly 40 million dollars and it reported more than 1.5 million members (Human Rights Campaign, 2015). These human and financial resources enable HRC to reach far and wide when it seeks to mobilize the public or lobby the government on behalf of its policy priorities. Recently, HRC brought its power to bear on behalf of trans* rights as an active player in the battle against HB2, North Carolina's discriminatory bathroom bill, including working with Equality North Carolina to coordinate the corporate boycott of the state and retaining former U.S. Solicitor General Theodore Olson to write an amicus brief co-signed by 68 corporations in support of the Obama Justice Department's intervention in the enforcement of HB2 (Olson, 2016). Due to its well-established connections to the corporate world and its vast reservoir of resources, HRC was able to quickly and effectively coordinate opposition to HB2.

Similarly, trans* individuals may benefit from the fact that the blueprints for rights mobilization, lobbying, and litigation are well established in extant liberal gay rights groups and legal advocacy organizations. In particular, litigation is an important strategy for many of these groups, as it has been for prior civil rights movements, because it "can politicize individual discontents and in doing so activate a constituency, thus lending impetus to movement for change" (Scheingold, 2004, p. 137). Groups such as Lambda Legal and GLBTQ Legal Advocates & Defenders are actively initiating litigation on behalf of trans* individuals, and the American Civil Liberties Union filed the lawsuit on behalf of Gavin Grimm, the transgender male high school student who challenged his school's refusal to allow him access to male restrooms as a violation of his civil rights as protected by the Fourteenth Amendment and Title IX of the 1972 Education Amendments, that the U.S. Supreme Court was scheduled to hear until the Trump administration declined to interpret and defend Title IX as prohibiting discrimination on the basis of transgender identity (*Gloucester County School Board v. Grimm* 579 U.S. ___ (2016)). The U.S. Supreme Court returned the case to the Fourth Circuit Court of Appeals in March 2017.

While the *Grimm* case is not likely to result in a landmark rights victory for the transgender community in the current legal environment, one could argue that trans* rights are advanced by the public awareness that accompanies this type of litigation. This case has received national media attention and has the potential to change the way that trans* individuals perceive daily injustices and increase constituent mobilization as well as increase the saliency of these issues within the broader public (Scheingold, 2004, p. 137). Understanding litigation as both a way to change the law and a tool for future political and legal mobilization demonstrates its utility for trans* communities seeking to combat institutional discrimination. As McCann (1994) explains, law is not simply a set of rules and norms that people learn to obey and follow but rather is a "complex repertoire of discursive strategies and symbolic frameworks that structure ongoing social intercourse and meaning-making activity among citizens" (p. 282). Given that liberal legal advocacy organizations are well-positioned to initiate litigation on behalf of trans* individuals and are actively doing so, these entities are likely to remain at the forefront of the fight for trans* rights moving forward.

Finally, working with liberal gay rights organizations and extant legal advocacy organizations that have broadened their commitment to trans* communities enables a small and marginalized population to connect to a larger group of allies. While it is extremely difficult to measure the portion of the population that identifies as trans*, a 2011 study by the Williams Institute suggests that 0.3 percent or approximately 697,500 adults identify as transgender (Gates, 2011, p. 6). Recognizing that there are significant challenges with getting an accurate estimate of the United States' trans* community, the fact remains that trans* individuals' collective political power is mitigated by their small numbers within the overall population. This limited democratic power is further complicated by the fact that, as previously mentioned, trans* individuals are among the most socioeconomically marginalized populations in the United States, and this is exacerbated for intersectionally-subjected trans* people (James et al., 2016, pp. 3–4). In contrast, the William Institute reports that approximately nine million people identify as LGBT in the United States (Gates, 2011, p. 6). As such, one could argue that working with liberal LGBT groups builds a collective identity that enhances the political power of trans* people by allying them with gays, lesbians, and bisexuals. Drawing on this collective identity, liberal gay rights and legal advocacy organizations may be able to harness their vast resources, established political and legal connections, institutional legitimacy and experience to effectively mobilize, lobby, and litigate to advance trans* rights.

The challenges of lgbt mobilization, trans* "rights" and collective identity politics

Despite the aforementioned benefits of working with existing liberal gay rights organizations and legal advocacy groups, there are compelling reasons why trans* interests may be better served by distancing themselves from mainstream gay rights groups. First and foremost, liberal gay rights groups have a history of discriminating against and marginalizing trans* people and their interests. In "(De)subjugated knowledges: an introduction to transgender studies," leading transgender scholar Susan Stryker describes listening to Jim Fouratt, a gay rights activist, Stonewall participant, and founding member of the Gay Liberation Front, attack transsexuals as "profoundly psychopathological individuals who mutilated their bodies and believed in gender oppressive stereotypes and held reactionary political views, and they had been trying for years to infiltrate the gay and lesbian movement to destroy it ... " (Stryker, 2006, p. 1). While this position may be extreme, the antagonisms within the LGBT movement are well documented, and this history complicates any attempts to forge new and viable alliances between trans* individuals and liberal gay rights groups.

There are numerous explanations for gay antipathy towards trans* individuals, including the fact that "in the legislative arena, gay advocates who are reluctant to include transgender people in gay rights legislation often argue that as a 'new' group, transgender people must wait their turn and cannot expect to 'piggyback' or 'ride on the coattails' of the gay movement" (Minter, 2006, p. 146). This reluctance is exemplified by HRC's ambivalence about a version of the Employment Non-Discrimination Act that did not include gender identity as a prohibited category in 2007; a position that culminated in the resignation of HRC's first and only transgender board member at the time (The Advocate, 2007). Put simply, trans* interests are not going to be furthered by alliances with groups that are not committed to those interests.

In 2014, Chad Griffin, the President of HRC, issued a public apology for the organization's mistreatment of trans* individuals. Speaking at the Southern Comfort Conference, Griffin stated:

> HRC has done wrong by the transgender community in the past, and I am here to formally apologize. I am sorry for the times when we stood apart when we should have been standing together. Even more than that, I am sorry for the times you have been underrepresented or unrepresented by this organization. What happens to trans people is absolutely central to the LGBT struggle. And as the nation's largest LGBT civil rights organization, HRC has

a responsibility to do that struggle justice, or else we are failing at our fundamental mission.

Human Rights Campaign, 2014

Recognizing the liberal gay rights movement's history of marginalizing transgender interests, it is difficult for some to imagine working within these organizations. Ryan Conrad, cofounder of Against Equality, a queer collective committed to "dislodging the centrality of equality rhetoric and challenging the demand for inclusion in the institution of marriage, the US military, and the prison industrial complex via hate crimes legislation" (Against Equality, 2011), stated that HRC's recent decision to prioritize trans* rights "shows how calculated [the HRC] has been with historically marginalized segments of the LGBTQ world" (Meronek, 2015). Conrad also criticized Griffin's apology at Southern Comfort as a "disingenuous PR move" (ibid.). Conrad's comments reflect the extent to which many individuals remain suspicious of HRC's commitment to trans* issues.

In addition to questions of trust and doubts about the sincerity of liberal gay rights organizations' commitments to trans* interests, hostility towards trans* people remains an issue within certain facets of the lesbian and gay community. As Denny (2006) notes, "Some gay men and lesbians have argued that gender-variant people are embarrassments to the movement, holding it back, that transsexuals have no commonalities with the gay and lesbian community, or, conversely, that they are gay men or lesbians in denial, or are tools of patriarchy" (p. 174). One need only view the video of Jennicet Guitérrez, a Latina transwoman, being publicly chastised by gay activists and allies at a White House gay Pride event to see first-hand the enmity that exists within the LGBT community (Democracy Now!, 2015). Guitérrez, a leader of Familia: Trans Queer Liberation Movement, interrupted a speech by President Obama in order to draw attention to the plight of undocumented LGBTQ individuals being held in U.S. detention facilities. As Gutiérrez asked the President to end "the abuse," the predominately White male crowd rapidly turned on her, audibly hushed and then booed her, and one individual can be heard shouting "It's not about you!" (Democracy Now!, 2015). This example is one of many that demonstrates the antagonisms that exist within the LGBT movement. To be clear, this is not to single out this movement for ridicule, but rather is intended to demonstrate the challenges that arise when diverse, and occasionally competing, interests are subsumed under a single collective identity that does not accurately capture the distinctions among orientations and identities (Stryker, 2008). In light of this contentious history and the ongoing marginalization of trans* individuals within the LGBT community, it is understandable that trans* individuals may see "collective identities [such as LGBT] as traps that distort complex realities, 'naturalize' labels, and deceive individuals about their goals and desires" (McGarry & Jasper, 2015, p. 4).

Similarly, liberal gay rights groups often prioritize gaining access to heteronormative institutions such as marriage and the military as opposed to challenging the hegemonic power structures that undergird and support said institutions.

The promotion of homonormative ideals and goals is not a top priority for many trans* people. In the recent 2015 "U.S. Transgender Survey Report" conducted by the National Center for Transgender Equality, one percent of respondents identified marriage recognition and one percent identified allowing trans* people to serve in the military as their most important policy priority (James et al., 2016, p. 239). In contrast, more pressing priorities include ending violence against trans* people (25 percent), gaining health insurance coverage for trans* related health issues (15 percent), racism (11 percent), and employment (7 percent) (Ibid.).

As trans* activist and legal scholar Dean Spade commented in 2014 when asked about the push by mainstream gay rights groups, including HRC, to end the ban on trans* individuals serving in the military:

> "There is a very conservative narrative in the US that eligibility for military services means a person can be considered a full citizen," says Spade. "Some people believe that gaining inclusion in the military changes the public image of marginalized groups, and that will change how they are treated." He disagrees. "Movements for social justice want people to be considered human, deserving of housing, food, education and everything else they need, without having to be connected to possibly the most destructive and dehumanizing force on earth, the US military." In over a decade working in trans communities, Spade says he's never heard military service raised as a key priority among trans people. Instead, "criminalization, poverty, unemployment and immigration enforcement are the priorities we hear again and again."
>
> *Meronek, 2014*

As such, the homonormative priorities of liberal gay rights groups as exemplified by the strategic calculations and discourses that informed the fights for marriage equality and military inclusion do not adequately capture the priorities of many within trans* communities.

In fact, the homonormative priorities and functional strategies of liberal gay rights groups come with significant costs for many trans* people. Notably, while litigation has the potential to raise the saliency and awareness of trans* rights, the use of litigation as a mechanism for gaining the recognition of rights is especially problematic for trans* communities and intersectionally-subjected individuals. Historically, successful rights-based litigation strategies emphasize the immutability of individual characteristics as a mechanism for gaining legal protection. This reflects the fact that one facet of the U.S. Supreme Court's equal protection jurisprudence extends the most rigorous protections to individuals who are targeted for differential treatment on the basis of their immutable characteristics. While *Obergefell v. Hodges* (574 U.S. ___ (2015)) was not decided on equal protection grounds, Justice Kennedy's majority opinion in the case discussed the "immutable nature" of sexual orientation as a justification for allowing gays and lesbians access to the institution of marriage (p. 4). While this recognition that sexual orientation is immutable may expand future opportunities for rights-based recognition for gays and lesbians, it obscures the fact that for many trans* individuals, gender identity is not a fixed or immutable characteristic. Individuals who are genderqueer, genderfluid and agender reject the binary operationalization of gender identity in favor of the ability to exercise self-determination across time and space. As such, accurately understanding gender identity as fluid as opposed to immutable will complicate future litigation implicating the rights of trans* individuals broadly defined as long as an emphasis on immutable characteristics continues to be one of the most direct means for securing legal protections and the recognition of rights.

Similarly, courts regularly operationalize identity as a binary. In fact, the growing popular use of the term cisgender to describe individuals who identify with their gender as assigned at birth as the antithesis of the term transgender reflects the extent to which identity politics privilege binary identity in contemporary U.S. society. Strategically, litigation challenging discrimination on the basis of gender identity may articulate a binary operationalization of gender over a more nuanced, accurate, and intersectional conception of gender. For example, in the marriage equality litigation, liberal gay rights groups argued that the state cannot treat gays and lesbians differently from heterosexuals, implicitly implicating a binary construction of sexual orientation (Daum, 2017). Yet, the articulation of a gay/lesbian-heterosexual binary identity erases bisexuals, pansexuals, queers, and trans* individuals from the legal lexicon and the protections of the law. Similar to Angela Harris's critique that White feminists perpetuate essentialism by "bracketing" or relegating Black women to footnotes, the complexity of gender identity is at risk of being relegated to the footnotes (Harris, 1990, pp. 592–3). For example, HRC's amicus curiae brief in *Obergefell v. Hodges*—which HRC referred to as the "People's Brief" because of its 207,551 signatories—stated in its second footnote:

> Although laws forbidding same-sex marriage fall most directly and onerously on gay people, it should be noted that to the extent a bisexual or transgender person seeks to marry a person of the same sex, these laws would also harm them. This brief generally uses the word "gay" to refer to anyone in the LGBT (lesbian, gay, bisexual, and transgender) community who might seek to marry a person of the same sex.
>
> *Kaplan, 2105, p. 1*

Regardless of its intent, HRC's attempt to articulate a collective "gay" identity in order to simplify rights discourse effectively subsumes and marginalizes bi- and pansexuals and trans* individuals. As McGarry & Jasper (2015) explain, "collective identities remain a central concept in explanations of mobilization, largely for supposed advantages that identities provide" (p. 4), but this discursive erasure of trans* people comes with costs and raises questions about the utility of rights litigation for advancing trans* interests.

At its worst, this reaction stems from a visceral and phobic antipathy to transgender people. More commonly, however, I believe this resistance reflects genuine confusion and concern about how to reconcile transgender issues with the modern, nontransgender model of gay identity that has dominated legal and political advocacy on behalf of lesbians and gay men for several decades.

Minter, 2006, p. 153

To Minter's point, litigation strategies benefit from straightforward unambiguous conceptions of identity, but the result is an essentialist and problematic conception of gender identity which complicates the assertion that there is a LGBTQ collective identity. If, as the evidence suggests, portions of the LGB community do not share a collective identity with trans* people, this problematizes collective mobilization around trans* issues, suggesting that trans* interests may be better served by working within smaller trans* or queer organizations.

Finally, given the current political climate, trans* individuals may find that pursuing rights-based strategies will come with real costs and few gains. With the election of President Trump and Republican control of both houses of Congress, the national political and legal environments have become antithetical to trans* rights. In his first few weeks in office, President Trump undermined legal protections for trans* individuals by refusing to defend the Obama administration's execution of Title IX's prohibitions on sex discrimination as covering gender identity and indicating that schools are no longer required to abide by the prior administrations' interpretation of this law. Furthermore, President Trump nominated Neil Gorsuch, a conservative appellate court judge, to the U.S. Supreme Court, and he will have the opportunity to fill numerous federal judicial openings in the years to come. Gorsuch's confirmation maintains the ideological split on the U.S. Supreme Court between five Justices nominated by Republican presidents and four Justices nominated by Democrats, and preserves a conservative ideological predisposition on the Court. Pending future retirements, the Court may tilt further to the Right if President Trump is able to nominate a replacement for one of the more liberal or moderate Justices on the Court.

Furthermore, despite the best efforts of liberal gay rights groups to advance the Employment Non-Discrimination Act (ENDA)—it would prohibit discrimination on the basis of sexual orientation and gender identity in the workplace—in Congress, the Republican Congress is not going to take up this legislation. ENDA is not a policy priority for Republicans, as exemplified by the fact that Republicans have regularly opposed since it was first introduced in 1994. In light of this hostile national political and legal climate, trans* interests may be better served by focusing their efforts and resources on local and regional mobilization and activism.

Moving towards a queer and trans* community resistance

Recognizing that there is incredible variation among the states (as exemplified by the fact that in 2017, 12 states and the District of Columbia are recognized as being high-equality states and 23 states are recognized as being low-equality states with respect to their state policies on gender identity), there is likely to be geographic variation in terms of the political and legal priorities within trans* communities (Movement Advancement Project, 2017, p. 6). In addition, socioeconomic, socio-cultural, geographic, racial, and ethnic variations across the United States intersect with trans* identities to produce incredibly nuanced and diverse communities with varying wants and needs. Due to the fact that local and regional organizations are products of the communities in which they are located, they may be more attuned to and better able to respond to the unique individual needs in their areas by help-ing trans* people navigate local services and bureaucracies; addressing issues related to local law enforcement and the ongoing criminalization and/or deportation of trans* people; responding to housing shortages, food poverty, and other issues related to economic insecurity; mobilizing for and/or against local and state political and legal issues; cultivating local leaders and advocates within trans* communities; building community networks and associations with other advocacy groups; raising public awareness and education; and so on in support of their trans* neighbors.

Given the challenges associated with working within liberal gay rights and legal advocacy organizations and the jurisprudential challenges associated with pursuing rights recognition for trans* people, trans* individuals may find that community-based queer and trans* movements predicated on the articulated and diverse needs and interests of trans* individuals are a more effective vehicle for advancing their interests. Local and regional organizations such as Southerners on New Ground (SONG), FIERCE and allgo are best situated in this historical moment to accurately and effectively advance trans* interests broadly defined. In contrast to national and/or liberal gay rights and legal advocacy organizations, entities such as SONG privilege intersectional identities and are premised on a commitment to individual self-determination of identities, priorities, and strat-egies. As Butler (1990) reminds us,

> The foundational reasoning of identity politics tends to assume that an iden-tity must first be in place in order for political interests to be elaborated and, subsequently, political action to be taken. My argument is that there need not be a "doer behind the deed," but that the "doer" is variably constructed in and through the deed.
>
> *p. 142*

Understanding that identities are often constructed through the processes of polit-ical mobilization (as individuals forge a connection with a larger community based on a collective identity and shared goals), trans* individuals are empowered through the process of crafting their own politics of resistance (or rights) as they see fit free from the constraints of prior liberal movements (Polletta & Jasper, 2001, p. 285). While these queer and trans* resistance groups do not receive the same attention as liberal gay rights and legal advocacy organizations, those local and regional groups that privilege the voices of trans* people, including trans* people of color and other intersectionally-subjected populations, are doing some of the most meaningful work on behalf of trans* people because self-determination of identities, priorities, wants, and needs is particularly important for intersectionally-subjected communities given the distinctive and intersecting modes of systemic oppression that operate on trans* bodies.

To that end, while SONG identifies as a queer people of color advocacy organization, its priorities cover a broad array of local and regional concerns beyond those which might be typically identified as LGBTQ concerns. SONG's 2016 annual report discusses its multi-faceted agenda which included mobilizing in opposition to anti-LGBQT policies and legislation including HB2 as well as protesting police abuse of and violence against Black people, ICE raids on immigrant communities, and the Dakota Access Pipeline near the Standing Rock Sioux Reservation (Southerners on New Ground, 2016). The history and lessons of the liberal gay rights movement's pursuit of marriage equality through the courts and the emphasis on assimilation and homonormativity over radical queer intersectional resistance and demands for socioeconomic justice came with great costs, particularly for intersectionally-subjected members of LGBTQ communities (Daum, 2017). SONG's local intersectional resistance stands as a vibrant alternative to the rights-based strategies promulgated by liberal gay rights groups. By abandoning the constraints of collective identity politics and the misnomer of LGBTQ politics in favor of the wants and needs of local communities as defined by the intersectionally-identified queer and trans* individuals in those communities, the discourse is expanded beyond the recognition of rights to include a broader array of trans* priorities and interests. In this way, local and regional queer and trans* resistance groups are free to speak truth to power in ways that are simply not possible when an organization is pursuing rights recognition through the same hegemonic institutions that are responsible for the oppression of its members.

In conclusion, while the increased attention to trans* rights is likely to continue (as exemplified by the ongoing legislative and legal battles for and against protections for trans* individuals occurring at the local, state and national levels of government), there are reasons to be cautious about the viability and efficacy of these strategies. While liberal gay rights and legal advocacy organizations are likely to continue to pursue the recognition of rights for trans* individuals, the national, political, and legal opportunity structures are not conducive to a successful quest for trans* rights at this time, and there is great variation among the states as noted above. At the same time, however, local and regional advocacy groups continue to cultivate a broad array of tools, coalitions, and strategies in response to the immediate and pressing needs of trans* and queer individuals as articulated by those individuals within their communities. Given the tremendous variation in local and state laws, norms, cultures, and demographics, these local groups may be better situated to facilitate meaningful intersectional community resistance while simultaneously responding to the immediate needs of their trans* members and neighbors.

Note

1   Throughout this article, I utilize the term trans* to signify that my discussion encompasses the broad array of people who identify as gender nonconforming or transgender to include non-binary as well as male-to-female and female-to-male transgender individuals. In those instances in which I utilize the term transgender I am specifically referring to individuals who were assigned the female sex at birth but identify as, or have transitioned to, male and those individuals who were assigned the male sex at birth but identify as, or have transitioned to, female.

References

Against Equality. (2011). Against equality: Queer challenges to the politics of inclusion. Retrieved from www.againstequality.org/.

Barclay, S., Bernstein, M., & Marshall, A. (2009). *Queer Mobilizations: LGBT Activists Confront the Law.* New York, NY: New York University Press.

Beauchamp, T. (2009). Artful concealment and strategic visibility: Transgender bodies and U.S. state surveillance after 9/11. *Surveillance & Society,* 6(4):356–366.

Bettcher, T. M. (2013). Evil deceivers and make-believers: On transphobic violence and the politics of illusion. In S. Stryker & A. Z. Aizura (Eds.), *The Transgender Studies Reader.* Vol. 2. New York, NY: Routledge, 278–290.

Beyond Marriage. (2006). Beyond same-sex marriage. *Beyondmarrige.org.* Retrieved from http://beyondmarriage2006.blogspot.com.

Butler, J. (1990). *Gender Trouble: Feminism and the Subversion of Identity.* New York, NY: Routledge.

Cain, P. (2000). *Rainbow Rights: The Role of Lawyers and Courts in the Lesbian and Gay Civil Rights Movement.* Boulder, CO: Westview Press.

Currah, P. & Moore, L. J. (2013). "We won't know who you are:" Contesting sex designations in New York City birth certificates. In S. Stryker & A. Z. Aizura (Eds.), *The Transgender Studies Reader.* Vol. 2. New York, NY: Routledge, 607–622.

Currah, P. & Mulqueen, T. (2011). Securitizing gender: Identity, biometrics, and transgender bodies at the airport. *Social Research,* 78(2):557–582.

Daum, C. (2015). The war on solicitation and intersectional subjection: Quality-of-life policing as a tool to control transgender populations. *New Political Science,* 37(4):562–581.

Daum, C. (2017). Marriage equality: Assimilationist victory or pluralist defeat? What the struggle for marriage equality tells us about the history and the future of LGBTQ politics. In S. Burgess, M. Brettschneider, & C. Keating (Eds.), *LGBTQ Politics: A Critical Reader.* New York: New York University Press.

Democracy Now! (2015, June 25). Undocumented trans activist Jennicet Gutiérrez challenges Obama on deportations at White House event. *Democracy Now!* Retrieved from www.youtube.com/watch?v=ER9_M002aQY.

Denny, D. (2006). Transgender communities of the United States in the late twentieth century. In P. Currah, R. M. Juang, & S. P. Minter (Eds.), *Transgender Rights.* Minneapolis, MN: University of Minnesota Press, 171–191.

Duggan, L. (2003). *The Twilight of Equality? Neoliberalism, Cultural Politics, and the Attack on Democracy.* Boston, MA: Beacon Press.

Epp, C. R. (1998). *The Rights Revolution.* Chicago, IL: University of Chicago Press.

Ettelbrick, P. L. (1992). Since when is marriage a path to liberation? In S. Sherman (Ed.), *Lesbian and Gay Marriage.* Philadelphia, PA: Temple University Press, 20–26.

Fogg Davis, H. (2014). Sex classification policies as transgender discrimination: An intersectional critique. *Perspectives on Politics,* 12(1):45–60.

Freedom for All Americans. (2017a). About. Retrieved from www.freedomforallamericans. org/about/.

Freedom for All Americans. (2017b). About the Education Fund Board. Retrieved from www.freedomforallamericans.org/about/education-fund-board/.

Freedom for all Americans. (2017c). How we will win. Retrieved from www.freedomforall americans.org/how-well-win/.

Freedom for all Americans. (2017d). About the team. Retrieved from www.freedomforall americans.org/about/team/.

Gates, G. J. (2011). How many people are lesbian, gay, bisexual or transgender? *The Williams Institute.* Retrieved from https://williamsinstitute.law.ucla.edu/wp-content/uploads/Gates-How-Many-People-LGBT-Apr-2011.pdf.

Goldberg-Hiller, J. (2002). *The Limits to Union: Same-Sex Marriage and the Politics of Civil Rights.* Ann Arbor, MI: University of Michigan Press.

Hale, C. J. (2009). Suggested rules for non-transsexuals writing about transsexuals, transsexuality, transsexualism, or trans. Retrieved from http://sandystone.com/hale.rules.html.

Harris, A. (1990). Race and essentialism in feminist legal theory. *Stanford Law Review,* 42:581–616.

Human Rights Campaign. (2014). Speaking at Southern Comfort. Retrieved from www.hrc. org/blog/speaking-at-southern-comfort-2014.

Human Rights Campaign. (2015). HRC Assets. Retrieved from http://assets.hrc.org//files/ images/general/FY16-HRC 990.pdf?_ga=1.10123125.1195779503.1487709146.

James, S. E., Herman, J. L., Rankin, S., Keisling, M., Mottet, L., & Anafi, M. (2016). *The Report of the 2015 U.S. Transgender Survey.* Washington, DC: National Center for Transgender Equality.

Kaplan, R. A. (2015). Brief of the Human Rights Campaign and 207,551 Americans as amicus curiae supporting petitioners, Vol. I. *Obergefell v. Hodges.* US Supreme Court. Retrieved from http://hrc-assets.s3-website-us-east-1.amazonaws.com//files/assets/resources/the peoplesbrief.pdf.

McCann, M. (1994). *Rights at Work: Pay Equity Reform and the Politics of Legal Mobilization.* Chicago, IL: University of Chicago Press.

McGarry, A. & Jasper, J. (2015). Introduction: The identity dilemma, social movements and contested identity. In A. McGarry & J. Jasper (Eds.), *The Identity Dilemma: Social Movements and Collective Identity.* Philadelphia, PA: Temple University Press, 1–17.

Meronek, T. (2014, July 21). Transgender activists speak out against campaign to end trans military ban. *Truthout.* Retrieved from www.truth-out.org/news/item/25015-transgender-activists-speak-out-against-campaign-to-end-trans-military-ban.

Meronek, T. (2015, January 11). Human Rights Campaign under fire in LGBT community. *Truthout.* Retrieved from www.truth-out.org/news/item/28430-human-rights-campaign-under-fire-in-lgbt-community.

Minter, S. P. (2006). Do transsexuals dream of gay rights? Getting real about transgender inclusion. In P. Currah, R. M. Juang, & S. P. Minter (Eds.), *Transgender Rights.* Minneapolis, MN: University of Minnesota Press, 141–170.

Movement Advancement Project. (2017). *Mapping Transgender Equality in the United States.* Denver, CO: Movement Advancement Project. Retrieved from http://lgbtqmap.org/ file/mapping-transequality.pdf 2017.

Murib, Z. (2015). Transgender: Examining an emerging political identity using three political processes. *Politics, Groups and Identities,* 3(3):381–397.

Olson, T. (2016). Unopposed motion for leave to file an amicus curiae brief in support of plaintiff. *United State v. North Carolina,* U.S. District Court for the Middle District of North Carolina, Case No. 1:16-cv-00425. Retrieved from http://assets.hrc.org//files/

assets/resources/As-Filed_-_Unopposed_Motion_for_Leave_and_Proposed_Amicus_ Curiae_Brief_by_68_Companies_in_Support_of_United_States.pdf?_ga=1.207231315. 1195779503.1487709146.

Polikoff, N. (2008). *Beyond (Straight and Gay) Marriage: Valuing all Families Under the Law.* Boston, MA: Beacon Press.

Polletta, F. & Jasper, J. M. (2001). Collective identity and social movements. *Annual Review of Sociology,* 27:283–305.

Rimmerman, C. A. (2002). *From Identity to Politics: The Lesbian and Gay Movements in the United States.* Philadelphia, PA: Temple University Press.

Scheingold, S. (2004). *The Politics of Rights: Lawyers, Public Policy and Political Change.* Ann Arbor, MI: University of Michigan Press.

Southerners on New Ground. (2016). *2016 End of Year Report.* Retrieved from http://southerners onnewground.org/2016/12/16endofyearreport/. Accessed on February 19, 2017.

Spade, D. (2004). Fighting to win! In M. B. Sycamore (Ed.), *That's Revolting! Queer Strategies for Resisting Assimilation.* Berkeley, CA: Soft Skull, 47–53.

Spade, D. (2011). *Normal Life: Administrative Violence, Critical Trans Politics, and the Limits of Law.* New York, NY: South End Press.

Stryker, S. (2006). (De)Subjugated knowledges: An introduction to transgender studies. In S. Stryker & S. Whittle (Eds.), *The Transgender Studies Reader.* New York, NY: Routledge, 1–17.

Stryker, S. (2008). Transgender history, homonormativity and disciplinarity. *Radical History Review,* 100:145–157.

The Advocate. (2007, October 4). Donna Rose on why she resigned as the only transgender member of HRC's board. *The Advocate.* Retrieved from www.advocate.com/news/ 2007/10/04/donna-rose-why-she-resigned-only-transgender-member-hrcs-board.

Vaid, U. (1995). *Virtual Equality: The Mainstreaming of Gay and Lesbian Liberation.* New York, NY: Anchor Books.

Cases cited

G.G. v. Gloucester County School Board, U.S. Court of Appeals for the Fourth Circuit, No. 15-2056 (2016).

Gloucester County School Board v. Grimm 579 U.S. ___ (2016).

Obergefell v. Hodges (574 U.S. ___ (2015)).

8

CENTERING INTERSECTIONAL POLITICS

Queer migration activisms "after marriage"

Siobhán McGuirk, Jara M. Carrington, Claudia Cojocaru, Jamila Hammami, and Marzena Zukowska

Editors' introduction:

In this chapter, five activists, researchers, and practitioners make the case for a vision of queer migration politics that is more critical and intersectional than the homonormative and homonationalist framings that drove marriage equality campaigns.

They address major issues of queer migration, making important links between those issues and larger social problems, including: neoliberal capitalism, labor, and poverty; policing and state violence; racism, Islamophobia, xenophobia, and imperialism. They explore the challenges that must be confronted by LGBTQ immigration activists and offer suggestions about how to overcome those challenges by centering intersectional politics.

Readers should consider the following questions: What are the advantages of making connections between issues that are often viewed as separate social justice concerns (immigration, labor, policing, etc.)? How has previous LGBTQ activism, such as the marriage equality campaigns, shaped the public understanding of which immigrants are considered deserving and acceptable? How should we decide who gets to live in the USA?

Introduction

Since the Naturalization Act of 1790, the United States has restricted entry, residency, and citizenship to people based on intersecting, normative categories of race, nationality, class, gender, sexuality, and perceived "moral character," among other criteria. Laws introduced in the nineteenth and twentieth centuries, for example, barred individuals who were deemed by officials to be promiscuous, dangerously procreative, or "mentally defective"—a category that included homosexuals (Luibhéid, 2002). The ban on "sexual deviants," a proxy category for lesbian and gay persons, stood until 1990. A travel ban on HIV+ people remained until 2010.

While LGBTQ[1] activists have been fighting discriminatory immigration policies for decades, the topic became a key feature of the "marriage equality" movement in one particular sense: the ability of a U.S. citizen or Lawful Permanent Resident (LPR) to sponsor the visa application of their non-citizen, same-sex spouse. In drawing attention to binational same-sex couples, many organizations supporting LGBTQ immigrants invested heavily in the family-centric rhetoric of committed, monogamous partners, "united by love, divided by law" (Rickard, 2011). Post-DOMA, advocates for LGBTQ refugees and asylum seekers have heralded same-sex marriage as proof of the country's liberal credentials, confirming its status as a "safe haven" for people fleeing homophobic persecution elsewhere.

These narratives erase historical and present realities faced by queer immigrants. International love stories, journeys "from fear to freedom" (Morris, 2013) and other, related moral geographic mappings of the United States vis-à-vis the rest of the world obscure the ongoing threats and dangers faced by LGBTQ-identified immigrants living within, or attempting to cross, U.S. borders. Advocacy strategies and rhetorics that prioritize certain immigrant categories—spouse, family-member, asylum seeker—work in tandem with the homonormative[2] politics of the marriage equality movement to narrow popular ideas about which LGBTQ immigrants can be seen as deserving and acceptable members of U.S. society.

The neoliberal "politics of belonging" promoted in mainstream marriage equality campaigns also reproduces Orientalist, specifically Islamophobic, discourses, which frame the ostensibly liberal West in opposition to an "East" that is imagined as inherently oppressive, intolerant, and dangerous (Said, 2003). The assertive claim by one organization that LGBTQ asylum seekers and other immigrants are, "rarely supported by their families or fellow expatriates. Because of their nonconforming sexual orientation or gender identity, they are often excluded from the[ir] religious and immigrant communities" (ORAM, 2012, p. 1) is just one example of this perspective. Orientalist narratives erase the voices of LGBTQ Muslims in the United States, and LGBTQ activists in the Middle East, among other groups. They also tacitly justify increasingly militarized border securitization measures at home, and imperialistic "interventions" overseas, such as the U.S.-backed occupation of Palestine by an Israel Defense Force celebrated for its LGBTQ-inclusivity (Ahmed, 2011; Spade, 2017).

A recent example of this maneuver can be found in the Executive Orders issued by President Trump in January 2017. One Order, dubbed "the Muslim ban" in the media, explicitly framed Muslims as homophobic in order to justify their exclusion from the United States (Trump, 2017). Another Order granted immigration officials greater powers to detain anyone they deem to be a "threat to public safety"—coded language that further sanctions their already disproportionate targeting of LGBTQ people (Gruberg, 2016). This political sleight of hand may be also described as "homonationalist" (Puar, 2007); it effectively deploys a veil of pro-LGBTQ rhetoric over exclusionary, often racist policies in the name of "securing the nation." In short, the post-marriage equality United States is only seemingly pro-LGBTQ. It continues to inflict violence against queer people, domestically and abroad, and particularly those who are marginalized within intersecting hierarchies of normative race, class, gender, sexuality, and immigration status. As we more fully explore below, LGBTQ migrants in particular experience disproportionate levels of violence within our society, especially within the criminal justice system, and the closely related U.S. Customs and Immigration System (USCIS) nexus of raids, detentions, and deportations.

During the marriage equality campaign, the majority of well-funded, high-profile LGBTQ-rights non-profits and non-governmental organizations (NGOs) invested heavily in these limited and limiting discussions of LGBTQ immigrants. It was left to smaller, local grassroots-led groups to address, and to commit resources to, advocacy on broader issues such as undocumented peoples' rights, detention, and deportation. Even "after marriage," notably few large LGBTQ rights NGOs have paid lasting attention or provided significant funding to immigrants' rights. Those that did, have frequently refused guidance and ignored calls for solidarity from grassroots groups such as Undocuqueer or Transcend Arizona. Indeed, they have often pursued advocacy strategies at odds with, and even occasionally damaging to, grassroots organizers' abolitionist and immigration reform goals (Gutiérrez, 2016).

Now, and especially under the Trump administration, it is vital that large LGBTQ rights NGOs follow grassroots LGBTQ immigrants' lead. In this chapter, we draw on our experiences as researchers, practitioners, and activists to argue for a more critical, intersectional vision of queer migration politics "after marriage." We focus on key topics informing queer migration activism today. We situate each theme in relation to broader social issues, including: policing and state violence; neoliberal capitalism, labor, and poverty; racism, Islamophobia, and xenophobia; imperialism, and pervasive ideas about who "deserves" to live in the United States. Keeping activism at the forefront of our discussion, we highlight the politics and practices of NGOs and grassroots organizing, and explain some of the challenges we face as LGBTQ immigration activists. We conclude by outlining ways in which we might overcome those challenges by centering intersectional politics.

Family reunification

Policies that define family are a crucial site for a queer intersectional analysis of migration and citizenship. Currently, family-based migration accounts for over two-thirds of documented migration to the United States (Kandel, 2014). According to U.S. immigration law, family is defined through marital and biological connections, which are divided into categories of spouse or fiancé, parent–child, or sibling. Immigrant visas for family members are differently prioritized, based upon the petitioner's status as a U.S. citizen or LPR. Importantly, these categories do not capture the complexity of kinship and other relations that are especially meaningful for LGBTQ-identified people.

Legal categories of family are figured through intersecting hierarchies of gender, sexuality, race, class, ethnicity, and nationality (Luibhéid, 2005, 2008; Yue, 2008). Only some people can take advantage of family-based immigration benefits—particularly those who already have a family member in the United States, are able to lawfully enter the country, possess economic and/or cultural capital, and can adhere to heteronormative standards of monogamy and marriage. Those whose identities, relationships, and immigration histories fall outside these normative parameters are often excluded.

Prior to *Windsor v. United States*, "binational same-sex couples" were not able to petition for the immigrant partner through the spousal relative category, and thus were denied access to a significant means of lawful migration—particularly important in a time of increasingly militarized border enforcement. Yet the advocacy efforts and policy measures that were developed to support rights for binational same sex couples are a fruitful site to think through the possibilities and pitfalls for current queer migration activisms "after marriage" (Carrington, 2016). Over the past 25 years, a number of high-profile NGOs formed around and focused attention on the immigration challenges faced by same-sex couples. This group became a prominent public symbol of LGBTQ immigrant politics more generally, pushing other LGBTQ immigrant populations and issues out of the spotlight. Advocacy efforts and strategies prioritized the inclusion of same-sex couples into existing immigration law as "family." Framed by this politics of inclusion, NGOs' proposed legal and legislative solutions to the challenges faced by binational same-sex couples, and employed a rights narrative that was tied to the U.S. citizen partner and the rights of marriage, rather than to the foreign national and their rights as an immigrant.

Advocacy campaigns developed by the most well-funded and visible LGBTQ immigrant rights NGOs frequently featured homonormative depictions of lesbian or gay immigrants, using images and narratives that marked couples as middle-upper-class families by highlighting their marital, professional, financial, and lawful legal statuses (Chávez, 2010). The NGOs Immigration Equality and The DOMA Project each developed advocacy campaigns around carefully vetted "spokescouples," whose images, stories, and statements to Congressional leaders relied on normative rhetorics to argue for their inclusion into "the nation." Photographs of binational same sex-couples in traditional wedding attire, standing in front of the nation's capital, became a prominent feature in NGO campaign materials, explicitly marking the relationship as safe, familiar, and reassuringly lawful. Other advocacy campaigns featured spokescouples playing with their children, always on a well-manicured, expansive lawn outside their large, single family home, implicitly locating them within a middle-upper-class position.

These types of rhetorics and visual representations worked to produce the binational same sex-couple as a normative, nuclear family, and as the primary site of the "good gay immigrant" who was most deserving of state protection. In doing so, advocacy strategies and tactics also directly and indirectly disqualified other immigrants from access to the rights demanded for the stereotypical binational same sex couple. Immigrants whose photographs and statements would not appeal to the conservative elites in Congress, who did not explicitly express appropriate nationalist sentiments, or who lived in low-income housing, for example, were all obscured by these campaigns. Immigrants unlikely to marry a U.S. citizen, or those with complex immigration histories and/or no lawful immigration status, were erased completely. Thus, campaigns that privileged this particular category of LGBTQ immigrant both worked to exclude already marginal immigrant persons and communities and validate state-sanctified marriage as the arbiter of rights, recognition, and national belonging.

Advocacy efforts focused on incorporating same-sex couples into existing immigration policies additionally failed to reflect critically on the relationship between marriage and immigrants' rights. Consequently, structural inequalities embedded in the law that impacted opposite sex couples are now similarly affecting same-sex couples. For instance, the rules and regulations regarding the spousal category of family reunification position the immigrant partner as dependent on the U.S. citizen/LPR partner in all interactions with the immigration service. This dynamic of dependency is open to abuse by U.S. citizen/LPR partners, who may use immigration status as a weapon against their significant others—coercing them to enter into, or to remain in, an unwanted or unsafe relationship. Existing frameworks do not adequately protect immigrant spouses, same-sex or opposite-sex, against intimate partner violence.

Finally, the inclusion of same-sex spouses as "family" does not disturb the class privilege that was already built into contemporary immigration law: in petitioning for an immigrant visa for any spouse, the U.S. citizen partner must prove that they have the financial means to support the immigrant partner, and sign a binding affidavit that they will do so until the foreign national partner naturalizes (becomes a citizen) or works for at least ten years. Further, if the immigrant partner receives public benefits during this period, the U.S. government can sue the U.S. citizen petitioner to recover the money. This means that spousal visa sponsorship is only accessible to those with significant economic capital. Those with few financial resources are, regardless of their partner's sex, denied the rewards promised to them by mainstream same-sex marriage campaigns.

A queer intersectional analysis of advocacy and policy for binational same-sex couples reveals how power is exercised through immigration regulation in a complex manner that goes beyond simple practices of exclusion. That is, immigration laws that define family also work to discipline those immigrants who are able to fit into existing legal categories, and compel them to fashion themselves in accordance with national norms that regulate belonging. Further, the dominant discourses and practices around binational same-sex couples unveil the exclusionary and productive power not only of immigration law, but also of advocacy efforts that overlook the nationalist and moralist implications of immigration regulation. Family reunification is, however, just one area in which intersectional interventions are required in order to disrupt initiatives that position "good" homosexual immigrants against "bad" queer intruders.

Asylum

The U.S. asylum system is another site in which LGBTQ immigrants are measured against homonormative expectations of "good gay" subjectivity. Intersectional analyses of statist logics (claims grounded in a belief that the nation-state is, and should be, the exclusive source of law, social order, and morality, and that state agencies must forcibly uphold these ideals) are useful for understanding asylum adjudication mechanisms, particularly as they relate to questions of authenticity, deservingness, and belonging. An intersectional approach is also necessary for creating effective justice campaigns and appropriate initiatives to support LGBTQ asylum seekers.

The United States, as a signatory to the 1951 United Nations Convention and 1967 Protocol on the Rights and Status of Refugees, is obliged to offer protection to foreign nationals fleeing persecution in their home countries. Unlike refugees, who enter the United States after being granted protected status overseas, asylum seekers apply directly to the U.S. government for protection after travelling to the United States. Also unlike refugees, asylum seekers are not eligible for federal aid or legal support, and are barred from legally working until six months after submitting their claim. As private immigration attorneys are costly, many asylum seekers rely on "pro bono" legal services. The few organizations that provide financial, housing, or other material support to asylum seekers are often under-funded and heavily reliant on volunteer staff.

Asylum seekers must prove that their fear of persecution is "reasonable" and "credible." Adjudicators frequently expect LGBTQ claimants to "prove" their non-conforming sexuality and/or gender identity in a manner that is legible within U.S.-centric norms and stereotypes about homosexuality (Kimmel & Llewellyn, 2012). This is an impossible task. Worldwide, people who do not self-identify as "LGBT" may nonetheless face persecution because of their non-normative sexual activity, desires, or gender presentation. For example, men who have sex with men but identify as straight can still face criminal charges where sodomy is illegal. Others may self-identify using culturally-specific identities and terminologies, such as *hijra*, *travestí*, *kuchu*, *muxe*, or *mashoga*, for example, which do not map easily onto Western identity categories. Even those asylum seekers who do identify as "LGBTQ" may struggle to produce verifiable "proof" of their identity.

LGBTQ claimants are not all equally situated to obtain documentation in support of their claim, such as medical reports, police statements, news articles, threatening messages, support letters, country profiles from reputable sources, and so on. For example, outspoken members of LGBTQ rights organizations overseas are often better able to provide compelling evidence of their public persona and the persecution they have faced than those who have experienced violent repression in private. Women's experiences of anti-LGBTQ violence are doubly concealed, as country-context reports, laws, and high-profile moral panics primarily focus on male homosexuality and gender nonconformity. The particular threats posed to LGBTQ women are consequently less known and understood by asylum adjudicators (Lewis, 2013). Additionally, where anti-LGBTQ prejudice is widespread, victims often do not report the full circumstances of hate-crime to police or medical examiners, if they report them at all. This makes official verification of events difficult. Asylum seekers who are estranged from their family, who have little formal education, or who have worked largely in the informal sector—all common experiences within LGBTQ populations—may struggle to prove even the most basic facts of their lives. Indeed, adjudicators frequently reject LGBTQ asylum claims on the subjective grounds that they believe that the claimant is "not really" LGBTQ, or that they have not suffered persecution for that reason. These decisions are informed by pernicious racial and religious stereotypes (Morgan, 2006), in keeping with Salvador Vidal-Ortiz's insight that, in the United States, "LGBTQ" is coded as White (Vidal-Ortiz, 2014, p. xi).

Emphasis on the "immutability" of sexuality in U.S. asylum law makes it especially challenging for bisexual or otherwise sexually fluid claimants to win asylum. Adjudicators generally pursue lines of questioning about childhood experiences and self-realization or self-acceptance that presuppose a fixed sexual identity, and those who have been in heterosexual marriages or who have children often arouse suspicion (Rehaag, 2009). Salient ideas about sexuality and gender identity as essential, fixed, and demonstrable are reinforced by advocacy efforts that frame LGBTQ asylum seekers as "persecuted because of who they are," but able to live as their "authentic" selves, if granted protection (McGuirk, 2016, pp. 95–99).

Campaigns for LGBTQ asylum seekers often also deploy homonationalist framings, which assertively present the United States as inherently safe and welcoming for LGBTQ people in contrast with "other" global locations. Ubiquitous examples include NGO slogans and magazine headlines that describe LGBTQ asylum seeker's journeys as ones "to freedom" or "to safety." This mapping of the United States vis-à-vis other countries echoes adjudicators' expectations that credible claimants should regard their homes and their fellow nationals as pathologically homophobic, and attest to feeling safe and liberated in the United States (Cantú, Luibhéid, & Stern, 2005). Consequently, asylum seekers who avoid mainstream U.S. LGBTQ scenes, retain ties to diaspora communities, maintain their religious practice, or are in regular contact with people back home may be regarded as disingenuous or "closeted"—in either case, as not "genuine" LGBTQ asylum seekers. Anxieties over so-called "bogus" claimants permeate government and non-governmental spaces alike, creating additional barriers to safety for those who do not conform to U.S.-centric norms and stereotypes about LGBTQ individuals. Service providers who share adjudicators' normative expectations can subject their clients to questioning, suspicion, and rumor—and often decline to support those they do not deem "genuine" (McGuirk, 2016, pp. 119–132).

Intersectional analyses of the U.S. asylum system reveal that LGBTQ claimants must appear to adjudicators as "gay enough" (Kimmel & Llewellyn, 2012), and suitably traumatized, in order to win asylum. Homonormative tropes—conspicuous consumption, unthreatening political views, a stated desire to assimilate to U.S. norms, and fixed and knowable "out and proud" subjectivity—heavily inform adjudicators' determinations. These tropes are notably raced, classed, gendered, and ethnocentric. Asylum seekers who fail to meet these limited expectations can struggle to secure NGO and pro bono support, and are more likely to face criminalization, detention, and deportation. Even those who are granted asylum often continue to encounter prejudice—racism, xenophobia, and Islamophobia, in addition to new forms of anti-LGBTQ sentiment—and exploitation.

Labor trafficking and labor migration

Some LGBTQ immigrants are spouses, while others are refugees or asylees. Yet, many more are students or workers and/or the siblings, children, or parents of people living in the United States. Of the estimated one million LGBT-identifying immigrants living in the United States in 2013, 30 percent were undocumented (Gates, 2013). Those 267,000 people are, as a result of U.S. policies, unable to access federal social service programs, denied workplace protections and subject to exploitative employment practices, and often separated from loved ones because their freedom of movement is restricted. As comprehensive immigration reform campaigns came to the fore in the late 2000s, Undocuqueer, #Not1More, and other undocumented youth-led groups sought to highlight the intersections between immigrants' rights and LGBTQ rights movements, and the diversity of immigrant experiences and struggles.

People migrate to the United States for a combination of reasons, ranging from personal and professional to structural factors. This often includes the search for a "better life," for themselves and/or for their families back home. While so-called economic migrants in the United States are frequently portrayed as a social problem, or so-called "public charge" (Fix & Capps, 2017), the movement of people—by force or by choice—can only be completely understood in the context of imperialism, globalization, and neoliberal capitalism. U.S. interventions, in terms of foreign policy, trade agreements, or support for pro-U.S. regimes (including by military coup) have forced millions of people in Central and South America (Gonzalez, 2011), Asia (Choy, 2003), and elsewhere to flee their homes in search of economic and social security. Yet upon arrival in the United States, millions of immigrants find employment in the informal economy in sectors such as domestic work, construction, farm work, hospitality, and others subject to minimal labor protections and systemically high rates of exploitation (Passel & Cohn, 2015; Cooper & Kroeger, 2017).

Immigrant workers in the United States are particularly subject to low wages, lack of employment benefits, adverse and unsafe working conditions, and varying forms of verbal, psychological, and physical abuse. Undocumented workers face the added vulnerability of discrimination due to their immigration status, and the threat of deportation or immigration enforcement; as a result, they may be less likely to report abuse or file a formal complaint against an employer out of fear of retaliation. These realities are compounded in sectors with already limited worker protections, like domestic work, where the legacy of slavery and systematic devaluing of women's (unpaid) labor, resulted in exclusion from most major labor laws in the United States (Burnham & Theodore, 2012). LGBTQ immigrant workers are further at risk of workplace discrimination, sexual assault, and harassment, due to their perceived sexual orientation or gender identity, yet may be hesitant to come forward or seek support in community spaces. Recognizing these challenges, organizations like Damayan and National Domestic Workers Alliance are working to address issues of homophobia and transphobia facing LGBTQ immigrant workers, both inside and outside of the workplace.

Mainstream LGBTQ rights organizations are, "after marriage," increasingly focused on securing workplace protections for their constituents, prioritizing policies such as the Employment Non-Discrimination Act, and resistance to the proposed "First Amendment Defense Act," which would sanction anti-LGBTQ discrimination on religious grounds. While important, these workplace protections often do not apply to, or fully cover, undocumented workers, who, if terminated from their jobs, may not be eligible for compensation or reinstatement. This reality also extends to workers (documented or not) who are employed in sectors of work that are largely unregulated or unprotected by the government, such as nannies, house cleaners, home health care workers, day laborers, and construction workers. They are also unlikely to protect those unable to readily access legal advice or counsel, or those working in sectors where filing a complaint could jeopardize one's job due to employer retaliation. An intersectional approach to labor rights reveals that a more expansive view of "work" is required, if LGBTQ rights organizations are to advocate for all LGBTQ workers, and not only those already somewhat protected by citizen rights and socio-economic status.

Another advocacy area that has obscured the widespread exploitation of undocumented and other migrant workers is human trafficking. As further explored below, high-profile, anti-trafficking organizations, particularly those focusing exclusively on "sex trafficking," have continued to base their efforts on "exceptional" categories of victims detached from the large immigrant rights and workers' rights spheres. Similarly, some immigrant labor organizations have been hesitant to include sex workers in their policy and other advocacy campaigns. Yet, the differentiation between sex work and other forms of labor overlooks the intersecting marginalizations that confront immigrant survivors of trafficking, and obscures that systemic oppression requires systemic solutions, not exception remedies.

Sex work and trafficking courts

Pervasive imaginaries about who can be considered an authentic and deserving trafficking victim, and who should be seen as a criminal—by virtue of immigration status and/or labor activities—both shape, and are shaped by, policing practices and judicial process. An intersectional assessment of recent initiatives within the New York Judiciary illustrates how moralistic ideas about race, sexuality, gender, class, and immigrant status impact courtroom outcomes for women categorized as *sex trafficking victims*.

In September 2013, the New York Judiciary announced the launch of the Human Trafficking Intervention Initiative. The project established special Human Trafficking Intervention Courts (HTIC) as part of a new approach to criminal justice promoted by the State of New York, "designed to intervene in the lives of trafficked human beings" in order to "break the cycle of exploitation and arrest" (New York State Unified Court System, 2013, p. 1). Notably, HTIC focus on sex trafficking is the most concerning manifestation of contemporary human trafficking.

HTICs are categorized as problem-solving courts, and are part of a broader movement focused on reforming the criminal justice system by providing alternatives to standard prosecution and incarceration (Nolan, 2003).To avoid jail time and lengthy involvement with the traditional courts system, HTIC defendants can be processed in such courts for misdemeanor offenses and violations. They enter a guilty plea in exchange for social services and benefits, and the opportunity to remove the arrest from their criminal record.[3] Many HTIC defendants have been arrested for so-called "quality of life" offenses such as congregating and/or drinking in public spaces, public urination, panhandling, littering, or unlicensed street vending—a policing strategy reliant on racial and gender profiling (INCITE! Women of Color Against Violence, 2014).Yet ethnographic study reveals that HTIC outcomes are quite different from the courts' stated intent. Rather than ending "the cycle of exploitation and arrest," the alliance between the judiciary and the police has had devastating consequences on the lives of the New York City's low-income communities and communities of color, including a great many LGBTQ immigrants (Howell, 2009; Steinberg & Albertson, 2016; Lieberman & Dansky, 2016).

An unsettling pattern of "status degradation" (Garfinkel, 1956) exists within the HTIC system, a process through which defendants are marked as morally corrupt, causing them social sanction and isolation, as well as feelings of shame, anxiety, and resentment. This particularly affects undocumented women, and "internally trafficked" Black and Latina sex workers. Notable contrasts are evident between the treatment of women seen by Judges as "rescued victims" and those seen as criminals. One example of discriminatory conduct is the habitual denial of representation to *unrepentant* sex workers by defense counsels affiliated with HTIC. These defense attorneys routinely claim scheduling conflicts, or lack of time and resources, when sex workers they perceive as "non-compliant" with the label of "sex trafficking victim" are present in court. This causes unnecessary delays in resolving cases. In contrast, the cases of individuals who have been "rescued" in police raids of massage parlors, the majority of whom are Korean or Chinese immigrants, are at the center of courts' activities.These women, labeled by court personnel simply as "the victims," are stripped of their identity but briefly granted a slightly different, somewhat elevated status compared with other sex workers.The differential treatment afforded to different nationalities is grounded in racialized and gendered tropes of Asian women as passive, quiet, and compliant, in contrast with black and Latina women, and most notably of transgender women, who are pathologized as sexually deviant—and therefore not deserving victims.

HTIC hearings can be read as performative spaces in which the state is configured as a "compassionate" protector of women that also upholds national moral values. This construction disguises the violence inflicted within the overlapping immigration and criminal justice systems. In HTIC courtrooms, defendants stand before a Judge, surrounded by defense attorneys, social workers and interpreters, while their existence and experiences are used to validate the court's mission to rescue exploited women and to restore their moral virtue through intervention. However, sex workers' testimonies repudiate the carefully crafted narratives of humanitarian state intervention, which is also (re)produced by mainstream feminists and anti-trafficking advocates (Vance, 2012). According to sex workers themselves, courtroom personnel, social workers and HTIC-affiliated service providers frequently accentuate the already visible social differences between themselves and defendants. Adopting condescending, paternalistic or discriminatory language and demeanors, these professionals reveal their class and race privilege in ways that reinscribe defendants' ascribed position within rigidly defined subaltern positions.

The HTIC affords these women a glimpse into the possibility of exercising citizenship, albeit couched in the language of U.S. ideals of justice and equality. This promise dissolves after the defendants plead guilty, and the Judge issues a ruling. Endowed with the power of the state, HTIC personnel use their discretion to delay the cases of women deemed "recalcitrant," "disobedient," or "arrogant," and make recommendations with which defendants would clearly have difficulty complying, given the limited secure employment options available to immigrant women in general and particularly those who have a criminal record. These recommendations effectively punish sex workers by placing them at higher risk of recidivism.

Proponents of HTIC claim that those eligible for a "second chance," specifically "victims of sex trafficking," receive much-needed benefits, such as social services and mental health counseling, and, eventually, a reduced or expunged criminal record. However, to be eligible, sex workers are required to comply with HTIC-mandated services, which means being present at all assigned sessions and participating in exit programs. The courts additionally make job training and immigration services, as well as temporary shelter and medical services, available to defendants. Yet these services are insufficient to replace the income lost by exiting sex work, and career readiness programs generally do not help people secure meaningful, long-term employment, nor do they remove structural barriers to employment faced by low-income immigrants of color. These already significant obstacles are especially difficult to overcome for those with criminal records, which, despite courtroom guarantees, are rarely cleared quickly, if at all (Kohler-Hausmann, 2014).

Immigrant sex workers deemed undeserving of a "second chance" are frequently placed into deportation proceedings and held in Immigration and Customs Enforcement (ICE) jails, rather than provided with social services and helped to file a T Visa application (Das, 2008). The spectacle of justice enacted by professionals at all the HTIC sites delivers a powerful, and rather intimidating message. Sex workers, whether willing participants in the sex industry, or victims of trafficking, are triaged and classified according to arbitrarily set standards of worthiness: some are punished and made into scapegoats, others are elevated to "rescued victim" status. Everyone in between remains in a liminal state, silenced and undermined, with limited resources and vulnerable to more violence and discrimination.

Criminalization, detention, and incarceration

LGBTQ migrants experience disproportionate levels of violence within our society, especially within the criminal justice system, and the closely related ICE system of raids, detentions, and deportations. As noted above, LGBTQ immigrants are subjected to acute profiling and harassment at the hands of ICE agents, who "overwhelmingly use their discretion to detain LGBTQ immigrants" (Gruberg, 2016). The Presidential Executive Orders of January and February 2017 promise further discretionary powers to ICE, and promote racial and religious profiling. Southern states are pursuing legislation to allow police to act as immigration officers (Schmitt, 2017), effectively sanctioning further targeting of immigrants, and particularly trans women who are already disproportionately harassed by police officers. These moves are deeply concerning for queer immigration activists.

It is important to understand the reality of extensive immigration detention and deportation systems within the prison industrial complex (PIC). Violating immigration law is not a crime, it is a civil violation for which immigrants must go through a process, overseen by the Department of Homeland Security (DHS), to determine whether or not they can remain in the United States. Yet, while the U.S. government separates its criminal justice system from its immigration systems, detention centers are practically identical to prisons, hence their inclusion with the PIC.

Only 14 percent of individuals in immigration detention have legal representation (Eagly & Shafer, 2016). This differs from the U.S. criminal justice system, in which defendants have rights and entitlements to legal representation. In addition, immigrants are subjected to prolonged, arbitrary incarceration, masked as "mandatory detention." They are jailed in detention facilities as well as in federal and private prisons, in beds purchased by ICE, where there is minimal oversight. "Immigration detention" should be called "immigration prison," as it is similarly focused on the criminalization of Brown, Black, LGBTQ and Muslim communities in the United States.

People that are incarcerated in immigration prisons can be apprehended by ICE agents at ports of entry, or as they go about their lives in the United States. Immigration detainers, which allow ICE to detain immigrants if they come into contact with law enforcement, are an important piece of the carceral system, often overlooked in the media but ever-present to those in the LGBTQ migrant community. Individuals arrested for misdemeanors, like jumping a subway turnstile, or driving under the influence, can be picked up by ICE post-release, and placed in immigration prison. Some people are apprehended many years after being charged with a crime. ICE's collaboration with local police departments allows this process to flourish—even in cities that have adopted "Sanctuary" status.

In immigration detention, LGBTQ people are subjected to elevated levels of bullying, physical violence, and sexual violence at the hands of peers and guards alike. They frequently suffer from medical neglect. LGBTQ people who seek support from ICE staff often face retaliation, specifically "administrative segregation," or solitary confinement. To add insult to injury, ICE claims that this punishment is designed to"protect them from the general population" (Gruberg, 2013, p. 6).

In *Lora v. Shanahan* (2015), it was held that non-citizens could not be subjected to prolonged periods of detention while their deportation cases were pending. Immigrants must therefore be granted a bond hearing within six months of their detention. However, this victory is not quite what it seems. While ICE does not control the amount at which bonds are set, it has created a "bond floor" of $1,500. Immigration judges often set bonds at even higher levels, which are unattainable for working-class citizens, let alone those who lack immigration status and employment authorization documents. These bond numbers can climb above $10,000.

In response to these extortionate bonds, the ACLU Foundation of Southern California (ACLU SoCal) and the national ACLU filed a class-action lawsuit, demanding that the government apply criminal case standards to immigration bonds (ACLU, 2016). A federal district court sided with the ACLU in November 2016. Celebrations have been tempered, however, by the acknowledgement that Trump appointees, particularly Attorney General Jeff Sessions, will pursue increasingly punitive future policies, justified by xenophobic, racist, and Islamophobic tropes.

The system of criminalizing LGBTQ migrants, then punishing them twice—through the prison system and then the immigrant prison system—then denying them adequate legal representation, and then requiring unattainable bonds, combines to form "the deportation pipeline."

Case study: the Queer Detainee Empowerment Project

The Queer Detainee Empowerment Project (QDEP), a community organizing initiative in New York City, was set up in response to the current state of the immigration system. I am Jamila Hammami, MSW, the founding executive director of QDEP, and the specific author of this particular section. We opened in January 2014 to provide post-release support, detention center visitation, and direct services to LGBTQ, Two Spirit, and HIV+ immigrant prisoners and their families, whether they are currently in, or have been recently released from immigration prison. A key component of this work is assisting folks coming out of immigration prison in securing structural, health/wellness, educational, legal, and emotional support and social services, while also queering the international dialogue around immigration, immigration prison, the prison industrial complex, and the varying forms of state surveillance and violence that lies in alternative-to-incarceration and alternative-to-detention programs, or the "industrialized punishment" complex (Gilmore, 2007). Project staff and community members organize around the structural barriers and state violence that LGBTQI immigrant prisoner/undocumented folks face related to their immigration status, race, sexuality, and gender expression/identity.

At present, the wait to receive employment authorization documents (EAD) is ever-climbing, making sanctioned employment unattainable for many immigrants.

Immigrants—especially LGBTQ workers, who experience compounded discriminations—are often forced to rely on alternative economies to survive. QDEP works closely with other organizations and has supported its members in joining workers' co-ops, radical, community-led, sustainable businesses that offer an alternative to exploitative and discriminatory labor markets.

The organization's mission is to create a world external to the capitalist status quo; to not just to imagine, but to build the structures necessary for all people to live safely outside of the system. Other QDEP projects include: the first LGBTQ/HIV+ immigrant bond-raising project, the Trans/Queer Migrant Freedom Fund; Host Homes, providing safe and stable housing by redistributing resources (housing and space) between community members; providing "wrap around" case management social services in collaboration with, rather than for, members; and building a volunteer base of co-conspirators, not allies, to support LGBTQ migrants. All of these initiatives are informed by ongoing discussion among the QDEP member base about creating concrete alternatives to immigration prisons and to the broader carceral state.

QDEP's member base plays an important role in the organization, comprising half of the advisory board and highly involved in decision-making at all levels. For example, QDEP members recently decided to pull out of the Close Rikers campaign, when NYC Mayor DeBlasio announced that closing the island jail would only prompt a relocation of the current population, including to segregative LGBTQ jail units across the city (Goodman, 2017). While the campaign discusses reducing the population, QDEP members, advisory board members and staff did not want to be a part of the campaign any longer. Many QDEP members and staff have been justice-involved (meaning that they have had direct contact with the criminal justice system through incarceration, or alternative-to-incarceration programs). Our first-hand experience of the justice system, including, for some of us, surviving the notorious Rikers institution itself, informed our decision to say: "not in our names."

Our sentiment was that QDEP absolutely could not be involved in any sort of a campaign that builds out additional facilities for our own community; our member base felt that this was against the prison abolitionist mission, values, and vision of the organization. While QDEP found that the Close Rikers campaign did not, ultimately, align with our values, we still support the campaign more abstractly. This experience reveals both the stakes and the complexity of grassroots community organizing, especially in the competing movement world of absolutist versus reformist ideologies.

Eschewing claims that LGBTQ people are equally "safe" and "free" in the United States, QDEP is one of a growing number of organizations are committed to assisting folks in building lives outside of detention at the same as organizing to end intersecting policing, ICE, detention, and deportation regimes. The QDEP motto, "we believe in creating a narrative of thriving, not just surviving," is informed by a deep understanding of intersectional oppressions, and points to the necessary strategy of queer migration activisms "after marriage."

Activism, at the grassroots and in the NPIC

As the discussions and examples above reveal, non-profit and non-governmental organizations, grassroots groups, community centers, and other coalitions have a central role within LGBTQ immigration activist work. They provide sites in which to organize advocacy campaigns, and often provide greatly needed legal and social services to directly impacted individuals. Generally regarded as having a veil of legitimacy, they also frequently produce particular narratives about constituent— and non-constituent—populations that can significantly shape policy outcomes and popular discourses alike. Queer immigration activism demands that we think through the impacts of various organizations, both on macro-level policies and laws, and on micro-level lived experiences.

In a time of increased political insecurity for marginal populations (such as LGBTQ immigrants) NGOs can become a crucial resource for individuals, particularly for those not protected by marriage or citizens' rights. This is as true for LGBTQ-based NGOs as it is for NGOs focusing on immigrants' rights and immigration reform. Just as the mainstream LGBTQ rights movement has often excluded non-citizens from its rhetoric and priorities, the mainstream immigrant rights movement has very often employed heterosexist ideals, claiming strength in the heteronormative, monogamous, nuclear family, while erasing the identities of LGBTQ people, who experience family in tremendously different ways. Yet, if those same organizations reinforce state practices of exclusion (whether in the form of promoting neoliberal homonormative values, or traditional heteronormative ideals), queer immigration activists are duty-bound to actively challenge their institutional structures and goals as part of our broader political strategy.

As the topics above also demonstrate, queer migration politics are already heavily informed by outside influences, including federal and state laws, government institutions and bureaucrats, private business interests, and public opinion. A radical counter-balance is sorely needed.

Contemporary LGBTQ political organizing is also impacted by internal struggles. Feminist and queer scholars and activists in particular have voiced concern about the "non-profit industrial complex" (NPIC). Critiques of the NPIC highlight how neoliberal economic and political norms and structures have created an uneasy relationship between non-profits and the state. Consequently, non-profit-led advocacy can be seen as working to "maintain politics and institutions of oppression" promoted by the state, "while pushing organizations to provide basic services that quell unrest" (Mananzala & Spade, 2008, p. 56). Organizations' reliance on philanthropic funding further privileges the voices and values of wealthy funders, while entrenching clientelist relationships between non-profits, the state, and private capital (Nair, 2013). The professionalization of non-profit work has additionally consolidated power in the hands of historically privileged populations, further excluding historically marginalized voices from high-profile, salaried positions within the hierarchically-structured NPIC (INCITE! Women of Color Against Violence, 2007).

The concept of the NPIC draws on transnational feminist analyses of the "NGOization" of women-centered social movements, especially in Latin America (Alvarez, 1999), as well as more recent critiques of the "mainstreaming" of early lesbian and gay rights politics (Vaid, 1995) and of the increased centrality of homonormative and homonationalist ideals within LGBTQ rights campaigns (Beam, 2016). Yasmin Nair, arguing that radical queer voices have been watered down and drowned out by large LGBTQ rights NGOs' "single issue" strategies, identifies the Gay Non-Profit Industrial Complex (GNPIC) as a significant barrier to queer liberation (Chávez, 2013, pp. 73–74).

For Nair and others, the rise of the GNPIC is directly linked to the rise of same-sex marriage as *the* pressing LGBTQ political issue, and to the privileging of certain identities, bodies, and histories over others. In prioritizing state-sanctioned recognition of erstwhile queer relationships, institutionalized and de-politicized LGBTQ social movements have effectively functioned to produce, and to police, the proper (civic, sexual, or laboring) gay and lesbian subjects of the U.S. state (Kwon & Nguyen, 2016, p. 4). In order to access state rights and recognition "after marriage," LGBTQ-identified persons must fashion themselves to fit the (normative) subject position that is produced by dominant NGO discourse.

Understanding the position of LGBTQ advocacy organizations in the United States as part of the GNPIC can usefully inform analyses of why particular bodies, issues, and experiences are prioritized by, or excluded from, advocacy efforts led by large NGOs. It is also important to recognize, however, that many LGBTQ immigration groups and organizations simply could not function without foundation grants or philanthropic support. It is also not possible for some groups to disengage entirely from state agencies and political processes, as their work is deeply embedded within existing oppressive systems. Indeed, queer immigration activists are often faced with the difficult choice between supporting an individual and refusing to engage with the systems in which they are trapped—paying a bail bond in order to free someone from an immigration jail, for example, or adopting adjudicators' language in order to win an asylum claim. The QDEP mantra of "reform to revolution"—working within the system without losing sight of radical goals—suggests one productive way of recognizing, and responding to, this tension in our work.

It is also important that we do not, in the shadow of the NPIC, overly romanticize grassroots organizations, which do not always or necessarily promote radical alternatives to dominant homonormative and neoliberal discourses—even if they have the potential to do so. Members of locally led, community-funded, or volunteer-run LGBTQ and immigrant organizations can—and do—embrace statist ideologies, hierarchical structures, and single-issue campaign strategies. They are not immune from promoting worldviews that are racist, xenophobic, classist, misogynistic, or informed by other prejudices, or from seeking to support only suitably deserving queer immigrant subjectivities.

In order to overcome these significant challenges to queer immigration activisms that are radical, inclusive, and free from moralist pronouncements, we must avoid complacency and be critically self-reflective of our work, and of our working relationships. Within and without the NPIC, there is much work to be done.

Conclusion: where next for queer migration activisms?

During the marriage equality movement, many LGBTQ immigration activists working at the grassroots found creative ways to boost and center the voices of people left out of mainstream narratives, and to situate their advocacy within broader justice campaigns. Established non-profit organizations and other affiliated networks of activists have already productively addressed some of the concerns we raise above, in their own work. Among others, QDEP, Queers for Economic Justice, the Audre Lorde Project, UndocBlack, Undocuqueer, Southerners on New Ground, and Transcend Arizona, for example, have all adopted different approaches to advocacy and service provision that do not acquiesce to dividing practices of the state. These and similarly attuned activists are making important connections between various, overlapping forms of oppression pervasive in U.S. society, and are pushing back on the structures that (re)produce them. Now, we must continue to build on these efforts to push for a more radical reconceptualization of queer immigrant rights, freedoms, and subjectivities.

Reflecting on our analyses and on the effective work of notable activist organizations, we close by underscoring three key areas of popular LGBTQ immigrant rights activism ripe for intersectional intervention. First, we need to push back against the productive and exclusive forms of power exerted by the state through the construction of campaign and policy initiatives that position "good" homosexual immigrants against "bad" queer intruders. Second, we need to center the deconstruction of systems of power in which certain identities, histories, experiences, class positions, and kinship relations are privileged over others, rather than focusing on the inclusion of some of us into the existing system. Finally, we must continue to acknowledge how the privileging of certain subjectivities and kinship relations can disguise important connections between labor, migration, and family rights, in the interests of state, and in the interests of the politically and economically powerful (Nair, 2011; Reddy, 2011). It is important to draw these lessons into mainstream organizing around family, to make sure all of our relationships, histories, and identities are honored—and are not selectively celebrated, or marginalized, in order to fit the state-promoted divisions between "good" and "bad" queers/immigrants.

Acknowledgement

The authors also thank Riya Ortiz, Community Organizer and Lead Case Manager at Damayan Migrant Workers' Association, for participation on the conference panel that formed the basis for this chapter.

Notes

1 We use the term LGBTQ throughout this chapter, to signify people who identify as lesbian, gay, bisexual, trans, and/or queer, as well and others who identify differently but who encounter similar discriminations and oppressions due to their sexual or gender nonconformity. Where organizations or speakers have used different acronyms or terminology, we have left their chosen language in place.

2 Lisa Duggan uses the term "homonormativity" to describe "a politics that does not contest dominant heteronormative assumptions and institutions, but upholds and sustains them, while promising the possibility of a demobilized gay constituency and a privatized, depoliticized gay culture anchored in domesticity and consumption" (Duggan, 2002, p. 50). Duggan's definition marks how gay and lesbian politics are not necessarily radical or oppositional to oppressive state practices and institutions, but rather, and importantly for our analysis, can work to reinforce them.

3 This manner of adjudication is known as Adjournment in Contemplation of Dismissal (ACD) and takes place the end of a six-month probationary period, on the condition that the defendant has no further contact with the criminal justice system.

References

ACLU. (2016, April 6). ACLU sues federal government seeking bond reform in immigration system. Retrieved from www.aclu.org/news/aclu-sues-federal-government-seeking-bond-reform-immigration-system.

Ahmed, S. (2011). Problematic proximities: Or why critiques of gay imperialism matter. *Feminist Legal Studies*, 19(2):119–132.

Alvarez, S. E. (1999). Advocating feminism: The Latin American feminist NGO "boom." *International Feminist Journal of Politics*, 1(2):181–209.

Beam, M. (2016). At the limits of "by" and "for": Space, struggle, and the nonprofitization of queer youth. *S & F Online*, 13(2):1–14.

Burnham, L. & Theodore, N. (2012). *Home Economics: The Invisible and Unregulated World of Domestic Work*. Chicago, IL: National Domestic Workers Alliance, Center for Urban Economic Development, University of Illinois at Chicago Data Center.

Cantú, L., Jr., Luibhéid, E., & Stern, A. M. (2005). Well-founded fear: Political asylum and the boundries of sexual identity in the U.S.–Mexico borderlands. In E. Luibhéid & L. Cantú, Jr. (Eds.), *Queer Migrations: Sexuality, U.S. Citizenship, And Border Crossings*. Minneapolis, MN: University of Minnesota Press, 61–73.

Carrington, J. M. (2016). Ambivalent subjects: Binational same sex couples and non-governmental organizations in the United States (Unpublished doctoral dissertation). University of New Mexico, Albuquerque, NM.

Chávez, K. R. (2010). Border (in)securities: Normative and differential belonging in LGBTQ and immigrant rights discourse. *Communication and Critical/Cultural Studies*, 7(2):136–155.

Chávez, K. R. (2013). *Queer Migration Politics: Activist Rhetoric and Coalitional Possibilities*. Champaign, IL: University of Illinois Press.

Choy, C. C. (2003). *Empire of Care: Nursing and Migration in Filipino American History*. Durham, NC: Duke University Press.

Cooper, D. & Kroeger, T. (2017). *Employers Steal Billions from Workers' Paychecks Each Year*. Washington, DC: Economic Policy Forum.

Das, A. (2008). Immigrants and problem-solving courts (Report). *Criminal Justice Review*, 33(3):308.

Duggan, L. (2002). The new homonormativity: The sexual politics of neoliberalism. In D. D. Nelson & R. Castronovo (Eds.), *Materializing Democracy: Toward a Revitalized Cultural Politics*. Durham, NC: Duke University Press, 175–194.

Eagly, I. & Shafer, S. (2016, September). Access to counsel in immigration court. *American Immigration Council*. Retrieved from www.americanimmigrationcouncil.org/sites/default/files/research/access_to_counsel_in_immigration_court.pdf.

Fix, M. & Capps, R. (2017). Leaked draft of possible trump executive order on public benefits would spell chilling effects for legal immigrants. *Migration Policy Institute*. Retrieved from www.migrationpolicy.org/news/leaked-draft-possible-trump-executive-order-public-benefits-would-spell-chilling-effects-legal.

Garfinkel, H. (1956). Conditions of successful degradation ceremonies. *American Journal of Sociology*, 61(5):420–424.

Gates, G. (2013). *LGBT Adult Immigrants in the United States*. Los Angeles, CA: The Williams Institute.

Gilmore, R. W. (2007). *Golden Gulag: Prisons, Surplus, Crisis, and Opposition in Globalizing California*. Berkeley, CA: University of California Press.

Gonzalez, J. (2011). *Harvest of Empire: A History of Latinos in America*. Revised Edition. New York: Penguin Books.

Goodman, J. D. (2017, March 31). Mayor backs plan to close Rikers and open jails elsewhere. *The New York Times*. Retrieved from www.nytimes.com/2017/03/31/nyregion/mayor-de-blasio-is-said-to-back-plan-to-close-jails-on-rikers-island.html.

Gruberg, S. (2013, November). *Dignity Denied: LGBT Immigrants in U.S. Immigration Detention*. Washington, DC: Center for American Progress.

Gruberg, S. (2016, October 26). ICE officers overwhelmingly use their discretion to detain LGBT immigrants. *Center for American Progress*. Retrieved from www.americanprogress.org/issues/lgbt/reports/2016/10/26/291115/ice-officers-overwhelmingly-use-their-discretion-to-detain-lgbt-immigrants/.

Gutiérrez, J. (2016). Liberation not deportation #not1more. Unpublished paper, presented at: After Marriage, October 2016; CLAGS: The Center for LGBT Studies, City University of New York, New York.

Howell, B. (2009). Broken lives from broken windows: The hidden costs of aggressive order-maintenance policing. *New York University Review of Law & Social Change*, 33(3):271–330.

INCITE! Women of Color Against Violence. (2007). *The Revolution Will Not be Funded: Beyond the Non-Profit Industrial Complex*. Cambridge, MA: South End Press.

INCITE! Women of Color Against Violence. (2014). *"Quality of Life" or "Zero Tolerance" Policing Factsheet*. New York, NY: INCITE!

Kandel, W. A. (2014). *U.S. Family-Based Immigration Policy*. CRS Report No. R43145. Washington, DC: Congressional Research Service. Retrieved from https://fas.org/sgp/crs/homesec/R43145.pdf.

Kimmel, M. & Llewellyn, C. (2012). Homosexuality, gender nonconformity, and the neoliberal state. *Journal of Homosexuality*, 59(7):1087–1094.

Kohler-Hausmann, I. (2014). Managerial justice and mass misdemeanors. *Stanford Law Review*, 66(3):611.

Kwon, S. A. & Nguyen, M. T. (2016). Nonprofits, NGOs, and "community engagement": Refiguring the project of activism in gender and women's studies and ethnic studies. *S & F Online*, 13(2):1–11.

Lewis, R. (2013). Deportable subjects: Lesbians and political asylum. *Feminist Formations*, 25(2):174–194.

Lieberman, D. & Dansky, K. (2016). The degradation of civil society and hyper-aggressive policing in communities of color in New York City. *Cardozo Law Review*, 37(3):955–1127.

Lora v. Shanahan (Court of Appeals, 2nd circuit October 28, 2015). (2015). 804 F.3d 601.

Luibhéid, E. (2002). *Entry Denied: Controlling Sexuality at the Border.* Minneapolis, MN: University of Minnesota Press.

Luibhéid, E. (2005). Introduction: Queering migration and citizenship. In E. Luibhéid & L. Cantú, Jr. (Eds.), *Queer Migrations: Sexuality, U.S. Citizenship, and Border Crossings.* Minneapolis, MN: University of Minnesota Press, ix–xlvi.

Luibhéid, E. (2008). Queer/migration: An unruly body of scholarship. *GLQ: A Journal of Lesbian & Gay Studies,* 14(2–3):169–190.

Mananzala, R. & Spade, D. (2008). The nonprofit industrial complex and trans resistance. *Sexuality Research and Social Policy,* 5(1):53–71.

McGuirk, S. (2016). LGBT asylum seekers and NGO advocacy in the United States (Unpublished doctoral dissertation). American University, Washington, DC.

Morgan, D. A. (2006). Not gay enough for the government: Racial and sexual stereotypes in sexual orientation asylum cases. *Law & Sexuality,* 15:135–161.

Morris, A. (2013, December 18). From fear to freedom. *Immigration Equality.* (Electronic mailing list message).

Nair, Y. (2011). How to make prisons disappear: Queer immigrants, the shackles of love, and the invisibility of the Prison Industrial Complex. In E. A. Stanley & N. Smith (Eds.), *Captive Genders: Trans Embodiment and the Prison Industrial Complex.* Oakland, CA: AK Press, 123–139.

Nair, Y. (2013). Gay Marriage Is a Conservative Cause. Retrieved from www.yasminnair. net/content/gay-marriage-conservative-cause.

New York State Unified Court System. (2013). Press Release: NY judiciary launches nation's first statewide human trafficking intervention initiative. Retrieved from www.nycourts. gov/press/pr13_11.pdf.

Nolan, J. L., Jr. (2003). Redefining criminal courts: Problem-solving and the meaning of justice. *American Criminal Law Review,* 40(4):1541.

ORAM. (2012). *Rainbow Bridges: A Community Guide to Rebuilding the Lives of LGBTI Refugees and Asylees.* San Francisco, CA: Organization for Refuge, Asylum and Migration.

Passel, J. S. & Cohn, D. (2015). *Immigrant Workers in Production, Construction Jobs Falls Since 2007: In States, Hospitality, Manufacturing and Construction are Top Industries.* Washington, DC: Pew Research Center.

Puar, J. K. (2007). *Terrorist Assemblages: Homonationalism in Queer Times.* Durham, NC: Duke University Press.

Reddy, C. (2011). *Freedom with Violence: Race, Sexuality, and the U.S. State.* Durham, NC: Duke University Press.

Rehaag, S. (2009). Bisexuals need not apply: A comparative appraisal of refugee law and policy in Canada, the United States, and Australia. *International Journal of Human Rights,* 13(2):415–436.

Rickard, J. (2011). *Torn Apart: United by Love, Divided by Law.* Ferrs: Findhorn Press.

Said, E. W. (2003). *Orientalism: Western Conceptions of the Orient.* London: Penguin Books.

Schmitt, S. (2017, April 25). Texas lawmaker on four-day hunger strike in protest of "Sanctuary City" bill. *The Washington Post.* Retrieved from www.washingtonpost.com/ news/morning-mix/wp/2017/04/25/texas-lawmaker-on-four-day-hunger-strike-in-protest-of-sanctuary-city-bill/?utm_term=.23331fdac06e.

Spade, D. (2017). The right wing is leveraging trans issues to promote militarism. *Truth Out.* Retrieved from: www.truth-out.org/opinion/item/40109-the-right-wing-is-leveraging-trans-issues-to-promote-militarism.

Steinberg, R. & Albertson, S. (2016). Broken windows policing and community courts: An unholy alliance. *Cardozo Law Review,* 37(3):995–1024.

Trump, D. (2017). *Executive Order: Protecting the Nation from Foreign Terrorist Entry into the United States. Executive Order 13769, Section 1.* Washington, DC: The White House Office of the Press Secretary.

Vaid, U. (1995). *Virtual Equality: The Mainstreaming of Gay and Lesbian Liberation.* New York: Doubleday.

Vance, C. S. (2012). Innocence and experience: Melodramatic narratives of sex trafficking and their consequences for law and policy. *History of the Present*, 2(2):200–218.

Vidal-Ortiz, S. (2014). Forward. In M. A. Viteri (Ed.), *Desbordes: Translating Racial, Ethnic, Sexual, and Gender Identities Across the Americas.* New York: State University of New York Press.

Yue, A. (2008). Same-sex migration in Australia: From interdependency to intimacy. *GLQ: A Journal of Lesbian & Gay Studies*, 14(2–3): 239–262.

PART III
Transnational perspectives

9

AFTER MARRIAGE, REDEFINING FREEDOM IN THE CROSSHAIRS OF EMPIRE AND DICTATORSHIP

Observations towards a new politics of sexuality

A presentation by Raha Iranian Feminist Collective

Editors' introduction:

This chapter is a transcript of the presentation offered by the Raha Iranian Feminist Collective at the After Marriage conference. Raha is a group composed of Iranian Americans, founded in 2009 to stand in solidarity with Iranians' democratic uprising while opposing U.S. military and economic interventions.

In this presentation, Raha offers a transnational perspective on this political moment by exploring the connection between U.S. nationalism and LGBTQ inclusion in the institutions of marriage and the military. They explain how the stereotypical married, nuclear family structure is central to America's image of itself, and how this image ("our way of life") is used to justify war when politicians decide "our freedom" must be defended from outside threats. The Middle East is often portrayed as the source of those alleged threats, and Iran, in particular, is frequently depicted as the antithesis of American freedoms. Reports about the treatment of women and LGBTQ people in Iran are often used as evidence of Iran's threat to freedom, and then as justification for military intervention.

The members of Raha explain how, as diasporic Iranian activists, artists, and scholars, they engage in a simultaneous battle to stand in solidarity with those fighting for gender and sexual rights in Iran, while also challenging those U.S.A. narratives about Iran that are being used to justify imperialism. Now that same-sex marriage equality is legal in the U.S.A., and in the larger context of an open-ended "war on terror," Raha is concerned about how some LGBTQ organizations and funders will further channel their activities towards expanding gay marriage rights globally as the litmus test of freedom. They are critical of how this agenda can dovetail with justifications for military intervention.

Questions for readers to consider include: In what ways are American values, such as marriage, connected to the military? How have Muslims been positioned in the American media as being anti-LGBT? How can American citizens support the efforts of Iranian activists working in their country for gender and sexual rights, without involving the U.S. government and military? Should gay marriage be considered a marker of freedom in Iran? In the U.S.A.?

Anywhere? Who gets to decide? How might a broader view of sexual liberation and freedom create greater solidarity among queer people in different countries?

Introduction

As people with intimate knowledge of Iranian and U.S. cultures and contexts, we are very interested in how this "after marriage" moment may reverberate internationally and domestically in the U.S. This collaborative presentation offers a transnational perspective on how to frame the problems and possibilities of this next phase of activism for gender and sexual justice. As Iranian and Iranian American feminists of diverse genders and sexualities, we examine the shortcomings of the mainstream U.S. LGBTQ movement's politics of inclusion, especially its increasing alignment with nationalism and imperialism. We then offer a vision of a more capacious politics of sexuality, love, and caring. We do this by drawing from a comparative, transnational understanding of the relationship between identity, state, and social institutions, in order to reanimate the concept of freedom. Instead of counterposing the US and Iran, as people from across the political spectrum do, we argue that there is much to be learned from engaging with the differences and similarities across both locations when it comes to thinking about what forms gender and sexual justice can take in the future.

"After marriage" is also "after military"

The same period in which the mainstream LGBT movement was focused on gaining equal access to marriage rights was also the period in which it was focused on gaining equal inclusion in the U.S. military as the other major national campaign, even while the US waged war across West and Central Asia and parts of Africa. While getting married is obviously very different than joining the military, both these institutions are central to how the U.S. constitutes itself as a nation to be defended. "Our way of life," "our freedoms"—all of these phrases that are continuously mobilized to justify war rely on a particular concept of the nuclear family, the monogamous married couple with children. Although there are many practical and economic reasons why people get married, especially at a time when the social safety net is being decimated and immigrants are under attack, it remains the case that marriage and the nuclear family privatize social reproduction and unpaid caregiving work. The financial burden of rearing new generations and caring for the old and the sick, all necessary social functions, is entirely placed on couples and families. While these conditions create huge savings for the wealthy, who don't have to contribute towards the costs of maintaining a healthy supply of workers or pay for the care of those no longer able to work, they place enormous strains on individuals. At the same time, those who do not live within a married couple or nuclear family are punished, like single mothers and single people who are elderly or sick. If you are a single parent, you have to work to pay rent and the cost of childcare at the same time, a reality that pushes many people into poverty. It is important to remember that, despite the romantic aura that surrounds it, the institution of marriage remains grounded in a set of private property relations that originated with feudalism, inheritance rights, and the need to control women's productive and reproductive labor. After the end of feudalism, these property and labor relations were adapted to the capitalist system, a system that relies on state violence domestically (police) and globally (military) to maintain extreme inequality.

The simultaneous campaigns for inclusion within marriage and the military reflect a massive retreat from the radical politics that launched the modern gay rights movement. One of the earliest gay rights organizations, The Gay Liberation Front that formed in 1969, took its name from the Vietnamese Liberation Front and was explicitly in solidarity with the fight against U.S. imperialism. The feminist movement of the 1970s also emerged out of the anti-war movement, with a significant anti-imperialist and revolutionary wing. These were not movements primarily oriented toward gaining inclusion in existing oppressive institutions, but were focused on transforming institutions as well as economic and social relations. It is our hope that in this "after marriage/after military" moment, we can re-incorporate the best traditions of the U.S. feminist and gay movements, in particular their overlapping critiques of marriage, monogamy, militarism and war, and of the socio-economic basis for sustaining gender and sexual oppression in this country.

"Gays" vs "Muslims"?

As *some* LGBTQ people have been more able to lay claim to their shared humanity and equal citizenship through their inclusion in these conservative institutions, they have also found themselves courted by right-wing movements. The new homonationalist formation is one that aligns LGBT rights with the violent exclusion of immigrants and people of color. We see this particularly clearly in Donald Trump's cynical inclusion of, as he said, "LGBTQ citizens" (which implicitly distinguishes citizens from other LGBTQ people) whom he vowed "to do everything in my power to protect."

During the 2016 presidential campaign, Trump used the devastating Orlando nightclub shooting as an opportunity to pit queer people against all Muslims. He has argued that Muslim immigrants to the U.S. must be subject to "extreme vetting," and said he wanted to ban Muslims who support the death penalty for gays. To understand the Orlando shooter, Omar Matteen, primarily through the frame of national origin and religion is to ignore the other significant elements of his identity and experiences that are, arguably, far more significant. For example, it is more significant that he was a man who was violent toward women including his two wives, that he had studied criminal justice and trained to be a corrections officer, eventually finding work as a security guard, and that he had a history of bullying and being bullied, and possibly of undiagnosed mental illness. To reduce the individual and social forces that produced Matteen to his religion is to fit the problem of violence into an ideological paradigm of U.S. exclusionary nationalism and military intervention in this particular moment. It also aligns with Trump's representation of Muslims as the primary group responsible for violence against sexual minorities. This conveniently serves to further deflect from Trump's own role in normalizing a toxic White masculinity that contributes to violence against women, queer people, and people of color.

The pitting of Muslims against LGBTQ people is not about protecting anyone but rather about erasing the multifaceted reality of the more than one billion Muslims in the world and the three million Muslims in the United States. The truth that all religions are diverse, and that the views of religious people are dynamic and shaped by a range of social, economic, and political forces in the societies in which they live, is quickly forgotten. Should we be surprised that a 2014 Pew study (Pew Research Center, 2015) found that Muslim Americans' level of acceptance of homosexuality (46 percent, 2014) is similar to that of all US Protestants (48 percent), and much higher than that of evangelicals (36 percent, 2014) and Mormons (36 percent, 2014)? Those of us who have experienced living, working, and organizing among Muslim communities are not surprised by these numbers, and yet it remains too easy for pundits and politicians to cast Muslims as uniquely homophobic.

Indeed, for many LGBT rights activists in the United States and Europe, Iran is known as the country that executes gays. The problem with this singular image of the status of gay people in Iran is that it creates an absolute division between Iran and "the West," and prevents us from seeing the continuities and connections between violence in Iran and in the U.S. or Europe. For one thing, state persecution of sexual minorities cannot be separated from other elements of repressive state power that affect many Iranians—such as the surveillance of political activities or the policing of public space, both of which also occur in different forms in the U.S. and Europe. Furthermore, the situation of sexual minorities in Iran is shaped not only by the criminalization of homosexuality (and again let us remember that sodomy was not fully decriminalized in the U.S. until 2003), but also by homophobia, and especially the social pressures to get married and abide by particular gender norms. The ability to resist marriage, to delay or avoid it, is still often the foremost issue for many men and women who desire more flexibility in their gender roles and sexual preferences. While there have been significant shifts in public opinion on marriage and gender roles in parts of Europe and the U.S. (although perhaps less than we sometimes imagine), it is worth remembering that homophobia and sexism are not particular to Islam or Iran, but rather are embedded in societies and cultures the world over.

Furthermore, the Iranian state uses homophobic laws as part of its larger apparatus of repression. Last year, Hassan Afshar was executed in Iran on a charge of rape of another boy, allegedly committed when Afshar was a minor. News headlines in the U.S. (Grindley, 2016) framed this as an execution of a gay teen, repeating the way other cases—particularly the 2005 execution of two teenage boys charged with rape of another boy—have been covered. This framing seems to discount the possibility that an actual act of violence (rape of another boy) instigated the criminal charges and implies that the young man's execution only warrants attention if he were gay. In any case, we condemn this egregious taking of human life. We also are concerned with how this execution is presented as epitomizing the status of gay people in Iran, and separated from the almost 1,000 executions in Iran in 2015 (Amnesty highlights "disturbing rise" in global executions, 2016; Rahimpour, 2015) the vast majority for drug-related convictions. The fact that Iran executes people at all, and at rates only second to China, and that it continues to execute people for crimes allegedly committed as minors, should provide sufficient fodder for our outrage. Furthermore, the framing of executions in Iran primarily in terms of homophobia obscures linkages between state violence in Iran and the U.S. Notably, the U.S. is the only developed country to be, along with Iran, in the list of top ten executing nations. The U.S. also imprisons more people than any other nation in the world (notably, disproportionately people of color), and the immense growth of this prison population in the last 40 years has corresponded with the expansion of the war on drugs (Drug Policy Alliance, 2016). The interest in Iranian executions as anti-gay persecution plays into a perception of Islam as uniquely homophobic, thereby reproducing a framework of vast civilizational difference between Iran and "the West."

Hence, we are concerned with how same-sex marriage rights could become yet another marker of "civilization" used to distinguish the U.S. and Europe from places perceived as in need of intervention on behalf of the oppressed. For one thing, we feel this representation fails to capture the reality of life in the U.S. for LGBTQ people and women—particularly those who are low-income and/or people of color. Considering the economic hardship, policing, and discrimination experienced by many LGBTQ people and women, we reject the notion that the US is a progressive haven. We also demand that the situation of sexual minorities in Iran be approached contextually in relation to other social and political struggles, including those of young people and feminists countering the regulation of sexuality and gender through marriage and divorce laws. While in the U.S. it is too common to draw strong distinctions between political issue areas (e.g., feminist versus queer politics), we recognize that agency in one realm buttresses agency in another—that the freedom to protect one's privacy, or to avoid marriage and pregnancy, for example, is essential to having more power in choosing one's relations and lovers. Therefore, we advocate a holistic non-identity-based transnational politics of sexuality that provides tools for addressing contexts that are different, yet interconnected.

Towards a transnational politics of sexuality

In fact, every society regulates sexuality and imposes hierarchies of sexual relations and behavior. In addition, all states endeavor to control sexual relations and gender roles in order to promote specific forms of intimacy and kinship.

Not everyone experiences life in the U.S. as liberating when it comes to gender and sexuality. For example, we have listened to Iranian male friends who are immigrants talk about experiences of homophobia in U.S. culture that are so normalized as to become invisible even to many avowedly non-homophobic men. These Iranian men speak of how their habit of casually touching a male colleague, friend. or classmate when talking to them or sitting next to them, as is common in Iran, elicited strong, negative reactions from American men. An Iranian male friend was complaining that his friend, another immigrant man from Iran, has begun avoiding the Iranian greeting of kissing on the cheek when in public, returning to this custom only when they meet at each other's homes.

Recognizing that sexuality is actually regulated in the U.S. is essential for the possibility of any transnational politics of solidarity that goes beyond rescue and aid to seek out common causes and mutual exchanges of experiences and strategies.

Here we want to bring in a few examples from the Iranian context that show how engaging with ways of living and struggles over sexuality in other parts of the world can be fruitful for struggles *within* the U.S.

- In Iran, there are a series of legal battles being fought over the institution of marriage (particularly against the laws that punish adultery and govern divorce, such as efforts to gain divorce rights for women, change the default custody rights for fathers, and secure material compensation for women). Thinking about these struggles raises questions for us about what new forms of regulations same-sex couples will experience by inviting the state to regulate their personal affairs according to the norms of a heterosexual monogamous nuclear family, for instance extra-marital relations, property and inheritance, divorce, and child custody. Even those who do not participate in marriage are affected by the assumption that queer people should fit themselves into this model. For example, laws based on a normative heterosexual couple do not readily recognize many queer family structures, such as a single lesbian parent with a known sperm donor (in some states such a donor cannot give up their parental status), or a family with more than two co-parents (where not all parents will be recognized as such by the law).

- When hearing the stories of our gay friends in Iran exerting all possible efforts to avoid military service, because they perceive the military as a dangerous place for queers, known for humiliating and sexually harassing feminine men, in particular, we ask ourselves what happens to gay and lesbian people after inclusion in the U.S. military? What does it mean to participate in an institution that promotes forms of masculinity that are based on domination and violence, where women recruits routinely experience sexual harassment and assault? According to the Department of Defense's own statistics, which only include reported cases, there were approximately 26,000 incidents of "unwanted sexual contact" among military personnel (12,000 targeting women and 14,000 targeting men) in 2012 and over 6,000 sexual assaults in 2015 (Department of Defense, 2015; Mesok, 2016). It should come as no surprise that institutions devoted to carrying out state violence produce internally violent cultures. A politics of sexual and gender liberation cannot be based on participation in the oppression of other peoples and nations—the role that the U.S. military has played in the Middle East—and the ability to assimilate into imperial institutions.

- Thinking about decades of people's resistance to morality police patrolling the streets in Iran, and the policing of the streets that we witness around us in the

U.S., makes us attuned to the dangers of basing sexual rights and freedoms on the idea of privacy. This policing criminalizes the most sexually marginalized, such as street sex workers, targets those who are visibly queer, such as gender noncomforming and transgender people, and targets those who cruise or have sex in public spaces. It threatens the freedoms of those who don't have access to private homes, those who are poor, and those who are racially profiled and targeted by the police on a regular basis. In this "after marriage" moment, we hope there can be a focused effort to decriminalize public space and sex work, and to roll back the militarization of the police.

- Thinking about how gender and sexual identity are experienced and narrated differently across cultural contexts allows us to imagine alternative notions of identity. A recent historical and ethnographic study of transsexuality in Iran by Najmabadi (2013) documents a concept of identity that is not anchored in a deep inner core, but is relational and situational. One of the people Najmabadi interviews explains, "I am perhaps 70 percent *lesbian* and 30 percent *trans*" (p. 275), suggesting that sexuality and gender identity are not necessarily distinct, as they are conceived in the U.S. context. Another person says: "When I am in masculine clothes, I enjoy doing manly things; when I am in feminine clothes, I like to do womanly things" (pp. 280–281), highlighting a self that is produced through conduct, rather than as a reflection of an inner core. We might wonder why narrations of identity differ so much from one cultural context to another, and question uncritical applications of Euro-American constructs of the self to other contexts. The recognition of how identity is formed relationally leads us to consider the role of various arenas of life—including family, work, public space and state institutions—and to examine the thick sociality of becoming sexed and gendered people, as part of a transformative politics of identity, in Iran, the U.S. and elsewhere.

- Reflecting on our experiences of more collective and extended forms of family and kinship in Iran has made us both acutely aware of the limits of blood-based patriarchal kinship, but also familiar with more capacious forms of intimacy and care than those which attend marriage in a nuclear family context. In our experiences in Iran, we have seen relatives beyond the couple take part in raising children, and elderly relatives respected and taken care of collectively. Rather than representing an ideal, these other ways of organizing social reproduction encourage us to think beyond the nuclear family and imagine other ways of living and loving, and caring for older people, disabled people, and children. This is especially important as neoliberal economic shifts place greater pressure on families and often push people towards the nuclear family as a new, if strained, global norm. LGBT people have a long history of valuing extended queer families of choice, and yet the focus on marriage has distanced us from this tradition.

These reflections lead us to ask the following questions: What is freedom, if you live in the fear of touching or being touched by another man? What is freedom if you feel obliged to enter the structures of marriage and the reproductive nuclear family out of fear of being alone and having no care or support? What does freedom mean when monogamous marriage, an institution that limits and ties sexuality to reproduction and property, comes to symbolize the pinnacle of self-actualization and equality for queers? What is freedom when alternative bonds of love and care become increasingly unimaginable and practically difficult? What is freedom when the choice to not participate in the two-parent-plus-children family model casts one as abject? What is freedom when you are supposed to declare a fixed identity, when you have to claim you were born this way, that it is in your genes, to be seen as authentic and worthy of rights?

In conclusion, if we begin to think about what it would take to create the social and economic conditions in which queer life could flourish outside the bounds of marriage, it seems to us that a broader politics of sexuality, including but not limited to LGBT rights, has a greater potential for crossing national and cultural borders and generating transnational dialog and solidarity. Such a politics would address state and cultural practices related to a range of issues that we have not had the space to address in this presentation, such as marriage/cohabitation/being single, sex outside marriage, the sexuality of children and the elderly, non-normative sexual practices, intimacies of various kinds, sexual violence and violence against the sexually marginalized, the organization of the family and childcare, birth control, abortion, sterilization, and other fertility practices. A broader, comparative politics of sexuality can productively engage with different national and cultural contexts that are often considered diametrically opposed—Iran is just one example. We hope this approach can lead towards a more robust vision of sexual freedom and justice not constrained by the regulatory regimes of marriage, nationalism, and global imperial power.

The Raha Iranian Feminist Collective is a group of New York Iranian and Iranian Americans founded in 2009 to stand in solidarity with Iranians' democratic uprising while opposing U.S. military and economic interventions. We gathered to collectively articulate a voice of solidarity with people's movements in Iran. We see this work as inextricably linked to a diverse range of grassroots movements for economic, racial, gender, and sexual justice with which we seek to build alliances. We believe that all genuine liberation comes from below.

References

Amnesty highlights "disturbing rise" in global executions. (2016, April 6). *BBC News*. Retrieved from www.bbc.com/news/world-35971623.

Department of Defense. (2015). Annual report on sexual assault in the military: Fiscal year 2015, p. 7. Retrieved from http://sapr.mil/public/docs/reports/FY15_Annual/FY15_Annual_Report_on_Sexual_Assault_in_the_Military.pdf.

Drug Policy Alliance. (2016, February 10). The drug war, mass incarceration and race. Retrieved from www.drugpolicy.org/resource/drug-war-mass-incarceration-and-race.

Grindley, L. (2016). Teen executed for gay sex in Iran is latest in long trend. *The Advocate*. Retrieved from www.advocate.com/world/2016/8/05/teen-executed-gay-sex-iran-latest-long-trend.

Mesok, E. (2016). Sexual violence and the US military: Feminism, US empire, and the failure of liberal equality. *Feminist Studies*, 42(1):57–58.

Najmabadi, A. (2013). *Professing selves: Transsexuality and Same-Sex Desire in Contemporary Iran*. Durham, NC: Duke University Press.

Pew Research Center. (2015, November 3). U.S. public becoming less religious. Retrieved from www.pewforum.org/2015/11/03/chapter-4-social-and-political-attitudes/.

Rahimpour, R. (2015, May 12). Iran hardliners cling to death penalty. *BBC News*. Retrieved from www.bbc.com/news/world-middle-east-32668950.

10

BETWEEN SECULARISM AND PRO-ISLAMISM

A historical review of LGBT activism during the pro-Islam JDP rule in Turkey

Caner Hazar

Editors' introduction:

In this chapter, Caner Hazar analyzes LGBTQ activism in Turkey. He explains how civil society in Turkey has been shaped by multiple historical changes in the economic and political spheres, and forces such as globalization and modernization. Drawing from interviews with activists and participant observation of LGBTQ activism, Hazar analyzes how LGBTQ activism in Turkey in the 21st century has been impacted by economic, political, social, and cultural history.

He argues that LGBTQ issues and people were invisible and oppressed under both a secular government and under the more religious authoritarian regime, in different ways and for different reasons that reflected the particular political coalitions of the time. This persistent invisibility and oppression under such varying and complex conditions cannot be understood through Eurocentric stereotypes that construct secularist as "modern" and free and believe that public religion (including Islam) are backward and oppressive.

By complicating those simplistic stereotypes, this chapter invites readers to consider the following questions: What are the political opportunities and constraints facing LGBTQ activism in Turkey, a predominantly Muslim country ruled by a political Islamist government? What lessons can be learned from activism in Turkey that might be instructive to activists in other Muslim countries? In the United States? How does LGBTQ activism in the context of political Islam in Turkey differ from the hegemonic Western framework of LGBT rights activism?

Introduction

Political ideologies can shape people's emotions, ideas, everyday interactions, social movements, and goals in crucial ways. States, state institutions, and non-governmental organizations take part in this production of dominant ideologies. To understand human rights in Turkey, it is necessary to examine how politics, economy, and social life shape social movements, civil society, and politics. In Turkey, religion, secularism, and modernization function in a way that is different from what modern Western observers would assume is important in shaping the current context. Before I explain these dynamics, I offer some brief historical notes.

The Enlightenment ideals influenced the predominant understandings of secularization. According to these predominant understandings, religion was at odds with modernization and democratization. However, scholars have argued that the dualist understandings that equate modernization with the disappearance of religion in the public space were reductionist (Casanova, 2011). The state-led understandings which equate modernization with the disappearance of religion have engendered contentions between secular and religious groups in various countries (Gorski & Altinordu, 2008, p. 70). Turkey is one of them. The Ottoman Empire functioned on pro-Islam principles from the fourteenth century until the foundation of the secular Republic of Turkey in 1923. I use the definitions pro-Islamism or Islamism from Gorski as "encompassing the pietistic movements that seek the increase the impact of Islam on everyday conduct and political movements and parties that reconstruct Islam as a political ideology and seek to take control of state power" (Gorski & Altinordu, 2008, p. 70).

The secular Republic of Turkey crafted its own ideology that is called "Kemalism." I use the definition of Kemalism from Kosebalaban (2007), who described it as an ideology of Westernization and "Turkish nationalism, historically developed as Islam-less Muslim communalism for the remaining members of the Ottoman Muslim millet [people] within the territory that could be liberated from the European occupation" (p. 90). Scholars argued that Kemalism had a top-down, authoritarian approach regardless of the strong presence of religion within some parts of the society (Yavuz, 2009).

One needs to see the rise of the Justice and Development Party (JDP) of Recep Tayyip Erdogan (the current Turkish President) in this historical context. The JDP has been in power as the sole owner of the government since its first election success in 2003 until now. The JDP and its opponent secular groups have waged ideological wars for hegemony. The JDP, in reaction to the Kemalist state, used the neo-Ottomanist ideology to understand and organize Turkish society. I use the definition of neo-Ottomanism from Yavuz as an ideology that "has a powerful ethnic Turkish amplitude by positioning Turkey at the center of a new imperial project to 'lead' the Muslim world" (Yavuz, 1998, p. 23). Because of these competing ideologies between Kemalists and Ottomanists, LGBT activists had to navigate political tensions carefully without falling into simple explanations of secularism as a modernizing force against religion.

This chapter provides an overview of secular and pro-Islamist phases of the Turkish state, and then examines how LGBT people are situated within them, whether secularism has meant recognition and rights for LGBT people in Turkey, and how the clear emergence of pro-Islamism at the state level affected the relationships between LGBT people and the state. I show that modernist understandings of secularization (which treat religion as antagonistic towards the development of a nation and advancement of freedoms) fail to understand how secularism in Turkey has been repressive against LGBT people as well. One needs to situate LGBT rights in Turkey in a context that considers the complexities of secularization and religion in a nation. By focusing on the example of Turkey, I demonstrate that secularization, or the retreat of religion, does not necessarily mean the advancement of rights.

Secularism and modernization in Kemalism in the twentieth century

The predominant secularization theory has become widely shared, common-sense knowledge. In general, it proposes that as a country becomes more modern, it also becomes more secular (Cannell, 2010). However, sociologists of religion found the inevitability of secularization in modernity as an unfounded idea given the continuance and rise of public religions (Cannell, 2010; Casanova, 2011; Gorski & Altinordu, 2008). Furthermore, Asad (1993) argued that the idea of secularization was built upon a Western perspective, and that secularization in other parts of the world takes place differently. He explained that religion was not in a process of retreat in the Middle East when Europe started to secularize its institutions and separate the church and the state. Thus, the predominant argument that secularization is inevitable in modernity will be reductionist, given the complex nature of secularization, modernization, and religion in non-Western contexts.

The founders of the secular Turkish Republic deployed a modernization project, which stressed the rupture with the Republic's Imperial Ottoman past that functioned based on pro-Islam and non-secular principles. The ruling class of the new Republic pursued a top-down conversion from a traditional nation into a modern society by promoting Western ideals of rationality and reason (Keyman & Gumuscu, 2014). The modernization process required four changes, including:

> (i) the transition of political authority from personal rule to impersonal rules and regulations, that is, the rule of law; (ii) the shift from divine law as the explanation for the order of the universe to positivist and rational thinking; (iii) the shift from a community founded upon elite-people cleavage to a political community; and (iv) the transition from a religious community to a nation-state.
>
> *Keyman & Gumuscu, 2014, p. 13*

However, the transition from a religious order to a secular one in Turkey created exclusions, and could not provide a fully-functioning alternative in which secular and religious groups could partake in democracy. The separation of religion and the state was not a full separation in which both parties maintained freedoms and democratic principles. The Turkish state interfered in religious affairs to contain the challenge to its authority as both camps aimed for power at the state level.

Turkish secularization did not contribute to the construction of a strong participatory democracy but to the battles between seculars and conservatives over state power. The new Turkish Republic saw religion as antagonistic to the modernization project because the founders of the Republic based their rhetoric on the Enlightenment idea that reason and religion are essentially different. While some can argue that some reforms were helpful in the overall secularization of the country, it is indisputable that some of those reforms were implemented in exclusionist ways against religious freedoms. The Kemalist regime abolished the caliphate—the rule of a chief Muslim leader—in 1924; put the schools—religious or not—under state control in 1924 rather than under the control of religious authorities; adopted the Latin alphabet and ended the use of the Arabic alphabet in 1928; changed the language of adhan (religious prayer in Islam) from Arabic to Turkish in 1933; and effectively prevented the use of headscarves by students, civilians, and government officers at most of state institutions as late as the 2000s (Aldıkaçtı-Marshall, 2013). Pro-Islamist groups in Turkey saw these reforms as rejections of their Ottoman Muslim past, values, and traditions. Secularists saw these steps as necessary to be on a par with industrialized Western countries in terms of financial, industrial, and cultural development.

Because of cleavages for political power, the early secular Republican regime maintained a single-party system that lasted from 1923 till 1945. The party in power implemented secularization reforms that the conservative camp challenged. Because of pressures for political liberalization in the 1950s, the strictly secular government legislated the transition into multi-party-based parliamentary democracy. Since political opportunities for the representation of conservative and pro-Islam parties were closed before, the transition into the multi-party system led to "the resurgence of Islam" in Turkish politics (Keyman & Gumuscu, 2014, p. 128). Since then, conservative politicians have mobilized their bases using the framework of religious tradition and conservative values compromised by the secular Western state that intentionally distanced itself from the Ottoman past.

Citizenship and nationalism in Kemalist Turkey in the twentieth century

The construction of citizenship in Kemalist Turkey in the early twentieth century was based on nationalist, patriarchal, and heteronormative assumptions. It was nationalist because the efforts to improve women's status—such as granting women the right to vote before the UK and other developed countries did—were used as "a means to cultivate Turkish nationalism" (Arat, 2000, p. 109). It was patriarchal and heteronormative because the state constructed gender roles in which women held traditional positions such as homemakers who were responsible for raising the nation's youth. At the same time, the hegemonic state ideology was purporting the idea that Turkish men were born to be soldiers (Gole, 2002, pp. 173–190). Contrary to the secular modernization claims at par with the highly industrialized secular Western European countries, the Kemalist state rebuilt patriarchy as a secular one rather than the religious one that they associated with the Ottomans. As a result, women had to "bargain with patriarchy" (Kandiyoti, 1988) through adhering to the Kemalist ideology that perceived them only as potential wives and mothers (Coşar & Yeğenoğlu, 2011).

Historically, the Turkish state did not criminalize homosexuality and trans identities. Instead, the state and its institutions had adopted an approach that ignored and made invisible LGBT citizens. State officials neither openly targeted LGBT people in politics nor recognized them. However, this lack of criminalization did not mean that LGBT people lived comfortable lives without the scrutiny of the state. The state indirectly disciplined LGBT people through the institutions of education, the military, health, law enforcement, and family. LGBT people faced discrimination in state institutions because of the lack of anti-discrimination laws regarding sexual orientation and gender identity. Everyday society policed masculinity and femininity performances regarding how they represent traditional heteronormative male and female gender roles and gender performance.

The formal disciplining without criminalization happened in various indirect ways: gay males had to provide visual documentation of sexual encounters in which they are the receptive sexual partner to be exempt from the military service (Basaran, 2014). Furthermore, the legal system decreases prison sentences based on an unjust provocation clause. This clause considers being asked to be the passive partner in a sexual encounter or not knowing that a woman was a trans woman as legal justifications for committing a crime against transgender people. The lack of hate crime laws and the presence of honor killings by the family—since the strong collectivist culture in Turkey means that being LGBT is generally perceived as a shame brought to the family—shape everyday lives of LGBT people and LGBT activism's priorities in Turkey (Ahmetbeyzade, 2008; Kogacioglu, 2004). Furthermore, LGBT people still have no legal protection against hate crimes and workplace discrimination.

These conditions disadvantaged LGBT people in Turkey without the legal criminalization of their existence. In this way, the state upheld the secular and modern image that it did not practice laws or religion in everyday affairs while it disadvantaged LGBT people and ignored the discrimination and hate crimes against them.

Economic restructuring and globalization as determinants of Turkish politics and social movements

Since 1980, globalization has been influential in shaping the political, economic, and cultural contexts in Turkey. Starting from the 1980s, Prime Minister Turgut Ozal (of the first democratically elected government after the 1980 military coup) continued restructuring the economy through opening it up to market forces (Hale, 1994). The Turkish state used to regulate and dominate the market, which increased the foreign debt. The debt decreased the confidence in the previous economic system in the 1980s (Keyder, 1987). As a result, the state had to opt out of state-led developmentalism to a market-oriented transnationalist developmentalism over which the state had less control. This change created more trade and economic opportunities for the excluded groups, such as Islamic ones (Gulalp, 1997).

As the state retreated more from the market, the Islamic middle class grew (Atasoy, 2005; Heper & Toktaş, 2003;Yavuz, 2003, 2009): the economic liberalization bene-fited local conservative businessmen who "felt excluded from an economical life that was dominated by large industrialists with the support of the secular Turkish state" (Başkan, 2010, p. 170).This emerging class of conservative Muslim economic capital was one of the forces behind the rise of the JDP to power later in 2003.

Globalization opened the country not only to new economic policies, but also to new political LGBT ideologies.The first LGBT Pride meeting in 1993 was initi-ated with the support of an LGBT activist from Germany who wanted to "do something in order to help LGBTs in Turkey" (Personal communication, July 8, 2013). Second, in Ankara and Istanbul in the 1990s, trans sex workers, lesbians and gays, mostly with college degrees, mobilized using the Internet as a means for both organizing and consciousness-raising (Görkemli, 2014). Later, in the late 2000s, mostly middle-class, educated parents in Istanbul mobilized for their LGBT chil-dren.These changes in LGBT activism were influenced by opportunities brought by globalization, economic liberalization, and Europeanization (Bereket & Adam, 2006; Görkemli, 2014).

The previously hegemonic Kemalist state ideology had alienated LGBT people by both ignoring them as political equals in the democracy and indirectly condon-ing everyday violence against them through inaction about discrimination and hate crimes.Turkey's particular secularization and modernization project aimed to invis-ibilize the differences within society in order to build a homogenous nation, which was built on Turkishness and secularism and allowed religion mostly only in the private sphere. The same aimed to invisibilize ethnic minorities (e.g., Kurds, Armenians), religious minorities (e.g., Alawites, a sect of Shii Islam), Christians, atheists, and political dissidents (e.g., leftists, conscientious objectors, feminists, and LGBT activists) as political actors.

In this political context of political oppression under a secular state, the rise of conservative democrats who criticize the practices of the previous secular govern-ment is not surprising. Erdogan and his conservative party had an agenda of curbing the influence of the previous Kemalist state ideology on civil society.At the same time, they promised to take democratizing steps such as granting equal rights to disadvantaged groups if they were elected.As a result, Erdogan's party, JDP, gained the majority of votes in the 2003 general elections. However, as Erdogan's JDP won three subsequent elections, it has also become more authoritarian by acting against its initial promises of equality and democratization.The following section examines the historical trajectory in which the JDP transformed from a supposedly demo-cratic political actor into an authoritarian anti-LGBT party.

Emergence of the JDP and the strategic use of democratization as a political tool

Contrary to secular Kemalists, whose ideal citizen was not only nationalist but also secular—distant from the Ottoman past—the JDP adheres to the Ottoman-Islamist past as an essential characteristic of Turkish national identity (Çinar, 2005) and neo-Ottomanist political goals. Neo-Ottomanism, coined by Barchard (1985), is a political ideology that aims to revive an idealized Ottoman multiculturalism that supposedly respects ethnic and religious differences under a pro-Islam government. Also, neoliberalism during the JDP period in Turkey manifests itself through "socio-cultural conservatism, liberal free-market discourse and nationalist reflexes" (Coşar & Yeğenoğlu, 2011, p. 55). As Duggan (2012) explains,

> neoliberal politics must be understood in relation to coexisting, conflicting, shifting relations of power along multiple lines of difference and hierarchy. Developing analyses of neoliberalism must ask how the many local alliances, cultural projects, nationalist agendas, and economic policies work together, unevenly and often unpredictably, rife with conflict and contradiction.
>
> *pp. 70–71*

As a result of pragmatically adapting to economic and political changes in conflictual ways for more political gain, the JDP has treated the topic of LGBT rights in pragmatic ways.

Prior to 2007, the JDP presented a face of conservative liberal democracy. The JDP government emerged as a reaction to the Kemalist state ideology, which repressed different ethnic, sexual, and religious minorities. Consequently, it garnered support from both the emerging conservative-identified business people and various groups alienated by the Kemalist homogenization of civil society and erasure of difference. As a result, before and in the beginning of its rule, the JDP government developed a rhetoric that presented itself as a moderate conservative democratic alternative to the democracy problem dating back to the 1920s under the Kemalist state. The JDP government's goal was also lessening the military and the Kemalist state ideology's influence on democratically elected governments, the state, and the civil society.

Pursuing democratization goals, the JDP's conservative identity affected the situation of LGBT people negatively. Legislated in 2005 under the JDP rule, the Misdemeanor Law furthered the problems of transgender people. This law aims to "protect the social order, public morality, public health, the environment and the economic order" (Resmi Gazete, 2005, para. 1). After the enactment of the law, police departments fined transgender people according to their list of misdemeanors which included begging, gambling, occupying the pavements, drunkenness, hanging posters in public places, failing to disclose one's identity to a public official, carrying an unlicensed gun, smoking where restricted in closed places, disturbing the peace, making noise, etc. (Resmi Gazete, 2005). This law greatly restricted transgender individuals' daily activities because the police could fine a transgender person more than once a day. The extent to which the police department enforced this law on transgender individuals was high because the Istanbul police force had a bonus system (in a scale called the "Preventive Services Superior Bureaus Bonus Scale") which awarded points to police officers for fining transvestites (Kaos, 2012, para. 5).

Some gradual liberalization occurred in Turkey, as a result of demands from both citizens and the European Union. After a change in the Law on Meetings and Protests (Resmi Gazete, 2002) was required for European Union membership in October 2002, LGBT activists started to organize public protests in 2003. Lambdaistanbul LGBT Association, founded in 1993, became official in 2006 as a result of the liberalization of the Law on Associations in 2004 (Cengiz, 2010). While this step was positive, the state offices designed by the government also initiated setbacks. In 2008, Lambdaistanbul LGBT Association was dissolved by Istanbul's 3rd Civil Court of Peace on the grounds that "the name and objectives of the group were offensive to Turkish 'moral values and its family structure'" (Human Rights Watch, 2008, para. 6). Later that year, the 7th Judicial Office of the Supreme Court of Appeals overturned this ruling in response to international pressure and protests. However, in their decision, they noted that:

> should the association go against its own regulations in future by carrying out activities to encourage lesbian, gay, bisexual, transvestite and transsexual orientations and to make them more common, Articles 30 and 31 of the Association Law would apply and an application for the dissolution of the association could be made.
>
> *Çakır, 2009a, 2009b, para. 6*

While LGBT people were scrutinized based on morality arguments, widespread both in secular and conservative phases of the Turkish state, LGBT activists saw this court case as a political opportunity, which brought more prominence to the LGBT movement that was previously ignored, to a great extent, by the media and the Kemalist state. It was the first widely known legal court case between LGBT associations and the state.

LGBT activists saw the JDP area as a new phase with new political opportunities due to promises of change in the constitution. The coup government in 1982 had prepared the current constitution in line with the previous secular Kemalist ideologies of the state. The new conservative JDP government initiated the efforts to prepare a new constitution. As a result, some LGBT associations moved their focus from social and cultural goals (such as gaining more visibility and awareness-raising) to mobilizing at the state level. This new form of mobilization at the state level focused on adding sexual orientation to the anti-discrimination clause in the constitution.

The new constitution preparation opened a new phase of political opportunities. Previously ignored LGBT activists saw this phase as enabling them to bring their demands to the parliament's constitution preparation committee, which oversaw the preparation of a new constitution. As a result of open channels to communicate demands with the state, LGBT activists adapted their strategies to the new reality. They pressured the parliament to address the issue of protection against sexual orientation and gender identity-based discrimination. In order to achieve these goals, they benefited from the central role of family in Turkish society: they organized individual meetings between politicians and parents of LGBT people in Turkey in an attempt to benefit from the cultural sympathy toward the family institution in Turkish culture. In other words, they communicated their activist agenda to old members of the parliament (MPs) through the empathy that was generated as a result of the common identity of parenting among both MPs and parents of LGBT people.

During this new phase of increasing interactions between the state and the LGBT movement, the emergence of anti-LGBT rhetoric was inevitable, since LGBT people were becoming visible and known political actors in Turkish politics. Contrary to the cooperation with the European Union countries and Turkey since 2003, the JDP found EU accession less appealing, starting from 2007, because of the economic boom Turkey experienced at the time (Shively, 2016). After 2007, the JDP government started to be more outspokenly authoritarian and anti-LGBT. Contrary to previous optimism in interactions between the LGBT movement and parliament over the issue of the new constitution, the post-2007 phase signaled a re-emergence of a state characteristic of ignoring the diversity of groups in order to pursue a homogenous citizenship idea.

LGBT mobilizations, from invisibility to becoming a political actor and target

After 2007, the JDP's more authoritarian approach to civil society and the new constitution started to alienate LGBT people. Dengir Mir Mehmet Firat, founder and a deputy leader of Erdogan's government, said that LGBT rights, similar to environmental rights, were not a part of a "21st century constitution but a 22nd century one" (Kaos, 2015, para. 7). The new citizenship ideal of the new state was neo-Ottomanist. It aimed to recreate Turkishness by drawing upon Ottoman traditions, which prioritized Sunni Islam as the most important fabric that constitutes Turkish society. Contrary to the previous Kemalist state's secular and Turkish nationalist model citizen, the new JDP government and the state it transformed prioritized the Ottoman, pro-Islam, Turkish nationalist model citizen. This state-level construction of what a Turkish citizen ideally is created further exclusions in terms of not only ethnicity, sexual orientation, and race, but also how people conform to general morality assumptions influenced by conservative pro-Islamism.

As a result of the gradual rise of conservatism and authoritarianism at the state level, internationally known and widely diverse Gezi Park protests happened in the summer of 2013. The obstacles to equal rights faced by Kurds, Alawites, LGBT people, and women—ranging from banning websites and apps including words such as "gay" and "lesbian" to institutional decisions that reinforce women's traditional roles in society—brought these alienated groups together. In addition, not only previously hegemonic Kemalist groups but also dissident religious groups (e.g., anti-capitalist Muslims) found themselves repressed by the authoritarian rule of the JDP, and they joined the protests. As a central state had been responsible for exclusions, excluded groups could come together, seeing the root of their exclusions: a central, strong state. One prominent activist strategy was building critical alliances against the state's authoritarianism. As a result, LGBT activists could strengthen their relationships with the Pro-Kurdish People's Democrat Party and the pro-secular, historically, Kemalist Republican People's Party out of the necessity to build more alliances against an authoritarian government that used state apparatuses to force civil society differences into conformism under their neo-Ottomanist ideal of ruling.

The new resistance front, after the Gezi Park protests the JDP's neo-Ottomanist conservative authoritarianism, mainstreamed the LGBT cause as part of the resistance to authoritarian conservatism in the psyche of the general population against JDP authoritarianism and conservatism. As a result, two opposing political parties, pro-Kurdish PDP, and pro-secular RPP, nominated high-profile LGBT activists from Istanbul for member positions at the city councils in local elections in 2014. Furthermore, the pro-Kurdish party nominated a gay activist to stand as a member of the Turkish Parliament in the general elections of 2015. These developments were completely unprecedented for Turkish politics. These new coalitions between LGBT people and opponent parties led to the beginning of LGBT politics' visibility in Turkish politics for the first time in Turkey's political history at this scale, contrary to Kemalist and conservative state traditions of ignoring them as political actors. This newly-achieved visibility in politics also brought new political propaganda that targeted LGBT people.

As a result of both the success of LGBT people at the local elections and the nomination of a gay activist in general elections, LGBT people were not only starting to become engaged political actors, but also targets of the JDP. During the 2015 general elections period, the JDP adopted various campaigning strategies in different parts of Turkey. The common tactic was their strategic use of LGBT people as a campaigning tool. During the general election campaigns in 2015, President Recep Tayyip Erdogan targeted LGBT people, saying "we do not nominate a müfti [religious legal expert] in Diyarbakır, or a gay in Eskişehir" (Kaos, 2015, para. 45). Also, Prime Minister Ahmet Davutoglu said, "homosexuals caused the destruction of the Tribe of Lot and yet the PDP nominates them" (Kaos, 2015, para. 45). These were strategic campaign messages tailored for their constituents. However, as they campaigned, they gave strategically positive messages that contradicted previous statements in different parts of the world to exemplify their neo-Ottomanist tolerance of minorities. Concurrent with the anti-LGBT discourse, the JDP used the LGBT movement as an example of the level of democracy that "shows tolerance" to minorities in Turkey. In their 2015 election brochure, it said:

> Turkey is a country that can hold a Gay Pride on Istiklal Avenue even in the middle of the month of Ramadan. The increased visibility of conservative people does not carry the meaning that there is an intervention against people's life styles.
>
> *Kaos, 2015, para. 46*

However, surprisingly, the JDP did a crackdown on the LGBT Pride March in 2015 after the general elections. It was the first crackdown on the LGBT Pride March since 2003. These conflicting political movements are understandable in terms of their pragmatic strategizing to garner more support. After the 2015 general elections, the JDP found strict conservative rejection of LGBT people an effective political strategy. In order to consolidate their power, they referred to the conservative values they wanted to instill in society and also strengthened their conservative alliance against opponents.

After the turn toward authoritarianism, the JDP's rhetoric started to revolve only around neo-Ottomanist Turkish nationalism and conservatism without any room for respecting the rights and freedoms of political opponents. Their neo-Ottomanist community logic is visible in their statements. For example, the JDP spokesperson based his argument about the first crackdown on the LGBT Pride March since 2003 on a framework stressing general morality and family values. Speaking about the reasons of for the crackdown on the LGBT march, the Deputy Prime Minister said:

> Unfortunately, I am ashamed to talk about this in a place where our lady sisters are present. But, some people, people with different sexual orientations, turn this into pride. But it is extremely saddening that they get completely naked in broad daylight, challenging and having fun in the middle of Istanbul. And, unfortunately, parliamentarians from the RPP and PDP supporting them. If our society likes and applauds those, they can continue to follow them. If our society finds this wrong, critiques it, and swear unreservedly at them, they can do what is necessary at elections!
>
> *Hürriyet, 2012, paras 4–6*

While positioning LGBT people as opposed to the moral values of society, JDP politicians also associated them with Western culture. For example, President Recep Tayyip Erdogan targeted LGBT people, saying "Shame on those who in the West divert their sensitivity to the so-called freedoms, rights, and law shown in the debate over gay marriage away from Syrian women, children, and innocents in need of aid" (Al Jazeera, 2016, para. 2).

As illustrated in these quotations, JDP has used a neo-Ottomanist general morality framework to target the existence of LGBT people. According to neo-Ottomanist logic, the state takes the role of showing tolerance to minorities—as long as they do not challenge the state's conservative pro-Islam authority—rather than recognizing them as citizens with needs for protections, freedoms, and rights. Based on this logic, the first statement critiques the LGBT movement for going against general morality in order to garner more support in elections, using and creating antagonism against LGBT people in society. The second statement stresses the so-called protectionism that the neo-Ottomanist state showed for Syrian refugees while the West— according to Erdogan—supposedly failed Syrian refugees over a non-Islamic freedom. This way, Erdogan presents himself as an exceptional leader who protects minorities—as long as they "stay in line"—rather than granting them basic political and social rights.

Conclusion

In this chapter, I described dilemmas faced by LGBT activism in Turkey under secular and pro-Islam regimes. Contrary to the predominant secularization thesis, a secular versus a religious order does not necessarily mean the advancement of rights. Indeed, traditional Turkish state secularism before the JDP did not advance LGBT rights or even recognize LGBT activism. Furthermore, secular ideology also violated human rights, either in the name of Turkish nationalism or a conservative approach to sexual rights. These violations gained a different and stronger form during the pro-Islam JDP period as it became more authoritarian. As a result, LGBT activists in Turkey know that no top-down approach to society—whether secular or pro-Islam—necessarily provides a viable alternative. Thus, rather than choosing between secular or religious options (knowing that seculars in Turkey were not necessarily different, contrary to general public belief), they have tried to transform groups with which they could interact. As a result, the secular and pro-Kurdish parties in Turkey have shown positive changes in their approach to LGBT rights. While JDP members had not been completely closed to change, due to their conservative democrat identity, as the JDP adopted an authoritarian pro-Islam and anti-LGBT rhetoric, the possibilities of interaction between the LGBT movement and JDP members diminished to non-existence.

The example of Turkey does not support the simple argument that seculars are better for LGBT rights than Muslim conservatives. In Turkey, the secular state has not been beneficial in terms of freedoms and rights for LGBT people and other minorities. On the other hand, the emergence of the conservative JDP as a power against the old secular rule forces seculars to transform as well. Seeing the increasing rights violations as the JDP became more authoritarian, traditional seculars opened up to new critical alliances against a non-secular political actor. Traditional seculars, who ignored the rights activism of LGBT people historically, started to change with regard to their views on LGBT issues as a result of a common experience of repression under an authoritarian regime. Furthermore, the JDP used the same strategy of constructing an ideal citizen as Turkish, Sunni, and conservative. As a result, seculars started to learn to recognize the diversity of civil society actors, rather than holding onto their idea of an ideal citizen who is secular and heteronormative. While the current authoritarianism in 2017 is beyond worrisome for the Turkish democracy, Turkish civil society continues to show unprecedented reactions to changing state ideologies. If the JDP government's current strong hold on the country weakens, civil society in Turkey will be able to mobilize due to its particular critical alliances across religions, sexual orientations, gender identities, and ethnicities.

References

Ahmetbeyzade, C. (2008). Gendering necropolitics: The juridical political sociality of honor killings in Turkey. *Journal of Human Rights*, 7(3):187–206.

Al Jazeera. (2016). Erdoğan: Hassasiyetini Suriyelilerden esirgeyenlere yazıklar olsun. Retrieved from www.aljazeera.com.tr/haber/erdogan-hassasiyetini-suriyelilerden-esirgeyenlere-yaziklar-olsun.

Aldıkaçtı-Marshall, G. (2013). *Shaping Gender Policy in Turkey: Grassroots Women Activists, the European Union, and the Turkish State.* Albany, NY: State University of New York Press.

Arat, Y. (2000). From emancipation to liberation: The changing role of women in Turkey's public realm. *Journal of International Affairs*, 54(1):107–122.

Asad, T. (1993). *Genealogies of Religion.* Baltimore, MD: The John Hopkins University Press.

Atasoy, Y. (2005). *Turkey, Islamists and Democracy: Transition and Globalization in a Muslim State.* London: I.B. Tauris.

Barchard, D. (1985). *Turkey and the West.* London: Published for the Royal Institute of International Affairs by Routledge & Kegan Paul.

Basaran, O. (2014). "You are like a virus": Dangerous bodies and military medical authority in Turkey. *Gender & Society*, 28(4):562–582.

Başkan, F. (2010). Religious versus secular groups in the age of globalisation in Turkey. *Totalitarian Movements and Political Religions*, 11(2):167–183.

Bereket, T. & Adam, B. D. (2006). The emergence of gay identities in contemporary Turkey. *Sexualities*, 9(2):131–151.

Çakır, B. (2009a). European parliament's Cashman "Worried about Lambdaistanbul court case." *Bianet.org.* Retrieved from http://bianet.org/kadin/gender/113986-european-parliament-s-cashman-worried-about-lambdaistanbul-court-case.

Çakır, B. (2009b, April 22). European parliament's Cashman. Retrieved from http://bianet.org/kadin/gender/113986-european-parliament-s-cashman-worried-about-lambdais-tanbul-court-case.

Cannell, F. (2010). The anthropology of secularism. *Annual Review of Anthropology*, 39:85–100.

Casanova, J. (2011). *Public Religions in the Modern World.* Chicago, IL: University of Chicago Press.

Cengiz, O. K. (2010). *Dernekler Mevzuatının Örgütlenme Özgürlüğü Açısından Değerlendirilmesi Raporu.* İstanbul, Türkiye: TÜSEV Yayınları.

Çinar, A. (2005). *Modernity, Islam, and Secularism in Turkey: Bodies, Places, and Time.* Minneapolis, MN: University of Minnesota Press.

Coşar, S. & Yeğenoğlu, M. (2011). New grounds for patriarchy in Turkey? Gender policy in the age of AKP. *South European Society and Politics*, 16(4):555–573.

Duggan, L. (2012). *The Twilight of Equality? Neoliberalism, Cultural Politics, and the Attack on Democracy.* Boston, MA: Beacon Press.

Gole, N. (2002). Islam in public: New visibilities and new imaginaries. *Public Culture*, 14(1):173–190.

Görkemli, S. (2014). *Grassroots Literacies: Lesbian and Gay Activism and the Internet in Turkey.* Albany, NY: State University of New York Press.

Gorski, P. S. & Altinordu, A. (2008). After secularization? *Annual Review of Sociology*, 34:55–85.

Gulalp, H. (1997). Modernization policies and Islamist politics in Turkey. In R. Kasaba & S. Bozdogan (Eds.), *Rethinking Modernity and National Identity in Turkey.* Seattle, WA: The University of Washington Press, 52–64.

Hale, W. (1994). *Turkish Politics and the Military.* New York: Routledge.

Heper, M. & Toktaş, S. (2003). Islam, modernity, and democracy in contemporary Turkey: The case of Recep Tayyip Erdoğan. *The Muslim World*, 93(2):157–185.

Human Rights Watch. (2008). Turkey: Court shows bias, dissolves Lambda Istanbul. Retrieved from www.hrw.org/news/2008/06/01/turkey-court-shows-bias-dissolves-lambda-istanbul.

Hürriyet. (2012). Bülent Arınç'tan LGBTİ yorumu. Retrieved from www.hurriyet.com.tr/bulent-arinctan-lgbti-yorumu-29445022.

Kandiyoti, D. (1988). Bargaining with patriarchy. *Gender & Society*, 2(3):274–290.

Kaos, G. L. (2012). Polisin "Bonus Sistemi" Soru Önergesi Oldu. Retrieved from www.kaosgl.org/sayfa.php?id=10647.

Kaos, G. L. (2015). 2001'den 2015'e AKP'in LGBTİ tarihi. Retrieved from http://kaosgl. org/sayfa.php?id=20109.

Keyder, Ç. (1987). *State and Class in Turkey: A Study in Capitalist Development*. New York: Verso.

Keyman, E. F. & Gumuscu, S. (2014). *Democracy, Identity and Foreign Policy in Turkey: Hegemony Through Transformation*. New York: Palgrave Macmillan.

Kogacioglu, D. (2004). The tradition effect: Framing honor crimes in Turkey. *Differences: A Journal of Feminist Cultural Studies*, 15(2):118–151.

Kosebalaban, H. (2007). The permanent 'other'? Turkey and the question of European identity. *Mediterranean Quarterly*, 18(4):87.

Resmi Gazete. (2002). Çeşitli Kanunlarda Değişiklik Yapılmasına İlişkin Kanun. Retrieved from www.resmigazete.gov.tr/main.aspx?home=http%3A%2F%2Fwww.resmigazete.gov.tr% 2Feskiler%2F2002%2F04%2F20020409.htm&main=http%3A%2F%2Fwww.resmigazete. gov.tr%2Feskiler%2F2002%2F04%2F20020409.htm.

Resmi Gazete. (2005). Kabahatler Kanunu. Retrieved from www.resmigazete.gov.tr/eskiler/ 2005/03/20050331M1-2.htm.

Shively, K. (2016). Pragmatic politics: The Gülen movement and the AKP. In U. Cizre (Ed.), *The Turkish AK Party and Its Leader: Criticism, Opposition and Dissent*. London: Routledge, 183–204.

Yavuz, M. H. (1998). Turkish identity and foreign policy in flux: The rise of Neo-Ottomanism. *Critique: Critical Middle Eastern Studies*, 7(12):19–41.

Yavuz, M. H. (2003). *Islamic Political Identity in Turkey*. New York: Oxford University Press.

Yavuz, M. H. (2009). *Secularism and Muslim Democracy in Turkey*. New York: Cambridge University Press.

11

FRENCH LGBT ACTIVISM AFTER MARRIAGE

Hugo Bouvard

Editors' introduction:

In 2013, France made same-sex marriage legal. In this chapter, Hugo Bouvard examines how this has impacted the demands and strategies of the French LGBT movement since then. The chapter starts with a description of the political climate in France at the time, and the battles and activism that surrounded the passage of this law. This is followed by an examination of the changes that occurred in French LGBT activism after same-sex marriage was won. Bouvard looks at the new political priorities that have emerged, the re-emergence of forms of protests from earlier social movements, and tensions between mainstream and radical activists.

The chapter raises a number of questions for readers, including: What happens to a social movement when it achieves one of its primary goals? How does it negotiate disagreements and divisions about priorities and tactics? How does political memory get sustained, and how can younger activists draw from the politics and strategies of earlier generations? What lessons can be learned by U.S. activists about what the legalization of same-sex marriage can do to existing LGBTQ activism?

Introduction

In the spring of 2013, same-sex marriage was legalized in France, after almost nine months of intense political dispute covered extensively by the media. On April 23, the French National Assembly approved the law, which also granted same-sex couples the right to jointly adopt children. The adoption of "gay marriage", or "mariage pour tous" (marriage for all) as it was phrased by supporters of the bill, had been the top priority of most French LGBT organizations for a decade, although it was certainly not their sole request. A month later, the first marriage between two men was held in Montpellier, in southern France. Since then, about 4 percent of all marriages performed in France have been between same-sex partners (Institut National de la Statistique et des Études Économiques, 2015).

This chapter aims to assess the extent to which the adoption of this law has impacted the demands and strategies of the French LGBT movement since 2013. First, it is necessary to discuss the period during which the bill was introduced and then debated in the French parliament, since the visibility of LGBT issues in the public sphere has been impacted by the social and political context in which the debate took place. Indeed, the right wing and the Catholic Church strongly opposed the bill, and these anti-same-sex marriage mobilizations have long-lasting effects on French politics in general and on LGBT politics in particular.

Next, this chapter will examine the changes that occurred in French LGBT activism following the passing of the law. First, some topics which used to be relegated behind the fight for marriage emerged, mostly trans[1] rights issues and reproductive rights for LGBT people. Second, mainstream French LGBT organizations had to face new challenges, as they were criticized by the more radical fringes of the movement. Finally, seemingly new practices arose among the LGBT movement in response to the perceived inaction of the government after the legalization of same-sex marriage and to the discrepancy between the government's "socialist" claims and its actual policies.

The following analysis is based on a combination of methods: extensive reading of both mainstream and community-based media reports, press releases from LGBT organizations (both mainstream and more marginal), and numerous informal discussions with activists and participant observation in many of the demonstrations discussed below. This chapter also deals exclusively with the Parisian-based LGBT movement, and it is possible that in the rest of France different dynamics are taking place. Nevertheless, as France is a very centralized country, what is happening in Parisian-based organizations is crucial to the understanding of the transformations of overall French LGBT activism.

Flashback to the "marriage for all" dispute

Even though the "marriage for all" bill was eventually adopted by the French National Assembly, the process was never smooth. Indeed, the Socialist government led by Prime Minister Jean-Marc Ayrault introduced the bill in February 2013 but could not conceal its hesitations and sometimes reluctance. For instance, as soon as the debates started, President Hollande proposed a conscience clause[2] to allow public officials who opposed gay marriage the ability to not perform them once the bill passed. Overall, few members of the government showed a great deal of support for the bill, with the notable exception of Minister of Justice Christiane Taubira. Mainstream LGBT organizations were enormously in favor of the law, and several polls showed that the vast majority of gay- and lesbian-identified individuals were as well. While the LGBT movement appeared to be united behind the slogan of "equal rights," some leftist organizations severely criticized the heteronormativity of the bill. Indeed, it extended pre-existing rights to include same-sex couples but did not challenge the legitimacy of the very codified state-sanctioned partnership that is marriage (Perreau, 2014). Furthermore, the occasion to raise a political debate on what it means to be a family was not seized by representatives on the left in the parliament. For instance, only married couples or single individuals can adopt a child in France, and some groups wished that unmarried couples, as well as individuals who do not conform to gender norms, including trans people, would be legally allowed to adopt a child. Furthermore, they called for the integration in the law of the notion of co-parenthood, that would allow more than two people to be legal parents of a child (Outrans, 2013). These questions were not discussed in the National Assembly during the "marriage for all" debate. Indeed, representatives of the government argued that it would be the focus of a different law, that would deal with the legal definition of what is a family. However, that law was never introduced by the government; originally planned to be discussed in 2014, it was indefinitely postponed under the claim of an over-packed legislative agenda (*Le Monde*, 2014).

On the other side of the dispute, there were many opponents of the law. Hundreds of thousands of them, mostly affiliated with the Catholic Church (Béraud, 2014) staged massive protests in Paris and throughout the country, which were among the largest demonstrations of any kind over the previous thirty years. The organization that staged the protests named itself "la Manif' pour tous" (Brustier, 2014), which can be translated as "Protest for All" a parody of the unofficial name of the bill, "marriage for all." France's main right-wing political party, then called the UMP, supported the demonstrations, and most of its leaders took part in them. They stated that their party would repeal the law if it won the next presidential election. In the Assembly as well as in the streets, homophobic slurs and statements were common. After the law was adopted, a few mayors, mostly affiliated with a right-wing party but also some with a left-wing party, refused to perform same-sex marriages but faced charges for doing so.

In the Assembly, granting same-sex couples the right to marry was opposed by right-wing representatives, but not as much as same-sex parenting. Indeed, the representatives voluntarily perpetuated the confusion between adoption, "Procréation Médicalement Assistée" (PMA, i.e. artificial insemination with sperm donor) and "Gestation Pour Autrui" (GPA, i.e. gestational surrogacy), even though the bill only dealt with adoption and said nothing about PMA and GPA. Allowing female same-sex couples to access PMA had been part of President François Hollande's campaign promises, but allowing male same-sex couples to access GPA was not. Nevertheless, opponents of the law played on the similarity of the acronyms to raise concern among the population and galvanize conservatives.

Although several ministers, including the Minister of Justice and the Minister of Women's Rights, personally supported allowing female same-sex couples to access PMA, they nevertheless stood behind the government's decision not to act on that matter (*Libération*, 2014), saying that the country was already split up on the issue of same-sex marriage and that such a project would only strengthen the "Protest for All" movement. After the law was adopted, "Protest for All" did not disappear from the political agenda. On one hand, the movement turned itself into a free-standing political party. In the local elections of 2014 and 2015, "Protest for All" did not present any candidates, but instead endorsed candidates from other parties who supported the repeal of the law. On the other hand, "Protest for All" infiltrated the UMP, called The Republicans since 2015, and managed to place several of its members in the governing bodies of the party. It transitioned into an official organization, "Sens commun," that claims to gather around 10,000 members and 200 elected officials (*Ouest-France*, 2017). As a result of the months-long political dispute over same-sex marriage, a new generation of conservative activists arose and became politically active.

In reaction to the protests staged by the political right and the Catholic Church, there were a few support marches, but supporters of the law were always largely outnumbered by opponents. As a consequence, SOS Homophobie, one of the most important French LGBT organizations, witnessed an 80 percent rise in reports of LGBT-phobic events (slurs, aggressions) between 2012 and 2013 (SOS Homophobie, 2015). If many LGBT organizations reported a rise in number of their members during the first months of 2013, the political violence (slurs, defacing of a building in which an LGBT event was taking place, aggression towards patrons in a gay bar in Lille, etc.) enacted by the opponents of the law and allowed by the lukewarm defense of the bill by the government had negative consequences on the immediate future of the LGBT organizations after the adoption of the law (Clavel, 2013; Huffington Post, 2013; Borillo, 2017; RTL, 2013).

Consequences for mainstream LGBT activism

There were several consequences of the adoption of the law on the demands of the mainstream portion of the LGBT movement. In particular, I will focus on a specific organization which claims to be representative of the movement. In the wake of the legalization of same-sex marriage, mainstream LGBT organizations were criticized for focusing too much on matters that pertained primarily to wealthy cisgender gay men (such as marriage) and not enough on issues that were faced by more marginalized members of the community such as lesbians and trans people. (For sure, these criticisms were also offered before and during the "marriage for all dispute," but they were more vocally voiced—and perhaps more heard—after the legalization occured, when it became clear that the window of opportunity for the LGBT movement was at least temporarily closed.) Two topics were thus brought to the foreground of the LGBT organizations after the adoption of the law which had been largely eclipsed by the fight for marriage.

The first one, mentioned above, is PMA, i.e. artificial insemination with sperm donor. Currently, it is only available to heterosexual couples medically unable to have children, although a large number of female same-sex couples do have children in France. However, for same-sex couples, the process is fraught with pitfalls: unless they are able to find a medical professional willing to break the law, they have to go to Spain or Belgium, making it a long and expensive process.[3]

The second topic that has become prominent since the passing of the law is the topic of trans rights. When it comes to trans rights, several European countries have more progressive policies than France, which has even been condemned in the past by the European Court of Human Rights for imposing sterilization on trans people if they want to change their birth certificate (*B. v. France*, 1992). Indeed, having one's birth certificate modified is a very long and complicated process in France, with psychiatrists and doctors having huge power in the final decision. Even when demands for a simpler procedure were consistently voiced by the trans community, they were seldom amplified by the mainstream LGBT movement. However, attitudes have been changing since the legalization of same-sex marriage. For example, the theme of the 2016 French Gay Pride March was exclusively focused on trans rights for the first time, with trans activists leading the demonstration. In October 2016, after several years of uncertainty, a bill was finally approved by the French National Assembly removing the requirement that individuals wishing to change the gender on their birth certificate had to be sterilized. If some trans organizations were satisfied, others regretted that the reform was incomplete: for instance, a judge's ruling was still required to have one's gender officially recognized.

The organization "Inter-LGBT" is a good case study to see how same-sex marriage impacted the most important LGBT organizations in France. A federation of LGBT organizations, Inter-LGBT played a big part in the fight for same-sex marriage and was considered to be a legitimate representative of the LGBT movement by public authorities throughout the debate. Its main goal is to organize the annual "Marche des Fiertés LGBT" in Paris (LGBT Pride March), considered by many to be the most important day of the year for the LGBT movement because of media exposure, and to come up with a motto supposedly summarizing the demands of the activists.

In its heyday, the federation used to assemble up to sixty organizations, but since the adoption of the law on same-sex marriage, almost half of them have stopped participating, including some of the oldest organizations, as well as several focused on lesbian issues. A number of criticisms were leveled by organizations who quit the federation. These critiques included complaints about Inter-LGBT's inability to foster good communication between its members or to choose between a radical or reformist line.

Furthermore, the federation's failure to convincingly criticize the government during the same-sex marriage debate was at the center of many critiques. Officially nonpartisan, Inter-LGBT was specifically targeted for its proximity to the Socialist Party, which was in power at the time. Indeed, several members of Inter-LGBT's board of directors are or have been public members of the party, and some activists saw the situation as a conflict of interest. They thought it was the reason why Inter-LGBT had not been, in their opinion, vocal enough in its advocacy during the same-sex marriage debate. Specifically, the federation was blamed for allegedly underreacting when President Hollande announced his idea of a conscience clause. Other criticisms of the federation's tepidity came when the Socialist government backed down on its campaign promise of expanding reproductive rights (PMA) to all women.

Finally, numerous lesbian organizations blamed Inter-LGBT for its lack of feminist commitment and its ambiguity on the subject of gestational surrogacy (GPA). Indeed, GPA is such a controversial issue[4] in France that some feminist and lesbian activists loudly opposed it during and after the same-sex marriage dispute, even though it was never included in the bill. Some claimed that gestational surrogacy was a capitalist and patriarchal practice that allows gay men to exploit women's bodies (Bastié, 2014). They chose to voice their concerns even though it meant temporarily aligning and allying themselves with homophobic and anti-feminist members of "Protest for All."

All these issues were brought up, sometimes vehemently, during the fight for same-sex marriage. As a consequence, many activists experienced demotivation and weariness after the passage of the bill, and a number of them even disengaged from their organizations. For instance, in Homosexualités & Socialisme, an LGBT group within the Socialist Party which has tight connections with Inter-LGBT, almost half of its active members left the organization or simply stopped coming to meetings, according to my ethnographic observations ranging from 2011 to 2016. Most of those people were middle-aged white men who were on the frontline in the fight for marriage but who felt that their concerns were met after the adoption of the law.

Another important issue that was highlighted during and after the fight for same-sex marriage is the almost non-existent professionalization of LGBT activism in France. In the United States, many scholars and activists criticize the ongoing professionalization of LGBT activism: they point out how the neoliberal system of private funding (also known by its detractors as "the nonprofit industrial complex") determines the political priorities of LGBT organizations (Duggan, 2003; Munshi & Willse, 2016). But in France, the issue of the professionalization of the LGBT movement is rarely publicly debated. The only example of any debate was when two prominent lesbian activists recently called for an autonomization of LGBT activism from public funding that would allow for the hiring of paid professionals (*Diacritik*, 2017). However, they didn't specify what these alternative sources of funding would be.

Most LGBT organizations' primary revenue sources are their membership dues and private individual donations, which usually enable them to function on a relatively tight budget but without permanent paid positions. Some public events such as the Gay Pride March or some LGBT movie festivals are subsidized by local authorities such as municipalities or regional councils. This becomes problematic when political power shifts: for example, in the wake of the 2015 regional elections that saw the main right-wing party, Les Republicains, win most regional councils, many government grants were reduced or eliminated.

While there certainly are some benefits to this non-professionalization, one consequence is that the great majority of activists are volunteers who may disengage very suddenly. This lack of funding also affects LGBT media, and the two major— and almost only—French LGBT news outlets (*Têtu* and *Yagg*) both went out of business in 2015 and 2016, respectively (Guilbault, 2015; Yagg, 2016).

Towards new forms of mobilizations?

Nevertheless, despite these setbacks LGBT activism is not declining in France since the adoption of same-sex marriage. In reaction to Inter-LGBT's crisis, for example, many LGBT activists developed practices or forms of mobilization that came as a breath of fresh air in otherwise routinized LGBT activism. These "new" ways of protesting have an intersectional agenda, as they oppose racism and xenophobia coming both from inside and outside the community. Moreover, they are often part of anti-capitalist and anti-fascist groups, which informs both their discourse and their repertoire of contention (the range of forms of protest or actions available to the movement at a specific moment). Two different dynamics can be distinguished.

The first one is a strategy that externalizes LGBT activism from already-existing forms of activism and creates a new space for action. In June 2015, the first "Pride de nuit" (Night Pride) was staged by an informal group of LGBT activists just a few days before the official Gay Pride March, and in obvious opposition to it. While the official March takes place on the Left Bank of Paris during the day, organizers of the Night Pride chose to march in the evening, and in the historical gayborhood of Paris, the Marais (on the Right Bank of Paris).

The Night Pride is explicitly critical of the government and of what these activists call its "treasons" on the topics of PMA and trans rights. They argue that same-sex marriage was only used as a token of progressiveness so that the government could claim the support of the LGBT community when election time comes. In the second edition of the Night March in June 2016, more than 3,000 activists marched, according to the police. Based on my observations, most of them were much younger, and less white, than mainstream depictions of the LGBT community by itself and the media. Their message focused on demanding reproductive rights for female same-sex couples and civil rights for trans people, but they also heavily criticized the "state of emergency" established by the government after the November 2015 terrorist attacks in Paris for threatening civil liberties and for participating in the xenophobic and Islamophobic political climate that they claim is reigning in France since the attacks.

However, one should not come to the conclusion that Night Pride is a whole new form of mobilization. On the contrary, a number of similarities with past forms of protest are worth pointing out. First, feminists have been staging nocturnal demonstrations since the 1970s, and among the organizers of the first Night Pride several of them volunteered as activists for feminist and LGBT causes (Mackay, 2014). Second, references to American LGBT history are a constant feature of the signs held by demonstrators in the Night Pride. In particular, many of them were direct references to the Stonewall riots, with an emphasis on its insurrectional character and the prominence of trans, black, and Latina activists. Third, ACT UP Paris, one of the French chapters of the New York-based advocacy group founded in 1987 in response to the AIDS crisis, played a central part in organizing the march as well as in framing the demands. ACT UP Paris had been declining for years and was facing financial struggle at the time, but nonetheless was at the center of the demonstration.

The second new practice is more internal to the already-existing social justice movement. Rather than staging new protests or demonstrations, it entails infiltrating and subverting mainstream LGBT spaces, or spaces already politicized but not specifically focused on LGBT issues. In the first case, these self-identified "radical" activists, who are often younger and more racially diverse, started taking advantage of the official Gay Pride March to gather and form a subgroup in the crowd, with the intent of being visible and thus "radicalizing" the March from within.

This initiative was called "pôle radical" (radical group) and was authorized by the march organizers. It aimed at criticizing the government and the Inter-LGBT, which were both seen as not proactive enough on many issues such as PMA and trans rights. It also called for more public funding for HIV research and care, as well as for authorizing undocumented LGBT and HIV-positive migrants to legally remain in the country. This radical group was formally endorsed by some political parties, such as the Pirate Party and the New Anticapitalist Party (NPA); unions, such as Solidaires Étudiant-e-s (students) and STRASS (sex workers); and leftist LGBT organizations, such as Outrans and Act Up-Paris. Based on my observations in 2015 and 2016, many participants in this "pôle radical" also marched a couple days earlier in the Night Pride. These activists were met with some hostility on the behalf of some more mainstream activists who conflated them with ACT UP Paris, an organization with which they have had many disagreements over the years. Moreover, for several years in a row, this group publicly clashed with FLAG, the French Gay Police Association, during the main Pride March, drawing more criticism from less radical activists and groups.

In the second case, LGBT activists have been forming so-called "Pink Blocks" in routine traditional protests staged by left-wing unions and political parties. Here again, "Pink Blocks" are not new practices in alter-globalization social movements (Farrer, 2002). As Kolářová (2009, p. 100) reminds us, Pink Blocks "[are] a continuation of the Reclaim the Streets! activities that connect political protest, rave parties and theatre." According to Farrer (2002), this practice first emerged in 2000 in Prague "as part of an international mobilisation against the International Monetary Fund and World Bank" and "is a temporary and informal coming-together of people espousing libertarian values of decentralised and leaderless organisation with [. . .] no membership, [and] no formal organisation" (para. 30). When people form Pink Blocks in demonstrations which are theoretically unrelated to LGBT issues, this practice demonstrates queer solidarity and claims the convergence of all struggles, thus making queer activists visible in those social movements centered on class-based identities.

Although not new, this form of mobilization has been noticeably more visible in Paris since the passing of same-sex marriage. For instance, in labor-related demonstrations in Paris in the spring of 2016, activists in Pink Blocks claimed that labor issues were also queer issues, thus expressing themselves in an intersectional framework. They adopted a non-confrontational attitude toward the police, defusing the tension between protesters and armed forces through a very flamboyant and campy aesthetics: members of the Pink Blocks usually sing, dance, and wear pink or shiny colors. As in the case of the Night Pride, the past is once again not absent from the present. For instance, some of the activists in the Pink Blocks knowingly re-enacted forms of protests that were staged by French gay activists in the early 1970s, such as members of the Homosexual Front of Revolutionary Action (FHAR), going as far as chanting the FHAR's hymns and slogans (Sibalis, 2005).

Conclusion

In the three years following the adoption of the law, younger LGBT activists and LGBT activists of color dug up forms of protests which originated in feminist, alter-globalization, and 1970s Gay Liberation activism. By doing so, they showed that LGBT activism in France could not unilaterally be said to be on the decline, thus countering the prevailing pessimism in the politicized fringe of the LGBT community.

These younger activists also showed that, despite the prevailing feeling among older LGBT activists that the process of passing down "activist memories" from their generation to the next one is highly dysfunctional, the transmission of their repertoire of contention is nonetheless ongoing. Future research may focus on the inevitable innovations that these younger activists originate, even when they appear to be mimicking their predecessors.

Recent political events show that this new generation of activists does not intend to soften its criticism of the government. Even though a new President, Emmanuel Macron, replaced François Hollande on May 7, 2017, the conflict among different factions of the LGBT movement remains salient. Leftist groups opposed Macron for being too vague: while his campaign and image revolved around his self-proclaimed modernity and progressiveness, and he vocally called for anti-discrimination measures, he was never very specific in how he would implement them. Moreover, his program was far from proactive on several issues: even if personally in favor of allowing lesbian couples to access PMA, for example, he never officially committed to changing the law. On trans issues, the newly elected President has said very few words but basically thinks that the October 2016 bill is sufficient, despite the dissatisfaction of several trans organizations. On the other hand, many members of the LGBT community supported Macron, in part because they saw him as the best alternative to his opponent, Marine Le Pen, and her homophobic far-right policies.

These divisions in the movement were evidenced during the 2017 Pride March, where radical activists attempted to physically deny Macron's LGBT supporters from participating in the march. Conflicts like this one will continue to fuel activist commitment until burning issues such as reproductive rights for all women and trans rights are properly addressed by those in political power.

Notes

1   Throughout this chapter, the term trans is used as an umbrella term that includes everyone who does not identify with the gender they were assigned at birth.

2   The clause, which was never part of the law, was evoked by François Hollande on November 20, 2012, in response to representatives of the Association of French Mayors who opposed the law (in France, only mayors and their deputies can perform marriages). Asked to rule on the matter, the Constitutional Council found that the measure would have been unconstitutional (Decision No. 2013-353, 10/18/2013). For more information, see the content of the decision: www.conseil-constitutionnel.fr/conseil-constitutionnel/francais/les-decisions/acces-par-date/decisions-depuis-1959/2013/2013-353-qpc/decision-n-2013-353-qpc-du-18-octobre-2013.138338.html.
3   Some lesbian couples self-inseminate at home, using sperm donated by a relative, a friend, or a man who wishes to be a co-parent of the child. See Descoutures (2010) for more information.
4   Gestational surrogacy is strictly forbidden in France. However, some French couples resort to it in other countries, even though the process of repatriating the child to France can prove a hassle due to obstruction from some French consulate services. The controversy over gestational surrogacy in France is complex and many-sided. Some call for its de-penalization, some for the upkeep of the ban but the legal recognition of children born abroad via a surrogate mother, while some are categorically opposed to any change in legislation. For a clearer depiction of the different sides, see (Mehl, 2011, pp. 90–116).

References

B. v. France. (1992). Application no. 13343/87. European Court of Human Rights. Retrieved from http://hudoc.echr.coe.int/eng?i=001-57770.
Béraud, C. (2014). Un front commun des religions contre le mariage pour tous? *Contemporary French Civilization*, 3(3):335–349.
Borillo, D. (2017). Mariage pour tous et homoparentalité: Les péripéties du conservatisme de gauche. In B. Perreau & J. Scott (Eds.), *Les défis de la République*. Paris: Presses de Sciences Po, 88.
Brustier, G. (2014). *Le Mai 68 conservateur. Que restera-t-il de la Manif pour tous?* Paris: Cerf.
Clavel, G. (2013, April 18). Mariage gay et violences … La Manif pour tous débordée. Comment en est-on arrivé là? *Huffington Post*. Retrieved from www.huffingtonpost.fr/2013/04/18/mariage-gay-violences-et-intimidations-manif-pour-tous-debordeee-extremes_n_3107123.html.
Diacritik. (2017, April 14). Politiques LGBT? Entretien avec Alix Béranger et Gwen Fauchois. *Diacritik.* Retrieved from https://diacritik.com/2017/04/14/politiques-lgbt-entretien-avec-alix-beranger-et-gwen-fauchois/.
Descoutures, V. (2010). *Les Mères Lesbiennes*. Paris: Presses Universitaires de France.
Duggan, L. (2003). *The Twilight of Equality? Neoliberalism, Cultural Politics, and the Attack on Democracy*. Boston, MA: Beacon Press.
Farrer, L. (2002). Dance around the G8: Archives of global protests. *Nadir*. Retrieved from www.nadir.org/nadir/initiativ/agp/free/genova/pinksilver/index.htm.
Guilbault, L. (2015). Paris court declares Têtu bankrupt. *WWD*. Retrieved from www.com/business-news/media/paris-court-declares-tetu-bankrupt-10191671/.
Huffington Post. (2013, April 10). Frigide Barjot et le collectif "La Manif pour Tous" annoncent une plainte contre "Le Printemps français". Retrieved from www.huffingtonpost.fr/2013/04/10/frigide-barjot-manif-pour-tous-printemps-francais-plainte_n_3049965.html?utm_hp_ref=france.
Institut National de la Statistique et des Études Économiques. (2015). Bilan démographique 2014. Retrieved from www.insee.fr/fr/statistiques/1283853.
Kolářová, M. (2009). Fairies and fighters: Gendered tactics of the alter-globalization movement in Prague (2000) and Genoa (2001). *Feminist Review*, 92(1):100.

Libération. (2014, February 5). Bertinotti: Le temps de la PMA n'est pas venu. Retrieved from www.liberation.fr/societe/2014/02/05/familles-touraine-d-accord-pour-des-avancees-parlementaires-mais-sans-pma_978001.

Bastié, E. (2014, July 18). Marie-Jo Bonnet, lesbienne, féministe, de gauche et opposée à la PMA et à la GPA. *Le Figaro*. Retrieved from www.lefigaro.fr/vox/societe/2014/07/18/31003-20140718ARTFIG00172-marie-jo-bonnet-lesbienne-feministe-de-gauche-et-opposee-a-la-pma-et-a-la-gpa.php.

Le Monde. (2014, February 3). Loi sur la famille: L'examen repoussé à 2015 au plus tôt. Retrieved from www.lemonde.fr/politique/article/2014/02/03/l-examen-du-projet-de-loi-famille-repousse-a-2015-au-plus-tot_4359399_823448.html.

Mackay, F. (2014). Mapping the routes: An exploration of charges of racism made against the 1970s UK Reclaim the Night marches. *Women's Studies International Forum*, 44:46–54.

Mehl, D. (2011). *Les Lois de L'enfantement: Procréation et Politique en France (1982–2011)*. Paris: Presses de Sciences Po.

Munshi, S. & Willse, C. (2016). Introduction: Navigating neoliberalism in the academy, non-profits, and beyond. *The Scholar and Feminist Online*, 13:2. Retrieved from http://sfonline. barnard.edu/navigating-neoliberalism-in-the-academy-nonprofits-and-beyond/soniya-munshi-craig-willse-introduction.

Ouest-France. (2017, April 19). Sens commun: quel est ce mouvement derrière Fillon? Retrieved from www.ouest-france.fr/elections/presidentielle/sens-commun-quel-est-ce-mouvement-derriere-fillon-4938284.

Outrans. (2013, January 24). Mariage pour tou-te-s: La grande arnaque! Retrieved from http://outrans.org/2013/01/24/communique-de-presse-outrans-24012013-mariage-pour-tou-te-s-la-grande-arnaque/.

Perreau, B. (2014). The political economy of 'Marriage for All'. *Contemporary French Civilization*, 39(3):351–367.

RTL. (2013, September 2). Agression homophobe dans un bar gay de Lille: Trois hommes jugés mercredi. Retrieved from www.rtl.fr/actu/societe-faits-divers/agression-homophobe-dans-un-bar-gay-de-lille-trois-hommes-juges-mercredi-7764205156.

Sibalis, M. (2005). Gay liberation comes to France: The Front Homosexuel d'Action Révolutionnaire (FHAR). *French History and Civilization: Papers from the George Rudé Seminar*, 1:267–278. Retrieved from www.h-france.net/rude/2005conference/Sibalis2.pdf.

SOS Homophobie. (2015). Rapport Annuel 2014. Retrieved from www.sos-homophobie. org/rapport-annuel-2014.

Yagg. (2016). Yagg, une Page se Tourne. Retrieved from http://yagg.com/2016/10/26/yagg-une-page-se-tourne/.

12

QUEERING THE *INDIGNADXS* MOVEMENT IN SPAIN

Conflicts, resistances and collective learnings

Gracia Trujillo

Editors' introduction:

In this chapter, Gracia Trujillo examines the role of queer and feminist activists in one of Spain's most important social movements. The Indignadxs movement, also referred to as the 15-M movement, is an anti-austerity movement that began in 2011. Like the U.S. anti-austerity movement Occupy Wall Street (which emerged shortly afterwards), the Indignadxs movement protested capitalism, high unemployment rates, welfare cuts, and the political system, while demanding stronger investment in systems such as health, education, and culture.

Trujillo has been an activist with the Indignadxs movement since its start, and here she reflects on what she has seen in its work. She describes the tactics and goals of queer and feminist activists that were part of the movement, and examines the tensions they experienced in their work.

This chapter raises important questions for readers, including: How can LGBTQ activists get involved in work focused on areas that are not typically considered LGBTQ issues? How can the definition of "gay issues" be expanded? How can activists bridge identity politics with class-based, redistributive politics? What lessons are applicable to U.S. social movements?

Introduction

The *Indignadxs* movement originated with the occupation of many city squares in Spain on May 15th, 2011. The massive takeover of public space lasted a few weeks but part of the movement (a constellation of assemblies, together with people involved in actions and initiatives in the different districts and on the streets) continues today, six years on. The aim of this chapter is to explain the tensions and conflicts that feminist and queer activists faced during the occupation of the *Puerta del Sol* square in Madrid and afterwards, and the labor of political pedagogy carried out by them in two directions: toward the inside of the movement itself, and toward the city/society in general. In doing so, I analyze the work carried out by the queer assembly of Madrid (the so-called Transfagdyke assembly) I have been part of from its beginning in 2011, through the analysis of its actions and discourses, and through participatory observation during these six years.

Activists and/or people who research social movements (in my case, both), know that these rarely come out of nowhere. The beginning of the 15-M/*Indignadxs* appeared in some media as a popular uprising that emerged spontaneously. We know that this was not the case; the 15-M was neither completely "new" nor spontaneous: it had to do with earlier movements that made it possible, such as the anti-globalization movement and the Arab Spring. The 15-M/*Indignadxs* movement inspired, in turn, other occupations such as that in Syntagma Square in Athens and Occupy Wall Street in New York. In addition to these processes of protests spreading transnationally, the 15-M has also a feminist and queer genealogy. This political genealogy is not 15-M's only one but one of the many that we can trace, although this one is usually forgotten or not taken sufficiently into consideration.

From the beginning, the 15-M made an important critique of a democratic system that inhibits or does not permit citizen participation to a political class *"que no, que no nos representan"* ("that does *not* represent us"), and refused to have leaders and spokespersons in the movement. Assemblies are open to everyone (that is, in fact, one of the major differences with the anti-globalization movement), and decisions are made by consensus or can be blocked by anyone sitting in the assembly on that particular moment. From the outset, the movement was very heterogeneous in terms of social class, age, sex and gender identities, ethnicity, legal status, etc., and also regarding ideologies, activist experiences, and political socialization. In addition to activists who came from previous movements, people without political experience in either social movements or political parties joined the 15-M too. This issue is important for understanding how sexist and homophobic attitudes in the assemblies and camps in general co-habited with very rich and transformative discourses. From the beginning, the *Indignadxs* movement showed an amazing diversity of individuals working together in coalitions between struggles, and included groups such as feminists, ecologists, *okupas* (squatters), lesbians, gays and trans★, republicans, students and sex workers, among others.

"Revolution will be (trans)feminist or it won't be!"

As expected, in the 15-M camps there were problems related to the fact that very different people, the majority of whom did not know each other, were occupying a public space. In this space, which was at the same time being collectively (re)created, people shared their beliefs about how to organize themselves, the goals or priorities for the movement, the strategies to follow, personal issues, etc. Not only that, but the camps were not free from tensions and conflicts, and even violent situations. This is similar to what happened in other Occupy movements, such as those in Wall Street and Tahrir Square in Cairo (e.g., many Egyptian women who took part in Tahrir reported that they had been victims of group sexual assaults). In Madrid, feminist activists reported violent and unpleasant situations too, which led them to decide to no longer spend the night in the feminist tent set up in the square; this space continued to be used for meetings, activities, etc., but not for sleeping.

What I am interested in analyzing here are, as I mentioned in the introduction, the conflicts and resistances that feminist and queer activists had to deal with while trying to get a space of their own at the Sol camp (*Acampada Sol*) in Madrid, and in the 15-M/*Indignadxs* in general.[1] These activists were present from the beginning of the occupation of the square and made themselves visible with their bodies, banners, slogans and rainbow flags … in what we could call the beginning of the *queering* of the camp. It was then that the conflict arose with the feminist banner that had been hung on one of the buildings in *Puerta del Sol*, draped with many other posters displaying 15-M's demands. The banner said *"la revolución será feminista o no será"* ("the revolution will be feminist or it won't be"). A group of men, spurred on by other men, tugged on the banner until they managed to pull it down. That conflict is one of the most well-known, but it was not the only one, not in Sol nor in other square occupations across the country. And there were not only sexist issues, but also homophobic attitudes, in the form of slogans alluding to anal sex as the epitome of political and economic oppression, insults, etc., or those referring to the stigmatization of sex workers through, for example, slogans against politicians such as "Rajoy (our president) is a son of a bitch" and the like.[2] The point here was that we could all, as part of the 15-M, share the same critiques of politicians, but not the way they were expressed. In other words, criticisms could not whatsoever include sexist, racist, or homophobic remarks like those alluding to the politicians' mothers as whores.

Following the conflict with the feminist banner, in Madrid, as in many other cities, *Feminismos Sol* (Sol Feminisms) and the *Asamblea Transmaricabollo de Sol* (Sol Transfagdyke Assembly) were created. Some activists who took part in both groups wanted the queer assembly to organize under the umbrella or tutelage of the feminist one, but the majority did not agree to this. This proposal was rejected for two reasons. The first reason was political: this "merger" in some way subordinated sexuality issues to those of gender, the latter being considered more important than, or encompassing, the former. The second reason was practical: because a merger was not operative (agreements reached in the Transfagdyke Assembly had to then go through Sol Feminisms before reaching the 15-M's General Assembly). This proves how, for feminist activism, occupying their own space was not easy against dominant sexism, whilst queer protest was not guaranteed a space from the beginning either, not only in relation to the 15-M movement as a whole but also to feminism itself. A space for sexual and gender dissidents was something that we could not take for granted at all, we actually had to fight for it. In this sense, and as Pérez Navarro has pointed out (Pérez Navarro, 2014, p. 91), the spatial politics of the camp gradually developed following a *matrioska* or Russian nesting doll structure.

People who are part of the Transfagdyke Assembly (this term was the translation of queer into Spanish we finally decided to use) do not share an identity (these are more diverse than is represented by that phrase), but they do share similar political goals. A previous organization, and one that was quite influential for us, has been the *Bloque rosa* (Pink Bloc) of the anti-globalization movement. It was created in 2001, in the context of the protests against the IMF in Prague and was inspired by queer and feminist movements, as well as by queer and feminist theories (Bísticas-Cocoves, 2003). The Transfagdyke Assembly, like the Pink Bloc, stands up for (1) non-violent actions (unlike Black Bloc, another group of the anti-globalization movement, more inclined to engage in violent acts); (2) the need for activism to be inclusive to all; (3) coalition politics with other struggles, and (4) a repertoire of activities that includes performances, parodies, music, and comedy (which have proved to be very useful tools for social movements)[3]. As Butler (2002) has pointed out, queer activism (much like feminist activism) breaks the distinction between the private and the public, and between the theatrical and the political. It does this through public die-ins or kiss-ins, strategies that the Transfagdyke Assembly has deployed on many occasions already in public demonstrations and protests.

Lessons in political action

Social movements are forms of collective action by a series of people based on defending common interests, which are *sustained* over time against elites, opponents, and authorities (Tarrow, 1998). Movements are also pedagogical spaces, whether we consider the political work done inside them or towards the outside; that is, aimed at media and society in general. We have seen this double direction in other movements, such as the occupation of Gezi Park, in Istanbul, where lesbian, gay and trans* activists battled against neoliberal policies (symbolized by the plan to build a shopping center in a park) and, *at the same time*, worked toward the inside of the movement (i.e., questioning sexist attitudes and LGTBI-phobia from the activists themselves). The Transfagdyke Assembly has been—and continues to do—doing a similar thing in Madrid: confronting the homophobic slogans inside the 15-M movement, while also engaging in social protests against austerity politics, building networks, and joining forces with other struggles.

Thanks to this pedagogical work within the 15-M, we can say today that the movement has improved a lot since the days when the camp was set up and people used to laugh nervously whenever they heard the name *Transmaricabollo* (Transfagdyke) in the General Assembly or when one of our *critically queer* manifestos was read. At the beginning of the camp, the Transfagdyke Assembly was attacked in the most significant virtual spaces of the 15-M, like the *Toma la plaza* (Occupy the Square) website, for discrediting the movement with its "marginal" and "particular" demands. Right-wing media tried to question the movement using this assembly, saying that it was a disorganized space for promiscuity and sexuality, which the Assembly itself ended up defending of course. The ridicule (and sometimes virulence) of the criticisms of this type of press finally resulted in greater support to this Assembly from the 15-M in general.

In an example of the educational work carried out by social movements, the queer Assembly has engaged in several activities that question sexist, racist, and homophobic attitudes reflected in language. Thanks to the work of feminist assemblies such as *Feminismos Sol* from Madrid, *Setas feministas* in Seville and *Feministes Indignades* in Barcelona, among others, the 15-M uses the feminine plural (in assemblies, texts, etc.) as a way of questioning sexism (and homophobia) in language.

Initially, the Transfagdyke Assembly in Madrid managed to bring together many people who were not organized at that time (at first the assemblies were very large, with 30– 40 people, at least), like other 15-M assemblies coordinated around issues like housing, health, legal issues, education, etc. In recent years, the number in our Assembly has fallen and we are now currently around 10–15 people, which is not insignificant at all if we consider the much lower numbers of the majority of 15-M assemblies. The assembly is still active on many fronts and it seeks to link up its activities with those of other social groups to combat cuts and austerity policies in the current context of the crisis of the neoliberal system. More than a decade after lesbian and gay marriage was approved in Spain in 2005 (see Calvo & Trujillo, 2011), this varied series of issues includes: depathologization of trans* identities; control and/or modification of our bodies and sexualities; reproduction rights; HIV/AIDS; sex education; the fight for legal citizens' rights for everyone; sex worker rights; and rejection of homophobic attacks and the depoliticization and commercialization of Pride marches.[4] An important issue here is that the Transfagdyke Assembly protests not *only* for these demands but also tries to take part in all demonstrations, rallies, and activities against cuts to public education, health and social services, the labour reform, the *Ley Mordaza* (Gag Law), etc. It is quite surprising to see that some people still today look at us quite amazed when they see us with our rainbow flags and queer slogans in a general strike, for example, or in a march to support public education or the Republic, to give a few examples, as if non-heterosexuals were not affected by cuts and austerity policies. As Butler said,

> In the case of public assemblies, we see quite clearly the struggle over what will be public space, but also an equally fundamental struggle over how bodies will be supported in the world – a struggle for employment and education, equitable food distribution, livable shelter, and freedom of movement and expression, to name but a few.
>
> *Butler, 2015, p. 72*

The sustained presence of this queer (and feminist) assembly in all the possible political spaces and the criticism, offered in ironic and humorous ways, of sexism and homophobia inside and outside social movements have contributed to the critical break with the hegemonic subject of social protests. As Pérez Navarro (2014), who is also a member of the *Transmaricabollo* Assembly, explained: if the prototypical subject of the workers movement was a heterosexual white man, and "new" social movements were characterized by a series of identity divisions, what we see in the 15-M is a complex articulation of identities and bodies on the streets. This has been possible through the intervention of feminist and queer groups in global protests, from their position of clearly gendered and sexualized (and racialized) subjects, and *at the same time*, committed to combatting different forms of exclusion. In my view, the *Transmaricabollo* Assembly has done important work in *queering* social protest and the 15-M as a whole (as the *Pink Blocs* did in the anti-globalization movement), with its performative use of insults and of feminized language ("*somos todas perras flautas*" – "we are all (female) crusties"), of street music and theatre (such as parodies to welcome *Frau* Merkel or the Pope), comedy (like in a demonstration in support of the Republic: "*para reinas, ¡nosotras!*"—"if you want queens, here we are!"), sit-ins in the middle of Pride marches (because they have been very depoliticized and commercialized in recent years), or kiss-ins (against attacks and during the Pope's "invasion"). Here I also share Perez Navarro´s idea (2014) that this *transversal* orientation of the discourse and constant activity within the general protest have few or no precedents in the history of queer activism in Spain (see Trujillo, 2008).

To sum up, the *Indignadxs* movement cannot be understood, at least not entirely, without considering the previous and current queer feminist activisms. From the outset, the *Transmaricabollo* Assembly has been taking part in all struggles possible and deploying its queer tactics to mobilize and disseminate demands. We, who are part of this queer assembly, are thereby questioning those identity politics which spin around LGTBI issues only, while defending the need to incorporate an intersectional perspective and political praxis, working in coalitions even if they are temporary. In other words, we claim that our transfeminist and queer demands and struggles in the context of neoliberal austerity policies are not marginal or particular at all, not secondary or any less important than those related to social class, ethnicity, race, etc.; rather, they intersect with each other. We cannot, therefore, consider them separately nor as adhering to any type of hierarchy. This was argued in the 1970s (the issues that were considered important were the class-related ones; the other ones, which had to with gender, sexuality and so on, had to wait), a type of discourse we have heard again in the context of the crisis in southern Europe.

Final thoughts

In this article, I have tried to question the idea that social movements arise spontaneously (it is vital, in this respect, to recognize the political genealogies of movements), and that protest spaces are homogeneous in terms of participation (it has been said that the 15-M is a movement of young, middle-class university graduates) and exempt from conflict. Even spaces that claim to be utopian, like the camps, are not free from sexist, homophobic, or racist violence, and can be at times a replica of what occurs outside these microcosms: in the city, in the media, and in society in general. The wide diversity of the 15-M movement since the beginning helps to explain why the insults and violent attitudes run parallel to critical and creative feminist and queer discourses and proposals. It would be interesting, in this sense, to investigate other Occupy movements to see similarities and differences; I suspect that maybe some patterns (those related to these internal conflicts, for example) can be found in other occupations of squares.

Analyzing the *Indignadxs* movement from queer and feminist perspectives (which have generally received little attention, both academic and activist, in writings about the movement so far) could shed light on several issues, such as those related to the why and how of the tensions and conflicts, which highlighted a series of resistances related to the feminist and queer change proposed *within* the camp spaces; those associated with the double political work of some assemblies like the *Transmaricabollo* Assembly, fighting (and surviving) the crisis, in defense of education, health and public services, against evictions, etc., and, *at the same time*, the educational work targeting the inside of the 15-M, in an attempt to implement another language (inclusive), other ways of doing politics, other repertoires of activities, other demands that are not particular or marginal but which affect all of us and/or that we should all be concerned about (such as HIV, lack of sex education, bullying at school . . . to name a few).

One issue that we must continue highlighting is that there is no hierarchy of discriminations and demands but rather different vectors of oppression, which overlap with one another. In this sense, one of the challenges we face is how to recognize and appreciate the differences (race, class, ethnicity, sex-gender, etc.) and build political coalitions around them. The AIDS crisis taught us a lot in this respect, about what was done in other contexts (and what we lacked in the Spanish one) in terms of solidarity, coalitions, and building or strengthening of sexual communities. These can be useful lessons for today's protest.

Thinking along more general lines, today there are quite a few queer and transfeminist groups in Spain (our assembly is just one of them), doing intersectional work between struggles, some also at fertile junctions between activism and art (as is the case with the transfeminist group *Post-op* and functional diversity (that is, people with different abilities) in the great project "Yes, we fuck").[5] In addition, we have made stronger links with Latin America in recent years (through, but not only, migrants in Europe and vice versa), who are building bridges between struggles and oceans, more necessary than ever, to continue resisting critically and collectively the global threats.

Notes

1   Regarding feminism's complex relations with the 15-M, see the collective works *Revolucionando. Feminismos en el 15-M,* and those by Bilbao (2011), and Ezquerra & Cruells (2013), among others.

2   The *Colectivo Hetaira*, a group that defends sex workers' rights, designed in response to these derogatory sentences a collection of posters with slogans such as "*Las putas insistimos: los politicos no son nuestros hijos*" ("sex workers insist: politicians are not our sons").

3   An example of many on using comedy, with a queer tone, is the following: http://madrid. tomalaplaza.net/2012/02/18/transmaribolleras-al-borde-de-un-ataque-de-nervios/ There is also an English version of this manifesto in our blog: www.asambleatransmar icabollodesol.blogspot.com.

4 See "Manifiesto Transmaricabollo", 2011. http://madrid.tomalaplaza.net/2011/09/12/orgullo/.
5 See http://postop-postporno.tumblr.com/Pornortopedia and http://vimeo.com/yeswefuck.

References

Bilbao, M. (2011), 15-M. Porque sin nosotras no se mueve el mundo, la Revolución será feminista. *Viento Sur*, 117:118–124.

Bísticas-Cocoves, M. (2003). Black bloc, pink bloc: Reflections on the tactics of the anti-globalization movement. Paper presented in the American Philosophical Association Eastern Division, Washington, DC.

Butler, J. (2002) *Cuerpos que importan. Sobre los límites materiales y discursivos del "sexo"*. Buenos Aires: Paidós.

Butler, J. (2015). *Notes Toward a Performative Theory of Assembly*. Cambridge, MA: Harvard University Press.

Calvo, K. & Trujillo, G. (2011). Fighting for love rights: Demands and strategies of the LGBT movement in Spain. *Sexualities: Studies in Culture and Society*, 14(5):562–579.

Ezquerra, S. & Cruells, M. (2013). Movilización, discursos y prácticas feministas del 15-M. In P. Ibarra & M. Cruells (Eds.), *La Democracia del Futuro. Del 15-M a la Emergencia de Una Sociedad Civil Viva*. Barcelona: Ed. Icaria, 131–151.

Pérez Navarro, P. (2014). Queer politics of space in the 15-M Movement. *Lambda Nordica*, 19(2):83–114.

Tarrow, S. (1998). *Power in Movement. Social Movements, Collective Action and Politics*. Cambridge: Cambridge University Press.

Trujillo, G. (2008). *Deseo y Resistencia. Treinta Años de Movilización Lesbiana en el Estado Español*. Madrid: Egales.

INDEX

Locators in **bold** refer to tables.